SAMBA

Integrating UNIX and Windows

John D. Blair
Samba Team

Published by:
Specialized Systems Consultants, Inc. (SSC)
PO Box 55549
Seattle, WA 98155
Phone: +1-206-782-7733
Fax: +1-206-782-7191
E-mail: sales@ssc.com
URL: http://www.ssc.com/

ISBN: 1-57831-006-7

Table of Contents

Chapter 8: Access Control Configuration Examples 221

Chapter 9: Service Configuration Examples 235

To Rachel and my not yet born son.

Preface

This is a book about providing Windows networking services from a UNIX machine using Samba. Unlike other Windows networking servers, Samba is completely free, available under the GNU Public License. Like the Linux operating system and all the various parts of the GNU project, Samba proves to me that the GNU Public License is a viable model for software development. Samba is competitive with commercial SMB servers, including those from Microsoft, but is available completely free of charge.

I first discovered Samba shortly after I was charged with running a Windows NT domain. Since I was running Linux on my own PC I needed an easy way to share files between both systems. Before long I had discovered Samba, installed it, and set up a simple configuration that let me access files in my home directory from the Windows machines I tended.

However, it was quite some time before I had a handle on everything that Samba could do. Samba is a large and complicated piece of software, and my ignorance of the protocols that implement what a user sees as the Windows Network Neighborhood didn't make matters easier. The documentation included with Samba has most of the answers you need, but it has been written in pieces as each new function was added to Samba. The result is that you may have to dig for quite a while to find the specific answer you are after. This book is the result of compiling all of this information into a logical presentation, and mixing in useful information from other sources and my own experience. To sum up, this is the book I wish I had when I first started using Samba.

Audience

This book is aimed primarily at UNIX administrators who are now also responsible for making their systems available to PCs running any of the various Microsoft operating systems or OS/2. I've also striven to include enough detail so that people who are not UNIX gurus will be able to install and administrate Samba correctly. However, this is not a book on UNIX administration. It is assumed that the reader will consult the appropriate documentation for general aspects of running and administrating a UNIX system.

Organization

The organization of this book reflects my own experience with Samba and Windows networking, and the reference needs I wish had been available. The contents are a combination tutorial, reference, and "configuration cookbook." Its organized so you can home in on the specific information you need and still discover important related information that might otherwise not be obvious. To accomplish these goals there are frequent cross-references and sidebars describing specific topics in detail.

Chapter 1 is an introduction to Samba and the GNU Public License for those new to either, as well as a discussion of the current and future state of the Samba suite.

Chapter 2 is an introduction to NetBIOS and SMB, as well as an explanation of the important components of a Windows network. This chapter could be skipped if you are in a hurry, but is useful for understanding what the various Samba configuration options are trying to accomplish. When I was first put in charge of a Windows NT domain I was unable to find a concise, yet detailed explanation of how all the relevant protocols in operation in a Windows network operated. The second chapter is my attempt to create the guide that I wish I could have found.

Chapter 3 is a guide to downloading and compiling Samba, describing each section in the Makefile and includes notes for many different flavors of UNIX.

Chapter 4 describes each component in the Samba suite. This includes my own versions of the Samba man pages. I've reorganized the information in the man pages in a manner I find more accessible and provided cross references to related information in other parts of the book.

Chapter 5 and 6 are really the heart of the book, describing each of the global and service configuration parameters. Unlike the `smb.conf` man page, which describes these parameters in alphabetical order, I have grouped the parameters by topic. This makes it easy to see related options and topics that you might have missed when you look up a specific parameter. Because this may make it difficult to find a specific parameter, an index of all parameters has been provided at the beginning of each of these chapters.

Chapter 7, 8, 9 and 10 cover configuration examples. Because Samba has so many configuration options it can be very difficult to write your first configuration file. These chapters describe small examples, many of which are simple on their own, but which can be assembled into a complex configuration without understanding the full meaning of all the configuration parameters. When a configuration requires settings outside of the Samba config file, these settings have also been described.

Chapter 11 covers techniques for isolating and diagnosing problems. While I can't predict the specific problems you will encounter, these procedures will help you get started and may point to an immediate solution to some of the more common problems.

Chapter 12 describes the Linux SMB filesystem which allows you to mount a filesystem shared from an SMB server on your Linux system. This is not really part of the Samba suite, but is related and very useful.

Conventions

The formatting and other conventions used in this book deserve a brief mention. Notes (or "sidebars") are embedded in the text, but marked with an icon, and formatted distinctively. The information contained in notes is considered useful, but not as important as the information in the main text. Readers in a hurry will probably want to skip these notes. Examples are also embedded in the text, appearing in a constant-width font. Occasional warnings, which mark potentially dangerous problems, are in located in the text margins and marked with a "caution" icon.

In command syntax descriptions, angle brackets ("< >") denote *required* fields. Brackets ("[ ]", sometimes referred to as "square brackets") are used to denote *optional* fields in command arguments. In other situations, the square and angle brackets may be used in other ways, though the meaning should be clear in context. For example, be sure not to confuse the optional command arguments with entries in configuration files that require using square brackets. Each section in the `smb.conf` file is marked with a heading name surrounded by square brackets, as in a typical Windows `*.INI` file. In no way are these headings optional.

The CD-ROM

The CD-ROM bundled with this book contains a complete copy of the Samba ftp distribution site. This means that not only does it include the latest versions of the Samba server available at the time this book was printed, you have a complete library of related contributed software, documentation, and pre-compiled binaries for most common version of UNIX.

I regret that I was unable to include a copy of the DES library needed to compile Samba to support encrypted passwords. Current export restrictions (known as ITAR) forbid exporting strong cryptography from North America and I didn't want to restrict this book's distribution to just North America. Luckily, there are no such restrictions on importing cryptography. The `contents.html` file on the CD-ROM includes an easy to follow link to the `libdes` ftp archive in Australia. Regardless, starting with Samba version 1.9.18, the DES archive is not necessary. Starting with 1.9.18, Samba takes advantage of the fact that SMB uses DES to implement a hashing algorithm, not an encryption system. 1.9.18 contains just this hashing algorithm, thus allowing Samba with full encrypted password support to be exported from North America!

The CD also contains a copy of the Samba mailing list digest archives. If you encounter a problem and you can't find an answer in this book or in the Samba documentation, consult these archives before you post a question to the Samba mailing list. The CD also contains all the example scripts discussed in this book, and some additional documentation from other sources. The contents of the CD are described in detail in the files `contents.html` and `contents.txt`.

Errata to Be

I've done my best to prevent bugs and mistakes in this book, but undoubtedly some problem has crept in under my radar. If mistakes are found you will find an errata list and perhaps updates on some sections at http://www.ssc.com/ssc/samba. If you find a problem, or just have a suggestion or criticism, please direct it to samba@ssc.com.

Acknowledgments

Any large project is impossible to complete alone, and this book is no exception. It was a conversation with Phil Hughes at the Atlanta Linux Showcase which started the ball rolling, and he put his hand in at a few later stages as well. The text was reviewed by David Bandel and Mark Ballinger, who both made excellent suggestions regarding mechanics and content. Nearly all of their suggestions have been incorporated into this book. My contact at SSC was initially Belinda Frasier, who first offered me a chance to write this book, and then Britta Kuybus, who has worked with me nearly through its completion. Clarica Grove took over in the final stages, uncovering countless typos and grammatical errors that had slipped through. Here in Birmingham, both John-Paul Robinson and Andrew Baker have provided much useful mid-day diversion, and more importantly, quick answers to obscure networking questions.

Andrew Tridgell, Jeremy Allison, and Luke Kenneth Casson Leighton, all members of the Samba Team, are responsible for many important last minute additions and error corrections. As a result of their work this book is, for the immediate future, actually more accurate than the documentation that accompanies Samba. Similary, Volker Lendecke, the creator of the SMB filesystem for Linux, suggested useful additions to Chapter 12.

I also owe many thanks to my employer, The University Computer Center at the University of Alabama at Birmingham, and my supervisor Phyllis Berk. It was there that I encountered Samba, and it was the freedom they give me to pursue projects I think are important that first let me work with Samba.

Many thanks are of course due to the entire Samba Team: Paul

Blackman, Andrew Tridgell, Luke Leighton, Dan Shearer, John Terpstra, Jeremy Allison, Richard Sharpe, Peter Kelly, Volker Lendecke, David Fenwick, Chris Hertel, Paul Ashton, Eckert Meyer, and Karl Auer. Without their hard work Samba would not even exist, much less be the useful tool that it is.

Lastly, thanks to my wife, Rachel, who had to deal with all the times I said "sorry, can't do that, I have to work on the book" over the last several months.

John Blair

Birmingham, Alabama

John has been a UNIX fanatic ever since he got his first shell account while he was a senior in high school in 1991. He learned the fine art of UNIX system administration while an undergrad at Miami University (Oxford, Ohio), where he earned a Bachelor of Philosophy from the School of Interdisciplinary Studies. He currently resides in Birmingham, Alabama with his wife Rachel and two cats, and excitedly awaits the birth of their baby boy in April 1998. John provides commercial Samba support contracts through `brainwell.com`. *Consult* `http://www.brainwell.com/samba` *for more information.*

Foreword

Samba has come a long way from the early days of decoding packet sniffs of a PC talking to a pathworks server. The protocol upon which it is based, SMB, is now one of the most widely used file sharing protocols in the world and is growing in use all the time.

Samba has now become one of the best known tools for bridging the gap between the "Microsoft Networking" world and Unix systems. Growing with user needs, Samba has become an extremely flexible system that can find application in a wide range of situations. The very flexibility of Samba can be confusing to a network administrator, however, so I was extremely pleased to see that a book is now being published that will accurately guide network administrators through the options and terminology.

John has done a great job in producing a very readable book that users are sure to turn to as a reference as they explore Samba's capabilities.

Andrew Tridgell

Canberra, December 1997

Chapter 1: Introduction

What is Samba?
Why You Should Be Interested in Samba
The GNU Public License
The Future of Samba
> *What's New in 1.9.18*
> *Future Roadmap*

What is Samba?

Samba is a suite of programs which allow a machine running UNIX or a UNIX-like operating system to provide services using the Microsoft networking protocol. This allows a UNIX host to act as a file server for machines running the DOS, Windows and OS/2 operating systems. [1]

Parts or all of the UNIX filesystem and its printers can then be accessed directly from the DOS or Windows machine using the native networking clients which Microsoft supplies. The remote UNIX filesystem will appear on the PC as a drive-letter or an icon in the "Network Neighborhood," depending on the specific operating system and client software you are using. Since it appears as an additional local drive, use of the remote filesystem becomes transparent to the user. This differs considerably from FTP, which is probably the most common method for transferring files between UNIX hosts and PCs. Rather than forcing one to copy a file from the remote system to the local hard-drive before one may work with it, Samba allows users to open a file directly inside a Windows program as if it really were locally stored.

---

1. From now on when I refer to a "Windows" machine, unless noted otherwise, I also mean to include machines running DOS or OS/2, as well as all types of Windows.

Samba provides these services by implementing the SMB, or Server Message Block networking protocol. Specifically, Samba implements SMB running on top of NetBIOS over TCP/IP. NetBIOS is a networking protocol which, like TCP/IP, provides techniques for naming services, establishing virtual circuits and sending datagrams. NetBIOS implementations exist on the NetBEUI, IPX, and DECNet protocols as well. By using NetBIOS over TCP/IP Samba is able to use the built-in networking API provided by UNIX systems. Since a network composed of UNIX hosts will already be running TCP/IP, running NetBIOS over TCP/IP simplifies the process of integrating Samba and other Windows Networking servers into an existing network. Exactly how SMB services are implemented is explained in more detail in Chapter 2: Windows Networking Protocols.

 SMB Compared with NFS

Most people familiar with UNIX are familiar with the Network File System (NFS). NFS, like SMB, allows the filesystem to be shared across the network to client machines. However, there are significant differences between NFS and SMB.

NFS is a stateless protocol. This means that each network transaction stands on its own, separate from previous and following transactions. This means that NFS is very robust— it is possible for a connection to survive a crash of the server computer with only a long pause while the server is rebooted. SMB is also supposed to be robust in the face of such failures, but relies on the client to implement proper recovery procedures and recover the session from the point of failure.

NFS is a much simpler protocol than SMB. NFS just implements a mechanism for sharing the UNIX filesystem. In contrast, SMB also implements services for sharing printer services and for simple network messaging. Even the way that NFS shares the filesystem is much simpler than SMB. Following the UNIX philosophy of building up complex tasks out of simple operation, NFS provides only a handful of file access commands. This can result in more network traffic for some tasks. SMB, on the other hand, in an attempt to reduce network overhead and simplify the role of the client, provides hundreds of commands. The result is that SMB servers must be large and complex. NFS is often implemented in the UNIX kernel. SMB is far too large and complex to do this.

NFS offers only host-based authentication. An NFS server can specify which hosts will be granted what types of access to files. User-based access controls are handled by trusting the security of the client machine and making sure that userids are uniform across both systems. Put another way, the NFS server doesn't know anything about user access rights—it only describes the access rights granted to a file and trusts the client machine to follow the rules. Since, until recently, UNIX machines were usually large multiuser systems with a trusted administrator, this system worked. This approach has problems now that computers are smaller and the user is usually also the administrator. SMB incorporates the task of identifying the user during the session setup. How this is done depends on the specific version of SMB that is used.

All in all, it probably isn't fair to compare NFS with SMB. An SMB server, like Samba, is more like a combination of NFS, lpd (the UNIX printer daemon), and a distributed-access control system (like Kerberos or DCE).

Using Samba is actually very similar to sharing a filesystem between one UNIX host and another using the Network File System (NFS). In fact, by installing an NFS client like PC-NFS on a Windows machine one could achieve roughly the same effect without installing additional software on the UNIX host. Using Samba is superior to this solution for at least two reasons.

First, the administrative overhead of installing and maintaining an additional software component on a server is significantly less than installing and maintaining a new software component on every client on your network. Because Samba speaks the native Microsoft networking protocols, your UNIX host will be available to any Windows machine with TCP/IP and the Microsoft Networking components installed. These components are often installed by default in Windows 95 and Windows NT, and are not difficult to install in Windows for Workgroups and even older computers just running DOS.

Second, many Windows applications rely on filesystem features that cannot be provided by NFS. Also, in many cases SMB is much faster, especially since SMB's opportunistic locks allow file operations to be cached locally.[2]

---

2. 4.4BSD does offer an NFS "leasing" option that presents NFS clients with the equivalent of SMB's opportunistic locking.

Samba would be a great software package if all it allowed you to do was share your UNIX filesystem to DOS, Windows and OS/2 clients. Yet, in addition to this core service, Samba provides other services useful for bridging the gulf between UNIX and Windows hosts. Samba allows printers available on a UNIX host to be shared with Windows machines. This means that, rather than setting up printer spools to run on a Windows server or locally on Windows machines, you can utilize the lp spooler provided with most flavors of UNIX.

Samba also provides a "browse server" which means that your UNIX host can register itself with the master browser on your network. Samba can even act as the master browser. Users will see your UNIX host in the "network neighborhood" on their Windows 95 and Windows NT machines just as if it were a Windows file server, or in the list provided by NET VIEW on older machines. A client utility provided with Samba means that files can be copied off of remote Windows machines in an ftp-like shell interface. The client also allows printers spooled on Windows servers to be added to your UNIX printcap file and used as if they were traditional UNIX remote printers accessed via lpd.

An extension of the Samba client allows one to back-up remote Windows volumes into tar files on disk or tape. There is even a filesystem driver for the Linux kernel that allows one to mount remote Windows shared volumes. The password authentication services in Samba provide techniques for unifying the very different authentication systems which Windows and UNIX use. If your network is composed of multiple subnets, Samba will properly utilize WINS, the Windows Internet Name Service. Samba can even be set up to be a WINS server. Samba is the Swiss-army knife of Windows-UNIX connectivity.[3]

Why You Should Be Interested in Samba

Observers frequently point out that proponents of operating systems often act as if they are followers of post-modern religions. While this is a result of many factors, I believe its chief cause is the fact that any operating system is the manifestation of a design philosophy. If one believes that the design philosophy of a specific operating system is superior to other operating systems, using these other systems can be, at

---

3.   And like any good knife, Samba can cut if you're not careful.

the very least, an annoying experience. On one level, this attitude is silly. Application can be written for any sufficiently powerful operating system. On another level, the attitude is perfectly understandable—while it may be possible to use any operating system, who would want to? Those of us in the UNIX world usually feel that UNIX is so flexible and powerful that developing applications is frequently quick, easy and fun.[4]

The OS and its accompanying tools feel like a sandbox or Lego Blocks. Making components work in concert is a joy rather than a chore. Other operating systems, especially Windows, can feel so alien and non-intuitive that one sees little reason to migrate unless forced to do so by what feels like the arbitrary will of the marketplace.

Of course, one of the battle lines most frequently drawn between rival sects in this holy war is between UNIX and Windows. Despite this battle line, even the most die-hard UNIX hacker has to concede that Windows, in its various forms, is here to stay. Surely every UNIX shop has at least some personal computers running Windows and would benefit from a tighter integration between the two systems. Work is almost always easier and more efficient to accomplish if there are as few barriers as possible to the movement of information between different systems. Samba is one tool that allows UNIX and Windows to act in a partnership, each providing the services that it does the best. Unless you haven't installed a computer running Windows on your network and never plan to in the future, Samba will be useful for you.

If operating systems are rival religious sects, then Samba is the translator and diplomat that makes interoperability possible. Samba can appear very complex because it is the translator between the different systems for file attributes, file naming, user authentication, and network architecture used between UNIX and Windows systems. Running Samba effectively requires a thorough understanding of the different ways in which Windows and UNIX view the world.

In every way Samba is Windows Networking done the UNIX way. Rather than hiding the complex issues of configuring the behavior of services on your network behind complex heuristics, cute graphic user interfaces, and often simply hard-coded defaults, Samba lays open all aspects of the behavior of the Microsoft Networking protocols for adjustment or modification. While this contributes to the perceived complexity of Samba, it also means that one can carefully tune the behavior of Samba to match the specific setup of your network. There are many possible solutions to the problem of translating between the UNIX and Windows views of the world. The fine granularity of

4. Is this a plug for the book, "All I Ever Needed to Know In Life I Learned From UNIX"?

Samba's configuration means you can set up the specific solution that works best for you, rather than the solution that a software design team thought would work best most of the time.

Also, like other complex UNIX applications, Samba can be learned in stages. Rather than needing to master all the complexity of Samba all at once, one can start with relatively simple configuration. Additional services and more careful configuration of obscure parameters can follow after one is more comfortable with Samba and Windows Networking. It is one goal of this book to simplify this process of configuring Samba's many settings by providing example configurations for numerous classes of networking problems.

The GNU Public License

Most UNIX users are probably already familiar with the GNU Public License, but this short introduction is provided in case you are new to it. Most software is provided under a restrictive license that limits the rights of a purchaser to copy, distribute, and reverse engineer the software. Usually the license sets different fees based on the number of machines the software will be installed on or the number of users who will be utilizing the software. Since the software producer stays in business by making a profit on the sale of the software, the license is designed to counter the relatively simple act of copying and running the software on more than one machine. Traditionally licensed software is supplied only in pre-compiled binary format, though a few manufacturers allow people to obtain a "source code license" that gives one the right to modify the software, but not to distribute the resulting modifications.

Samba is supplied under the terms of the GNU Public License (GPL). This means that Samba is "free software." Releasing software under the GPL is also often referred to as "copylefting" rather than copyrighting. Don't confuse the term "free software" with "zero cost software." "Free" in this sense means free from restriction, not cost. The intention of the GPL is to encourage the cooperative development of new software. The GPL, like other software licenses, is a rather long document filled with legalese. You should read it yourself, but the gist of it is to encourage the further development of software by specifically granting the right to use the software for any purpose, and further distribute the software, even for a fee. It also grants the right to modify the software, use its source code as a base to derive other software, and to distribute this resulting software. In return for these rights, any redistribution of the original software or derivations of that software must be accompanied by the source code to the software, and distributed under the same licensing terms. The practical up-shot of this is that most copylefted software is produced by students or other members of research institutions, rather than commercial corporations, though this is beginning to change. For example Jeremy Allison, a member of the Samba Team, is paid by his employer, Whistle, to work on Samba. Samba provides the main file service for the InterJet, an "Internet appliance" sold by Whistle. Several other commercial products also use Samba. If you have an embedded CD-ROM or print server, you may be using Samba without even knowing it.

The biggest advantage of free software, other than its low cost, is that it is frequently superior to its commercial counterparts. A commercial company will, understandably, budget its programming time based on the market for new features. This means that uncommon features or ports to obscure operating systems are unusual. However, since free software makes it possible for programmers to make these changes on their own, all that is needed is the will and time of a skilled programmer.

Further, bugs in free software are often found and corrected more quickly than their commercial counterparts. To illustrate why this is true, consider the process of discovering and fixing a bug in a piece of commercial software. Someone is using the software and discovers a bug. Let's assume that this person wants to have this bug eliminated from the software. He or she isolates the conditions which cause the problem and communicates this diagnosis to the software producer. If the software has a large user base, the user may also communicate the problem to other users via the Internet to see if it has been noticed or if a work-around has been concocted. If this company is unusually responsive, our valiant user will hear back from them immediately, though will often be billed for the support time. A lively series of communications will result during which the bug is tracked down, fixes are incorporated into the software, and new versions are distributed to beta testers for evaluation. Eventually this new software is released.

It is more likely that, since the commercial software engineers have limited time and are already swamped with other projects, they will not be able to work on the bug-fix very quickly. Sometimes, if the bug occurs rarely and under strange conditions that exist under only a few installations, the bug will simply be ignored or a kludgy work-around will be distributed. Sometimes the bug-fix is provided free of charge to people who already own licenses. Often it is distributed for a fee, or only to those who have purchased a special maintenance contract.

Now consider the process of fixing a bug in a piece of copylefted software. Again, lets assume that a person finds a bug and wants to have it fixed. He or she again isolates the conditions which cause the problem and tracks down the source of the bug. If the user is a programmer he or she can use the source code to aid in finding the problem, even re-compiling the program with debugging hooks in place so it can be analyzed. Since most free software has a large user base, he or she can communicate the discovery to other users via the Internet to see if other people are having the problem, or if others are already working on a fix. Most free software has a specific person or group of people responsible for maintaining the software, and the diagnosis will also be communicated to them. The user may be able and have the time to determine where the mistake occurs in the source code and work out a fix. This fix can be quickly distributed to other users via the Internet and, if it is effective, will be incorporated into the next release of the software.

The GNU Public License was created by Richard Stallman, who founded the Free Software Foundation. The Free Software Foundation primarily develops and maintains the library of GNU tools. GNU is a recursive acronym standing for "GNU's Not UNIX." The GNU project's eventual goal is the creation of a complete UNIX-like operating system composed of free software including editors, a compiler, and a complete set of development tools. With the release of their own UNIX-like kernel, called the GNU HURD, the FSF has nearly reached this goal. The free operating system known as Linux was made possible by the GNU project. Technically, Linux refers only to the kernel—it was the complete set of GNU tools which made a workable operating system possible. Because of this some people refer to Linux as GNU/Linux, though, except for being released under the GPL, the Linux kernel itself is not associated with GNU or the Free Software Foundation.

You can learn more about the GNU Project and the Free Software Foundation at `http://www.fsf.org`. You can learn more about Linux at `http://www.linuxresources.com`. If you use free software in a commercial setting you should consider making a donation to the Free Software Foundation or one of the other free software organizations, like Software in the Public Interest, who maintain the Debian Linux distribution. If at all possible, make some of your own software available under the GPL.

At the very least you should thank the Samba team for developing and maintaining Samba. One way to express these thanks is to order Andrew Tridgell, the original developer of Samba, a pizza. This is rather difficult to do for most Samba users since Andrew lives in Australia. However, the Samba FAQ supplies a few suggestions, including mailing him a gift certificate for a multi-national pizza chain. You could also contact the Samba Team to see if any of the other developers of Samba live closer to you than Andrew. Another way to thank the Samba Team is to provide programming time, equipment, or monetary support, especially to attend conferences. International travel costs to attend Microsoft's CIFS conferences aren't cheap!

The Future of Samba

What's New in 1.9.18

At the time of printing, Samba version 1.9.18 is the current stable release. The Samba Team refers to this version as the "Browse Fix Release." The significant new features in version 1.9.18 are:

Support for Real Opportunistic Locking

All previous versions of Samba did not support SMB's opportunistic locks. This resulted in Windows NT Server being significantly faster in some situations, such as the sharing of Microsoft Access databases. This support added the `oplocks` service parameter, which is explained on page 197. With oplock support, Samba provides performance comparable to Windows NT.

New DES Code

Rather than linking against libdes, version 1.9.18 includes a special implementation of the DES algorithm which is only usable for authentication. This means that both the source code and binary of this version of Samba with full support for encrypted passwords can be exported from the United States without violating ITAR restrictions. As a result, encrypted password support is no longer a compile-time option. Only run-time configuration is necessary. See page 57 for more information about ITAR.

New Internationalization Support

Starting with this release Samba includes full Kanji (Japanese character) support without requiring special compile-time settings. A new client code-page implementation provides more flexible support for international character sets. Full UNICODE support is slated for the future, which will allow Samba to support multiple code pages at the same time.

Very Experimental Primary Domain Controller Support

Based on Paul Ashton's effort to reverse-engineer the Microsoft NT domain controller protocol, Samba now includes very experimental code allowing it to act as a Windows NT primary domain controller. This is one of the most difficult, and most promising areas of effort by the Samba development team. This is difficult because Microsoft refuses to publish the information needed to implement an NT domain controller. If successful, this feature will allow a UNIX server to completely replace the authentication role of Windows NT Server. Since this code is very experimental and the behavior of parameters that control it subject to change, no documentation of the feature is included in this printing. These features are not enabled by default in this release. If you wish to experiment with the PDC support you will have to compile Samba yourself.

A Prototype Web-Based Configuration Tool

A web-based graphical configuration utility is included with this release. It includes its own mini-web server so a separate web server is not required to run it. This tool is intended as a prototype to rough out the design for a GUI configuration tool. Because it is experimental, this tool is also not described in this book.

Future Roadmap

The Samba Team has distributed a "roadmap" explaining the features they plan to implement in future version of Samba. While they have no date set for any future releases, and reserve the right to release features out of sequence, the roadmap at least provides some sense of their plans for the immediate future.

Version 1.9.19, dubbed the "Auth Code Release" will include improved security and authentication code as well as password synchronization capability. Version 1.9.20, the "GUI Config Release" will include Samba's first official GUI configuration tool, as well as improved international support (maybe full support for UNICODE?). Version 2.0, called the "DSA Release," will contain "next generation Directory Services." It will probably also be when the experimental NT Domain Controller code stops being experimental and is announced as a production feature. Check the Roadmap file in the top level of the current Samba release for the latest details.

Remember that the best way to help these new features get incorporated sooner is to contribute code to the Samba project, or provide some sort of financial support to the Samba Team so they can spend more time working on Samba.

Chapter 2: Windows Networking Protocols

This chapter describes the operation of Windows Networking, from its foundation in NetBIOS to the higher level protocols used to form workgroups and NT domains. After reading this chapter you should understand:

- The services provided by NetBIOS and the relationship of NetBIOS over TCP/IP to other forms NetBIOS.

- The services provided by SMB and how it has changed with the evolution of Microsoft operating systems.

- The difference between workgroups and NT domains.

- How the network browse list is constructed and maintained.

If you are in a hurry (who isn't?) you should skim the first section and focus on section two. This section covers top-level network structures like Workgroups, NT domains, and browse lists which you need to understand to properly integrate a Samba server into a Windows network.

 The OSI Reference Model

The design and operation of a computer network is typically organized in terms of layers in a model. Each layer in the model represents a particular networking process and is responsible for shielding the layers above it from knowing how the layers below it function. The effect is to isolate each networking process in a specific software subsystem which can be designed, tested, and even replaced without affecting the other layers. Defining specific protocols to implement each layer allows different software implementations to interoperate as long as each properly implements the protocol.

The OSI (Open Systems Interconnect) Reference Model was defined by the International Standards Organization (ISO). It is presented here because it is generally seen as a good way to visualize the operation of computer networking. Besides, every book on computer networking mentions the OSI model somewhere, and I certainly don't want to break the tradition.

An important disclaimer: while the ISO has defined a protocol for each layer, no networking system in common usage has components which map directly to every layer in the protocol. In reality, the session and presentation layers are seen as expendable and are often dropped from discussions. The TCP/IP reference model doesn't contain either layer, relying on the equivalents of the transport and applications layers to accomplish the same task. The TCP/IP reference model is explained on page 15.

7	Application
6	Presentation
5	Session
4	Transport
3	Network
2	Data Link
1	Physical

1) Physical: The physical layer represents the actual physical medium in the computer network. It is concerned with defining the tangible aspects of networking like the type of cable, the pins on the connectors and how they're used, and the voltages which represent data.

2) Data Link: The data link layer is concerned with the error-free transmission of a stream of unstructured bits. It transforms the raw media in the physical layer to a useful transmission medium for the network layer.

3) Network: The network layer describes how to route information through the network from a sending host to a receiving host.

4) Transport: The transport layer is responsible for accepting messages from the session layer, breaking these messages into smaller pieces if need be, and then ensuring that the network layer properly delivers the message to the destination. It also processes incoming messages from the network layer and delivers them to the appropriate session. While the network layer has no awareness of a destination other than a specific computer, the transport layer is aware of multiple processes on each host and properly delivers each message to the correct process.

5) Session: The session layer allows the establishment of a session between processes on separate machines. This layer delivers information much like the transport layer but provides additional services, like allowing a user to log into a remote machine using a virtual terminal. The SMB protocol used by Samba, as well as the network file sharing protocol (NFS) are considered session layer protocols.

6) Presentation: The presentation layer is used for data translation services common enough to warrant finding a shared solution. Typically these are translating from one character representation to another (e.g., ASCII to EBCDIC or Unicode) or data encryption.

7) Application: The application layer is concerned with the meaning of the data that is transmitted and the actual user interface to network services. The Samba daemons smbd and nmbd both inhabit the application layer. So do applications like Netscape, ftp, telnet terminals, and e-mail servers.

The TCP/IP Reference Model

It is instructive to compare the OSI and TCP/IP reference models. The Internet community views the OSI reference model and its accompanying protocol standards as bloated and poorly designed—an example of the worst kind of design by committee.[5] TCP/IP was designed and tested in the real world rather than designed in the abstract and then mandated. On the other hand, the TCP/IP reference model was really an afterthought used to explain protocols that had already been developed and is not useful for studying other networking systems. OSI is good for explaining networking in the abstract, but its important to compare it with reality.

There are only four layers in the TCP/IP reference model. TCP/IP was designed to glue together separate networks, called subnetworks, into a larger internetwork.

OSI		TCP/IP
7	Application	Application
6	Presentation	not present
5	Session	not present
4	Transport	Transport (TCP, UDP)
3	Network	Internet (IP)
2	Data Link	Host-to-network
1	Physical	

1) Host-to-network: This layer concerns the physical connection between a host and the network and the transmission of data across this local subnetwork. The specific protocol is left up to the implementation. The only requirement is that it properly communicate with the internet layer.

2) Internet: This layer is the glue that holds the entire TCP/IP system together. It allows a host on any subnetwork to transmit packets, called datagrams, to another host on any subnetwork without knowledge of the underlying networking system. These datagrams provide "best-effort connectionless service," meaning that there is no guarantee that a datagram will arrive, or that multiple datagrams will arrive in the order they were transmitted. Remember that the word "internet" is used in the generic sense—the world-wide network known as the Internet is only one possible internetwork.

3) Transport: This layer allows two hosts to carry on a conversation with each other. It provides two modes of operation: TCP and UDP. TCP, or Transmission Control Protocol, establishes a reliable connection-oriented

---

5. Q: What do you get when you cross a gangster and an international standards-making organization? A: Someone who makes you an offer you can't understand.

two-way data stream between distinct processes on two hosts. UDP, or User Datagram Protocol, provides an unreliable connectionless means of communication. TCP is used to implement session oriented services, like telnet, where reliable delivery is important. UDP is used to implement services where prompt delivery is more important than accuracy, such as real-time data like audio and video.

4) Application: The application layer is responsible for implementing the application-specific protocol, such as SMTP for mail, NNTP for netnews, or HTTP for the world wide web. The need for the presentation and session layers was not perceived to be necessary—their role is shared partly by both the transport and application layers.

NetBIOS

Samba, like any other implementation of Windows Networking, uses a protocol called SMB, for *Server Message Block*. This protocol was built on top of the NetBIOS network interface. It is certainly possible to be a very effective network administrator without understanding anything about these protocols. However, since NetBIOS limitations are SMB limitations, and therefore Windows Networking limitations, a little bit of background can build the conceptual toolkit that will make it easier for you to diagnose the problems you will inevitably encounter.

The important concepts to understand are:

- Every service is referenced by a unique name existing in a flat namespace.

- Services communicate using the session service or the datagram service.

- NetBIOS is independent of the transport layer protocol and has been implemented over NetBEUI, IPX, TCP/IP and DECNet. Samba uses NetBIOS over TCP/IP.

- SMB, for Server Message Block, is a session layer protocol analogous to NFS.

When two machines negotiate an SMB connection they decide on a common protocol level to use between them. Samba implements all SMB protocols except for platform specific protocols, like the Xenix protocol extension. Some SMB servers only implement some protocol extensions, which limits the usefulness of the server with some clients.

NetBIOS Services

The NetBIOS interface itself establishes a set of services for identifying and managing connections between computer systems. These three services are the Name Service, the Session Service, and the Datagram Service. Most Windows networking services are built from these three fundamental building blocks.

 WINS Doesn't Use NetBIOS

An example of something that is an integral part of Windows networking but is not implemented using NetBIOS is the Windows Internet Name Service (WINS).

 NetBIOS Name Types

CAUTION!

The NetBIOS namespace is flat across your entire organization.

Values surrounded by < and > are hexadecimal representations.

Group Names

Group Names can be shared by more than one host.

WORKGROUP<00>: Registered by all servers in a workgroup

WORKGROUP<1E>: Registered by all potential master browsers. Elections packets are sent to all hosts who have registered this name.

WORKGROUP<1C>: This is registered by domain logon servers. This is also treated specially by WINS. It is the only group name that does not send an IP address in reply to a WINS query. Instead the list of machines that have registered this name is returned.

`<01><02>__MSBROWSE__<02><01>`: This name is registered by master browsers. It is used to announce workgroups so that other master browsers know they exist.

Unique Names

Unique Names can only be registered by a single host.

`HOST<20>`: All servers register this as their normal SMB server name.

`USER<03>`: This is used primarily by winpopup and similar apps. It is registered when a user logs in. All clients also register HOST<03> so winpopups can be sent to a host.

`HOST<00>`: Registered by all clients and subsequently used as the source name on normal NetBIOS connections.

`WORKGROUP<1D>`: Registered by the local master browser. It is treated specially by WINS to overcome the fact that it is unique but registered by lots of hosts. Registration is always accepted but a negative reply is always sent to WINS queries.

`WORKGROUP<1B>`: Registered by the domain master browser. It's a pity that Microsoft also chose to use this for the NT domain primary domain controller (PDC), preventing the roles from being easily split between hosts.

Name Service

All NetBIOS services are referenced by name. Any lower level representation of a service, such as the IP address in NetBIOS over TCP/IP, is unavailable to a NetBIOS application.[6]

The name space is flat, meaning it is not hierarchically organized. Each name consists of 16 characters and may not start with "*" (an asterisk). There are two types of names: exclusive names, unique to specific applications, and group names, which are shared among a group of applications. No two applications on the NetBIOS network may use a unique name at the same time. An application is considered to own a name until it requests that the name be deleted, or the host is powered

---

6. Some IP specific services have been added to CIFS, the latest incarnation of SMB.

off or reset.

The three primitive operations provided by the Name Service are:

Add Name: Requests use of a unique name by an application. Implicit permission to use a name is granted to a host if it receives no replies to a bid during a set period of time.

Add Group Name: Requests use of a name that the application is willing to share with other applications.

Delete Name: Requests deletion of a name that an application will no longer use. This name is then available for use by other applications.

Session Service

Sessions are reliable full-duplex sequenced data connections between two NetBIOS applications. A NetBIOS session is analogous to a TCP virtual circuit. More than one simultaneous session may exist between any two applications. Both applications participating in the session have access to the name of the remote application. No specification is given for resolving session requests to a group name into a data connection. A service is provided for the detection of a session failure by an application.

The six primitive operations provided by the Session Service are:

Call: Initiates a session with a NetBIOS service listening under a specified name.

Listen: Accepts a session from a calling application.

Hang Up: Gracefully terminates a session. The data connection is properly flushed before termination.

Send: Transmits one message over the session. A time-out after a send forces a non-graceful termination of the session.

Receive: Receives data. Like *Send*, a time-out after a receive forces a non-graceful termination of the session.

Session Status: Obtains information about all the application sessions under a specified name. No network activity takes place.

Datagram Service

The Datagram Service provides unreliable (best effort), non-sequenced, connectionless communication between two NetBIOS applications. Datagram Service is analogous to UDP service under TCP/IP. Each datagram is transmitted under the cover of the NetBIOS name registered to the sender. Datagrams are broadcast if sent to a NetBIOS group name. Datagrams sent to a unique name, if received, are received only by the named application the datagrams are addressed to.

The four primitive operations provided with this service are:

Send Datagram: Sends an unreliable datagram to the application associated with the specified name.

Send Broadcast Datagram: Sends a broadcast datagram to any NetBIOS application with a *Receive Broadcast Datagram* command posted.

Receive Datagram: Receives a datagram sent by a specified name to a specified name.

Receive Broadcast Datagram: Receives any datagram sent as a broadcast.

 Oddities of NetBIOS Over TCP/IP

Normally broadcast NetBIOS packets are transmitted using broadcast UDP packets and unicast NetBIOS packets are transmitted using unicast UDP packets. However, what defines a NetBIOS packet as broadcast or unicast is a Net-BIOS flag that is independent of the transport protocol. As a result it is possible to unicast a broadcast NetBIOS packet and broadcast a unicast NetBIOS packet.

The Three Prominent Flavors of NetBIOS

NetBIOS, or Network Basic Input Output System is a vendor-independent network interface originally designed for IBM PC computer systems running PC-DOS or MS-DOS. Counter to intuition, NetBIOS is a software interface, not an actual networking protocol. Put another way, it specifies the services that should be available while placing no requirements on the protocol used to implement those services. NetBIOS was intended to separate the basic network operations accessed by software from the specific underlying transport protocol. In this respect it is analogous to the BSD socket programming interface.

There is no officially defined NetBIOS standard. Instead, the original IBM PC-Network version, first described by IBM in 1984 in the "IBM PC Network Technical Reference Manual," is treated as the *de facto* standard. Since NetBIOS is just a software interface it assumes an underlying transport protocol but puts no restrictions on the specific protocol to be used. Since its introduction three main flavors of NetBIOS, each with their own transport protocol, have emerged: NetBEUI, NetBIOS over IPX, and NetBIOS over TCP/IP. Digital Equipment's DECNet implements SMB over DECNet.

NetBEUI

NetBEUI, or *NetBIOS Extended User Interface*, was the original PC networking transport protocol designed by IBM for their LanManager server. Microsoft later adopted the protocol for use in their own networking products. The protocol is optimized for local network segments. It is not routable, so is not usable over wide area networks. Microsoft has continued to improve NetBEUI since the original IBM implementation, shipping NetBEUI version 3.0 with Windows NT. Some of the enhancements from earlier versions include allowing more simultaneous sessions on the same network card and automatic self performance tuning. This latest version provides significantly better performance over slow links than earlier versions of NetBEUI and, due to its extremely low overhead, is the fastest protocol over a local network segment available for Windows NT. NetBEUI is often referred to as NBF, meaning *NetBIOS Frame*.

NetBIOS over IPX

In the early 1990s Novell realized that LanManager-based systems and Novell systems would need to be able to coexist on the same network. As a result, they developed NetBIOS over IPX. This implementation preserves the NetBIOS API, but uses IPX as the transport protocol. Since IPX is routable, NetBIOS over IPX could actually operate over larger networks. NetBIOS over IPX was quickly noticed by Microsoft and incorporated into Windows for Workgroups, Windows NT, and subsequently Windows 95. IPX support for Samba would not be very hard to do and will probably be added in the future.

NetBIOS over TCP/IP

NetBIOS over TCP/IP was first proposed in RFCs 1001 and 1002, which were submitted to the Internet Engineering Task Force in 1987.[7] This version of NetBIOS is sometimes referred to as RFCNB, for *RFC NetBIOS*. It is this flavor of NetBIOS which is used by Samba. These RFCs describe an implementation of NetBIOS using TCP for connection oriented session services and UDP for datagram services. This design has some significant advantages over the previous two protocols. First, it uses the existing TCP/IP protocols, so it is routable across the global Internet and any other wide area networks using TCP/IP. Secondly, software implementing the NetBIOS interface can be built using existing TCP/IP implementations—no new network drivers need to be written. Since any operating system worth its salt supports TCP/IP nowadays, any operating system could also support NetBIOS services with a minimum of effort. This is also why Samba is easily ported to new types of UNIX, as well as other operating systems.

RFC 1001 also included a proposal for a central NetBIOS name server, modeled on DNS, which would allow NetBIOS names to be registered across multiple subnets when broadcasting is impractical or impossible. The system proposed in the RFC has morphed into Microsoft's Windows Internet Name Service, which is described in detail in its own section towards the end of this chapter. The RFC also included an as yet unrealized proposal to utilize IP Multicasting to implement NetBIOS broadcasting.

---

7. These documents are included on the CD-ROM which accompanies this book.

SMB

What is SMB?

The Role of SMB

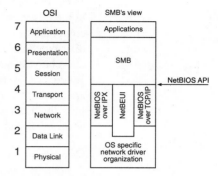

SMB fills roles assigned to the session, presentation, and part of the application layers of the OSI reference model. SMB is implemented using the NetBIOS API. This API, as pointed out in the diagram, defines the interface between the layers inhabited by SMB and the network and transport layers assigned to the specific NetBIOS implementation.

This diagram is not strictly correct, but draws a general picture useful for understanding the relationship between components. Remember that, while NetBIOS over TCP/IP fills the functions of the network and transport layers, strictly speaking, it is contained solely within the application layer of the TCP/IP reference model. This is because, from the perspective of the TCP/IP reference model, NetBIOS over TCP/IP is just another application specific protocol. This arrangement is reflected by the fact that Samba is implemented completely in user space. Also remember that these distinctions are mostly academic—don't get too hung up on them.

SMB, which stands for Server Message Block, is the protocol used to implement windows file-sharing and print services. Its name comes from its internal structure—commands are encoded as packets called *server message blocks*. The protocol is implemented on top of the NetBIOS API. Each server message block consists of a fixed-sized header followed by a variable-sized parameter and data component. The various types of SMB messages can be broken into four types: session control, file, printer, and message. Session control messages start, authenticate, and terminate sessions. File and printer commands (obviously) control file and printer access. Message commands allow an application to send messages to or receive messages from another host. The most common type of messages are called "WinPopup messages" after the common Windows application used to process them.

The protocol is functionally analogous to a combination of NFS and lpd in the UNIX world. The Windows NT Domain Controller Protocol complements, but is not part of, SMB. It is functionally equivalent to a distributed authentication framework like NIS+. However, in contrast to the relatively simple design of NFS, SMB is a behemoth of a protocol. Where NFS defines a relatively simple set of file access functions which are used to transparently replace a normal local filesystem, SMB has literally hundreds of different commands and offers many ways to accomplish the same file access operation.

One reason SMB is so complex is because it allows the definition of *protocol extensions.* When an SMB client (called a "consumer" in the Microsoft/Intel documentation) negotiates a connection with an SMB server, the two parties decide on a common protocol to use for communication. This functionality allowed Microsoft to "externalize" new capabilities as they were added to Microsoft operating systems while maintaining backwards compatibility with older implementations of the protocol. Andrew Tridgell explains the effect of this in the Samba documentation:

> This means the protocol is very "rich", offering many ways of doing each file operation. This means SMB servers need to be complex and large. It also means it is very difficult to make them bug free. It is not just Samba that suffers from this problem, other servers such as WinNT don't support every variation of every call and it has almost certainly been a headache for MS developers to support the myriad of SMB calls that are available.

> There are about 65 "top level" operations in the SMB protocol (things like SMBread and SMBwrite). Some of these include hundreds of sub-functions (SMBtrans has at least 120 sub-functions, like DosPrintQAdd and NetSessionEnum). All of them take several options that can change the way they work. Many take dozens of possible "information levels" that change the structures that need to be returned. Samba supports all but two of the "top level" functions. It supports only eight (so far) of the SMBtrans sub-functions. Even NT doesn't support them all.

Samba implements the latest protocol extension, which is called NT LanManager 0.12. This protocol extension contains a "capabilities" field which allows an implementation to explain which of these commands it actually supports. This lets Samba, and other SMB servers and "consumers" avoid implementing every commands in the spec.

To be fair, one reason there are so many commands in SMB is to be able to optimize for use by small computers on a slow network. This seems paradoxical (a large complex protocol runs faster on small computers?) but it makes some sense. The Microsoft design philosophy was that any file operation that could be done by the local computer should be able to be done by SMB. Many of the unusual commands allow complicated commands to be issued remotely using one network message. The many protocol extensions allow a powerful server to tune its behavior to the needs of a slow client. Another reason SMB is so large is that performance gains were made by combining commands, like file open and file read, into a single network message. Since each of these refinements were made in their own protocol extensions, a server must implement both the old and the new versions to be complete. Add to this all the commands added to implement all manner of file locking and caching schemes, as well as the numerous various security frameworks available under Windows, and you end up with SMB as we know it.

An Example SMB Exchange

After requesting a session at the NetBIOS level, a client will use SMBs to request services. The following exchange demonstrates the process of connecting to a filespace service.[8]

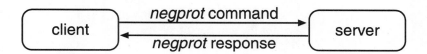

The first step in the process after the connection has been established on the NetBIOS level is to decide on a protocol extension to use for all following communication. The client sends a `negprot` SMB to the server, listing the protocol extensions that it understands. The server responds with the index of the extension that it wants to use, or `0xFFFF` if none of the dialects were acceptable. Dialects newer than the Core and Core Plus protocols supply information in the `negprot` response to indicate their capabilities, such as the maximum buffer size.

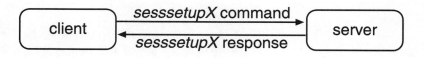

---

8.   Thanks to Richard Sharpe for allowing me to reproduce this example from his document "Just what is SMB?"

What happens after the client and server have decided on a protocol extension depends on whether or not the server is using user level or share level security. User level security associates access rights with specific users, so a client must provide both a username and password. The client does so by transmitting a `sesssetupX` SMB. The server's response indicates whether or not the client supplied a valid username/password pair and, if so, can provide additional information. One of the most important pieces of information in the response is a unique value that must be submitted with all subsequent SMBs transmitted to the server. Note that the Core and Core Plus protocols do not include a `sesssetupX` SMB.

 How Samba Chooses the Unique Identifier

Samba chooses the unique user identifier by mapping the userid of the authenticated user, which can be up to 32 bits in size, to the 16 bit value that must be returned to the client. This was done out of expediency, not necessity. The server can return any value it wishes to use to identify the user for the duration of the session.

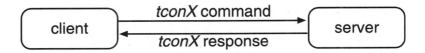

After the client has properly logged in it can proceed to connect to the file tree by sending a `tcon` or `tconX` SMB to the server. This stands for "tree connect" and is analogous to a mount request in NFS. Either SMB specifies the name of the share the client wishes to connect to. If there are no errors, the server responds with the TID (tree identifier) that the client will use to associate additional SMBs with this service. The client may now manipulate files within the share using additional SMBs.

If the server is using share level security, the client is expecting a password to be associated with each service, rather than with a username. As a result the `sesssetupX` SMB is not required, though modern clients send one anyway. This `sesssetupX` SMB, if sent, is not used for authentication, but does contain a username that Samba uses as its first guess when attempting to authenticate subsequent tree connect authentications. Instead the client must authenticate itself each time it mounts a service by including a password, but no username, in each "tree connect" SMB. As in server level security, the server returns a tree identifier that will be used by the client to associate subsequent file operations with this service.

Important Protocol Extensions

 SMB Protocol Extensions

SMB contains a new protocol variant for almost every new Microsoft operating system. Each protocol extension adds options supported by the new operating system version as well as refining (and fixing bugs in) the operation of previous protocols. Some of these protocol extensions are little more than dialects that Samba partially or fully supports. The six most important variants are: Core, Core Plus, LAN Manager 1.0, LAN Manager 2.0, and NT LM 0.12 and CIFS 1.0.

PC NETWORK PROGRAM 1.0 (Core):

The very first protocol variant. The original spec refers to SMB as the MSNET/PCNET file-sharing protocol. Some versions were called PCLAN 1.0. It came to be called the "core" protocol and is the lowest common denominator supported by any SMB implementation.

MICROSOFT NETWORKS 1.03 (Core Plus):

Added some combination commands like Lock&Read and Write&Unlock, as well as some new versions of raw read and write.

XENIX 1.0:

This protocol extension added support for the UNIX specific requirements of the LAN Manager server for Microsoft's XENIX flavor of UNIX (remember that?). It allowed pathnames to be delimitered by either "/" or "\" which appears in no other extension. Instead of supporting long file names, it allowed the ". " that in DOS delimits the extension to appear in an arbitrary location. This extension seems to have disappeared with XENIX. Samba does not support this extension since few clients support it.

LANMAN1.0 (LAN Manager 1.0):

This is the full LANMAN 1.0 protocol, designed to support the new capabilities of OS/2. Some additions allow for processing more than one request at the same time (since OS/2 allows multitasking), long file names, better support for user level authentication, and support for encrypted password authentication. It also adds support for opportunistic file locks.

MICROSOFT NETWORKS 3.0 (DOS LAN Manager 1.0):

This is identical to LANMAN 1.0, but must translate OS/2 error messages into DOS error messages.

LM1.2X002 (LAN Manager 2.0):

This is the complete LANMAN 2.0 protocol, designed to support additional capabilities of OS/2. Some augmentations support additional filesystem types, allow transmission of larger blocks of data in a single request, and refine the operation of commands added in LAN Manager 1.0. Like LAN Manager 1.0, this level supports long file names. This protocol has come to be called LANMAN 2.0 even though the protocol extension is called LM1.2.

DOS LM1.2X002 (DOS LAN Manager 2.0):

This is identical to LAN Manager 2.0, but translates OS/2 error messages into DOS error messages.

LANMAN2.1 (LAN Manager 2.1):

This extension adds some refinements and bug-fixes to the LAN Manager 2.0 protocol, as well as adding support for authenticating users as members of a security domain. It also allows the server and consumer to negotiate which new-fangled options they both actually support, simplifying implementation of the increasingly complex protocol.

NT LM 0.12 (NT LM 0.12):

Adds new commands to support new Windows NT concepts, such as new encryption techniques and full support for the NT domain security model.

Samba (NT LM 0.12):

This is the variation of NT LM 0.12 supported by Samba. It supports all required commands and a significant subset of the remaining optional commands.

CIFS 1.0 (Common Internet File System):

This is Microsoft's proposal for a protocol to fill the same role in the Windows world that NFS fills in the UNIX world—transparent file access anywhere on the Internet. It is still under development, but resembles a cleaned up version of NT LM 0.12 restricted to using NetBIOS over TCP/IP as a transport protocol. Microsoft has proposed using CIFS as a more efficient replacement for HTTP. Sun has responded by proposing WebNFS. The pace of change boggles the mind.[9]

There are currently at least eight distinct protocol extensions in the SMB spec—there may be more, but will be trivial variations on these extensions. Luckily, there are really only six important protocol extensions: Core, Core Plus, LAN Manager 1.0, LAN Manager 2.0, and NT LM 0.12 and CIFS 1.0. Samba supports all of these to one extent or another.

Core

The SMB protocol was first described in a 1987 Microsoft/Intel document called Microsoft Networks/OpenNET-FILE SHARING PROTOCOL, which defined the "PC NETWORK PROGRAM 1.0" protocol extension. This definition became later known as the "Core Protocol." It defined a simple client/server file and print sharing protocol. Some of the commands it defined were:

Negotiate Protocol: Allows the client and server to negotiate a specific "protocol extension" to use. Because of the large number of protocol extensions, this is perhaps the more important command in the protocol.

Tree Connect/Disconnect: Requests a connection to a shared block (disk) or character (printer) device from a server using a plaintext name/password pair for authentication and returns a Tree ID. A valid Tree ID is required for all subsequent commands.

File Access Operators: Open File obtains a file handle for accessing an existing file. Create File obtains a file handle for creating a new file. The file handle returned can be used in subsequent read, write, lock, unlock, flush and close requests.

---

9.   This may have happened the other way around, with Microsoft announcing CIFS in response to WebNFS. I found accounts explaining it both ways.

Other File Operators: File operators which don't require an open file handle, or require that there not be an open file handle are file create, file delete, directory create, directory delete, get file attributes, and set file attributes.

Other miscellaneous commands: Search for file in a directory, check a file path's validity, open printer file, close printer file, write printer file, create temporary file, get server attributes, message delivery commands and more.

 The Madness of SMB

The madness of SMB is illustrated by the fact that although print specific commands are defined they are not actually used by clients! Instead clients use open, read, write, close and some undocumented IPC calls to do printing. Samba supports both methods.

Core Plus

Core Plus was introduced a year later and describes a few relatively trivial modifications to the Core protocol. It allowed the combination of separate operations into a single SMB, which reduced network load. Examples of such calls are Lock&Read and Write&Unlock. The rawread and rawwrite SMBs were introduced.

LAN Manager 1.0

According to the official Microsoft/Intel document, Lan Manager 1.0 defined "extensions to the OpenNET/Microsoft Networks File Sharing Protocol (sometimes referred to as the 'core' protocol) that are required to support Operating Systems richer in function than MS-DOS 3.x." Yes, believe it or not, Microsoft saw the need to support operating systems richer in function than MS-DOS.

Lan Manager 1.0 defined new capabilities necessary to provide complete support for OS/2. These include recognition that OS/2 is a multitasking operating system and may wish to have more than one simultaneous network connection open at the same time. It also recognizes that processes should always be able to clean up after themselves properly. In contrast, the Core protocol had to recognize the possibility that the client process, which ran under DOS, had crashed and that no remaining process would be present to properly close all open connections.

Lan Manager 1.0 provided a richer set of authentication options, including support for encrypted passwords. In particular Lan Manager 1.0 extends the concept of user level authentication by providing a user id token. The core protocol allowed for user level authentication, but left the process of actually implementing it to the specific server. Each client connection was still required to authenticate itself with a username/password pair. Under Lan Manager 1.0, a client will authenticate once during the session setup operation, then use the user token to authenticate future connections in the same session.

 More SMB Madness

The addition of the `rawread` and `rawwrite` commands was actually a step towards the deterioration of the SMB protocol. They are headerless (a bad idea) and are allowed to be up to 64k in size even if the client and server specifically negotiate a smaller size. Later protocol extensions have paid the price for this by making many operations more complex and difficult to implement.

Lan Manager 1.0 also added the "opportunistic lock" file locking option. Opportunistic locking is explained in more detail on page 197

Additional file path semantics were added, such as supporting the " . " and " . . " as parts of a file pathname with their usual meanings. Additional error facilities were provided to cover errors unique to OS/2. Some variants of this protocol extension require that these error conditions be translated into a DOS error.

LAN Manager 2.0

The Lan Manager 2.0 extension added support for long file names. In typical SMB fashion it did so by adding a totally new set of SMBs, rather than extending the existing SMBs. This extension also added the ability for a server to specify whether or not it uses case sensitive pathnames. Unfortunately, no existing Microsoft client properly deals with a case insensitive server.

Lan Manager 2.0 also fixed bugs and refined parts of the Lan Manager 1.0 protocol, adding compound commands which can be used to reduce network load by performing more than one operation in a single network call (i.e., file open and read, or session setup and tree connect). All of these compound commands greatly increases the complexity of a LAN Manager 2.0 implementation, but do provide some optimization of network usage. Other additions provide more options aimed at OS/2, such as allowing the transmission of larger data blocks and supporting additional file system types.

NT LAN Manager 0.12

This protocol extension contains all of the Windows NT specific extensions to the protocol. These include support for new encryption policies, 64 bit file and locking offsets, unicode strings, NT error codes, and additional protocol optimizations.

 Not All Optional SMBs are Really Optional

In principle all of the additional commands provided by NT LAN Manager 0.12 are negotiated and optional. However, Samba implements many of the optional commands because, regardless of what is stated in Microsoft's own SMB spec, they are not really optional. Microsoft clients break if some of these "optional" commands are not implemented.

Common Internet File System (CIFS)

The Common Internet File System is Microsoft's effort to create a standard method for sharing filesystems across the Internet. The draft of CIFS has been submitted to the Internet Engineering Task Force for consideration as an Internet standard. CIFS is basically NT LAN Manager 0.12 with some of the redundancy cleaned out and some additional functions, such as symbolic links, needed to support UNIX filesystems.

CIFS Specification is Incomplete

Jeremy Allison, one of the Samba developers, notes that the CIFS spec is still woefully incomplete and inaccurate, failing to specify everything that you need to know to get a server up and running.

Functional Units of a Windows Network

Workgroups and NT Domains

 An NT domain is not an Internet domain

Resist the urge to confuse an NT domain with an Internet domain. An Internet domain is a host naming convention used to ensure that no two individual hosts on the global Internet have the same hostname. For example, the host *frodo.tucc.uab.edu* is located with the *uab.edu* domain, which is assigned to the University of Alabama at Birmingham.

An NT Domain is an administrative grouping of hosts on a Windows Network which allows for centralized administration of user accounts. Despite the hierarchical organization of domains in Microsoft's network browser, NT Domains have nothing to do with unique namespaces. I frequently wish that Microsoft had chosen a word other than Domain, like "Realm" (of course, then people would get confused with Kerberos Realms). Just remember that in dealing with UNIX and Microsoft, Microsoft's definition will likely differ from the more commonly-used computer science jargon definition, so be sure to check your point of reference.

The roles that workgroups and NT domains fill on a Windows network overlap and, as a result, the two terms are often mistakenly used interchangeably. Both workgroups and NT domains are administrative groupings of computer systems which usually represent political or managerial units in an organization. This grouping is used to provide the organization which is displayed in network browsers like the "Network Neighborhood" under Windows 95 and Windows NT 4.0. To a user Workgroups and NT domains look the same in the Network Neighborhood.

This confusion between the terms exists because the structure of Windows Networking has evolved as Microsoft's operating systems have become more powerful yet has remained backwards compatible to the original simple design that was part of Windows for Workgroups. For example, machines running Windows NT Workstation can be configured to be part of a workgroup or an NT domain and behave differently in either situation. A Windows 95 computer cannot strictly be part of an NT domain, but can ask users to log into an NT domain and can retrieve a list of users for access control. The subtle relationship between workgroups and NT domains also affects browsing, explained in more detail beginning on page 38.

 Samba Support Windows 95 Network Logons

Samba now fully supports the Windows 95 method of logging into an NT domain, or "logging into the network." This means that a Windows 95 machine can behave as if it is logging into an NT domain, but actually log into a Samba server.

 NT Domain Controller Protocol

The NT domain controller protocol is deliberately undocumented, but is based on running the Distributed Computer Environment (DCE) protocol over an SMB named pipe.

The most significant difference between workgroups and NT domains concerns the administration of access control information. Within a workgroup access control is configured locally on each host. Windows

NT Workstation computers in a workgroup must maintain an independent list of users and the corresponding passwords. Stated in Windows lingo, each Windows NT Workstation host has an independent *Security Account Manager* (SAM). Users may need to remember a different username and/or password for each network service provided by different hosts. A Windows 95 machine, if not configured to log into an NT domain, also uses distributed access controls. Each user must control access to resources using *share level security*. This means a password is assigned to each access mode on each shared resource. This password must be distributed amongst all users who must be granted access to the resource.

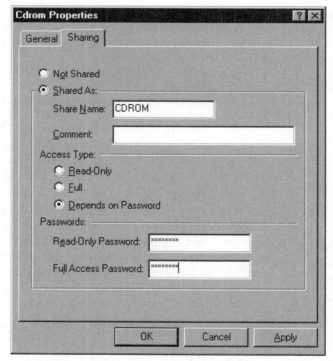

A Windows 95 share control panel configured to use share level security

In contrast, an NT domain stores user account information in a central location. Specifically, the information is stored on the *primary domain controller*, which must be a computer running Windows NT Server.[10] Another host, also running Windows NT Server, can act as a *backup*

---

10. Samba version 1.9.18, which came out as this book was in the final production stage, provides limited support of the NT domain authentication protocol.

domain controller. This host periodically synchronizes its SAM with the primary domain controller. When accessing a resource in a Windows NT domain, a user's username and password are verified by checking against the SAM stored on the primary domain controller or a backup domain controller.

This means that a user's username and password are consistent across all hosts in the NT domain. In general, this makes administration of access policies on the network significantly easier. Users only need to log in once and only need to remember one username and one password. It is less likely that a user will forget a single password, and thus less likely the password will be written down in some place that might be seen by an intruder. The organizational benefits of an NT domain can be extended to Windows 95 machines if they are configured to ask users to log into an NT domain. Resources are then shared to the network using *user level security*. Access controls are granted by assigning access rights to specific users while the job of authenticating the identity of a user is pushed off to the primary domain controller.

Please make note of the confusing fact that an NT domain is really just a special kind of workgroup. A workgroup and an NT domain with the same name refer to the same group of computers, except in subtle situations caused by multiple network segments. A host can identify itself as a member of an NT Domain without participating in its authentication structure. This host will view the NT domain as a workgroup and show all members of the NT domain/workgroup grouped together in its network browser. This behavior provides backwards compatibility to hosts running Windows for Workgroups, older versions of OS/2, and UNIX hosts running Samba. It also allows any version of Windows to be organized with an NT domain on the network even if it is not participating in the authentication structure of the NT domain.

 Security Through Obscurity is No Security!

Microsoft has chosen not to publish the protocol used to implement centralized access control from Primary and Backup Domain Controllers. There are two possible reasons they have chosen to do this: 1) They wish to make it difficult for non-Microsoft products to participate fully in an NT domain, or 2) They believe that access controls for an NT domain can be kept more secure if the protocol used to implement this is not publicly known.

While I find the first possibility extremely annoying, it would not be anomalous behavior for Microsoft. However, I find the second possibility especially troubling. The consensus in the computer security and cryptography community is that an algorithm can only be considered secure if it is open to public scrutiny. That is, the only way to know a protocol is secure is to show that an attacker still cannot break a specific application of the protocol even though the algorithms used by the protocol are published. For example, the security of a good cipher is a function of the secrecy of the specific key used, not the secrecy of the algorithm. Access control systems like Kerberos and NIS+ stand up to this challenge. Both have been examined, and in some cases, improved through thorough examination throughout the computer science community. Further, because they are completely open protocols, any OS vendor can choose to implement them.

Kerberos will be available as an access control protocol in Windows NT version 5.0, though, as usual, Microsoft has added their own "extensions and enhancements" to the protocol. Also note that a lively effort is underway to reverse-engineer the domain authentication protocols. Samba version 1.9.18 contains experimental code that will eventually allow Samba to fully participate in an NT domain.

A UNIX Machine running Samba cannot (yet) participate in the authentication framework provided by the NT domain. There have been many requests to incorporate this ability into Samba. Unfortunately, Microsoft will not publish the protocol for participating in an NT domain. However, Samba can be configured to use a Windows NT server to authenticate the identity of users. If usernames on the UNIX hosts are different from the NT domain for the same user, Samba can be configured to map one username to another. While the user may need to know another username and/or password to access other services on the UNIX host, Samba shares will be seamlessly available.

Further, Samba can be configured to authenticate a user when he or she "logs into the network" on a Windows 95 machine. This does not mean that Samba can act as a primary or secondary domain controller, it does mean that the benefits of central access control management can be extended to Windows 95 machines without the use of a Windows NT Server. In other words, a Linux machine running Samba can be used as a low-cost replacement for an NT Server in many contexts. These configurations are explained in detail on page 228.

Browsing

 Summary of Browser Response Time

As much as 45 minutes may pass after a primary domain controller is shut down before its NT domain will be removed from the browse list in other NT domains and workgroups.

In a NetBEUI, IPX, or non-routed TCP/IP environment, as much as 36 minutes may pass after a host has been shut down before it will be removed from the browse list.

In an environment with multiple TCP/IP network segments, browser synchronizations between the domain master browser and local master browsers will take place at least every 15 minutes. If your network spans two segments and a computer is added or removed from the network, it may take as long as 51 minutes for the change to be propagated to the browse list in the other network segment. This is because, in the worst case scenario, it will take 36 minutes for the change to be reflected in the local browse list, and then an additional 15 minutes for the local master browser to synchronize the browse list with the master browser on the other segment.

If you have three or more network segments you will have one segment containing the domain master browser and two segments containing local master browsers. It can take as long as 30 minutes for the two local master browsers to synchronize their browse lists. As a result, it can take as long as 66 minutes for a change in a segment containing a local master browser to be reflected across your entire network.

Viewing the resources available on a Windows Network is known as *browsing*. The list of other hosts and domains available on a network is called the *browse list*. Maintaining the browse list allows Windows to present other hosts offering network services through a point-and-click user interface rather than asking users to remember the names of remote hosts and services. Under Windows 95 and Windows NT 4.0 the browse list is used to construct the view of the network in the "network neighborhood" and Windows Explorer.

The Windows 95 "network neighborhood."

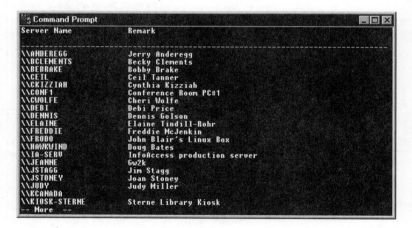

Output from the NET USE *command.*

The browse list is also accessible from the command line using the NET VIEW command. When a menu of other hosts on the network is presented to the user it was probably generated from the browse list.

The browser system is designed to save network bandwidth by reducing the need to use broadcasting for NetBIOS name resolution, as well as dynamically maintaining a list of available servers for users to browse. The browser protocol is designed to operate correctly without explicit configuration across a wide variety of network structures. As you probably expect, there are situations where the protocol can exhibit undesirable behavior. The system has become especially critical now that Windows networks can operate over TCP/IP where all hosts in a domain may not be accessible by broadcasting. Understanding how the protocol works will help you eliminate these problematic situations.

The Master Browser and Backup Browsers

The browse list for a workgroup or NT domain is maintained on a computer called the *master browser*. Whenever a computer offers a network service for the first time it broadcasts a server announcement packet. The master browser receives this packet and adds the computer's name to the browse list. In response, the master browser transmits a list of *backup browsers* back to this new computer.

Each domain or NT group will contain at least one backup browser. Maintaining a copy of the browse list on the backup browser eliminates the need to rebuild the browse list if the master browser goes down. When the master browser receives a server announcement packet from a new computer that is a potential master browser the master browser may notify the computer that sent the packet to become a backup browser. The master browser will maintain 1 backup browser for every 32 NT Workstation hosts or every 16 Windows 95 hosts in a workgroup or NT domain.

If the network is using NetBEUI or IPX as a transport protocol only one master browser will exist for each workgroup or NT domain. This is possible because every host on the network can be contacted by a broadcast packet. Windows networking over TCP/IP, where Samba operates, is slightly more complex. Since a broadcast packet will not reach all members of a workgroup or NT domain that spans more than one TCP/IP subnet, one master browser must be maintained on each network segment.[11] To maintain the proper number of master browsers on a network, a master browser will demote itself to a backup browser, and call a browser election if it receives a packet from a host claiming it should be the master browser instead.

11. With the exception of networks where routers are configured to forward broadcast packets.

Samba Cannot Act as a Backup Browser

Samba does not have the ability to function as a backup browser, even in the new version of nmbd that will be released with Samba version 1.9.19.

When a master browser comes on-line it will ask all hosts in the workgroup or NT domain to identify themselves by sending a RequestAnnouncement datagram. Each host that receives the RequestAnnouncement must reply after a random interval of up to 30 seconds. The randomized delay prevents the network from suddenly being overwhelmed by a flood of server announcements.

A host sends a server announcement to the master browser once every minute immediately after its SMB networking service is started, which usually occurs at boot time. The time interval between announcements increases until the announcements occur every 12 minutes. If a master browser hasn't received an announcement from a specific host for 36 minutes the host is removed from the browse list.

A master browser in an NT domain is also responsible for advertising the NT domain to master browsers in other NT domains. It does this by broadcasting a domain announcement packet every minute for the first five minutes after it becomes a master browser. After five minutes it issues a domain announcement every 15 minutes. The domain announcement contains three fields:

1. The name of the domain.

2. The operating system of the master browser.

3. Whether or not the master browser is also a primary domain controller.

The master browser is also responsible for receiving these broadcasts from other master browsers and adding the corresponding domains to the browse list. If a master browser has not received a domain announcement for 45 minutes, it will remove the NT domain from the browse list.

The browse list is limited to a size of 64K, which sets a limit of approximately 2000 to 3000 hosts per workgroup or NT domain. Realistically, if you have more than 100 hosts in a workgroup or NT domain, you should probably consider splitting it into separate groups.

The Browser Election Protocol

The master browser is selected through a process called the *browser election protocol*. The election protocol is biased to favor hosts running Windows NT Server and Workstation, but it is also possible for a Windows 95 or UNIX host running Samba to become the master browser.

A browse election is initiated when any computer broadcasts an election packet. The election packet contains a number representing the sender's operating system "level," the length of time the sender has been on-line, and the sender's name. An election packet will be broadcast under any of these three conditions:

1. A browse client is unable to contact a Master Browser.

2. A Backup Browser attempts to update its browse list and cannot find a Master Browser.

3. A Preferred Master Browser comes on-line.

 Details: The Election Criteria

The browse election is decided primarily on the basis of the *election criteria*. This criteria is really a four byte number composed of three parts.

The first (most significant) byte encodes the operating system type. The second and third bytes encode the election protocol version. The fourth (least significant) byte encodes the per version criteria, which identifies specific features about the browser.

Operating System Type:
Windows NT Server 4.0: 33
Windows NT Server 3.51: 32
Windows NT Workstation 4.0: 17
Windows NT Workstation 3.51: 16
Windows 95: 1
Windows for Workgroups: 1

Per Version Criteria (sum):
    Primary Domain Controller: 128 (bit 7)
    WINS client: 32 (bit 5)
    Preferred Master Browser: 8 (bit 3)
    Running Master Browser: 4 (bit 2)
    MaintainServerList=yes: 2 (bit 1)
    Running Backup Browser: 1 (bit 0)

When a browser receives an election packet the winner is decided by the following criteria:

1. **Election protocol version**: The browser running the highest election protocol version wins the election. Currently all system types set this value to 1. Some descriptions of the election protocol don't even mention this value since it doesn't yet have any effect on the outcome.

2. **Operating system type:** The browser running the highest operating system type wins the election. Operating systems are rated in this order, from lowest to highest: Windows for Workgroups, Windows 95, Windows NT Workstation, Windows NT Server. A newer version of an OS always beats an older version. Samba allows the value representing its OS type to be set with the `os level` configuration option. It is set to 0 by default, which causes it to lose all elections. It can be set to any value from 0 to 255.

   A server that is a "preferred master browser" has an edge of another server with the same OS level. Normally, only an NT server is a preferred master browser, though Samba can be configured to be one.

3. **Time On-Line:** If the election still has not been decided, the host which has been on-line the longest wins the election.

4. **Hostname:** If the election still has not been decided the host with the lexically lower name wins the election. (i.e., Aardvark beats Ziggy).

If a browser receives an election packet indicating that it has won an election it attempts to notify other browsers. After a delay based on the browser's current role, the browser broadcasts an election packet. A host becomes the master browser if, after broadcasting four election packets, it does not receive another packet indicating it has lost an election. If the host does receive a packet indicating it has lost an election it becomes a backup browser.

Cross Subnet Name Resolution

The first problem to be solved with using NetBIOS over TCP/IP is the resolution of names. This is necessary because a server will not necessarily be able to reach all other servers using broadcasting. WINS, for Windows Internet Name Service, provides a dynamically updated central database which can be used to resolve hostnames into IP addresses. The second solution is to define specific IP addresses for each host in the LMHOSTS file (which is described on page 45).

CAUTION!

Using a WINS server is the easiest way to allow for cross subnet name resolution.

Windows Internet Name Service

RFCs 1001 and 1002, which originally described NetBIOS over TCP/IP, described four possible name resolution environments. The "b-node," for *broadcast node*, environment used broadcasts to resolve and register NetBIOS names. This is the same mechanism used by hosts on NetBEUI and NetBIOS over IPX networks. The "p-node," for *point-to-point node*, environment used NetBIOS Name Service (NBNS), a service running on a specific known IP address. Hosts in a p-node environment register themselves with the NBNS when their networking service is started. The NBNS is responsible for storing the address of this machine and ensuring that no name is duplicated on the network. The service is something like a dynamic version of Internet Domain Name Service (DNS). Rather than being hard coded, hosts register and de-register themselves with the service as they go on and off-line. Unlike DNS, the namespace managed by NBNS is flat. The other environments, called "m-node" for *mixed node* and "h-mode" for *hybrid mode* allow both NBNS and broadcasting to be used to resolve names, depending on the specific situation a host finds itself in. The difference between the two modes is the order with which they try broadcast and unicast for name resolution. A mixed-mode client uses broadcast first, then unicast. A hybrid-mode client uses unicast, then broadcast. Microsoft hosts use this mixed method for resolving hostnames over TCP/IP.

Windows Internet Name Service (WINS) is based on and is compatible with the NBNS protocol, and is therefore compatible with other implementations of these RFCs, like Samba. This would seem to be a rare instance of Microsoft using a publicly defined protocol, yet they modified NBNS quite a bit to create WINS. When a new service is made available on the network, such as when a Windows machine boots or when Samba is started, the service must be registered with a WINS server if it is to be available to clients located on other subnets. The

WINS server records the name of the host, the NT domain the host is part of, and the IP address of the host. Whenever a machine attempts to resolve a hostname it first checks with the WINS server. If the host is not registered with the WINS server it will attempt to find the host using a broadcast. If the host is still not found, a "computer or sharename could not be found" error is returned. Samba includes an implementation of WINS that can be queried by Microsoft networking clients. Samba will also properly register itself with any WINS server.

WINS also includes a method for replicating its database of hostnames with other WINS servers. The provides a method for creating a backup WINS server that hosts can query if the primary WINS server is unavailable. It also allows large networks which are linked by slow links to distribute WINS servers closer to clients to provide faster name resolution.

Unfortunately, there are problems with WINS replication. The protocol only provides for replicating changes in the database on regular intervals. This means that there will always be a period when the WINS servers are out of date. Unlike DNS the protocol does not attempt to query other WINS servers if it can't resolve a name, and has no concept of authoritative data. In our environment here at UAB we originally tried to run a WINS server for each NT domain. Unfortunately, there were so many separate WINS servers that they were never completely in sync with each other. It was finally realized that setting up two WINS servers, a primary and a backup, for the entire campus was a simpler and perfectly adequate solution.

A final problem with WINS replication is that it is a proprietary Microsoft protocol. This means that the implementation of WINS included with Samba can't replicate its database with a Microsoft WINS server. There is some talk of implementing a system for replicating information between Samba WINS servers, decoding the Microsoft replication protocol, or using LDAP (Lightweight Directory Access Protocol). None of the possibilities were available at the time this book was written.

LMHOSTS

The LMHOSTS file, which stands for LanManager Hosts, is analogous to the UNIX /etc/hosts file. The LMHOSTS file allows specific hostnames to be mapped to IP addresses. It also provides a syntax for defining the domain a host resides in as well as loading a LMHOSTS file from a shared directory on a server. The syntax of the LMHOSTS file is discussed in the implementation section of chapter 7 (page 218).

Cross Subnet Browsing

Windows 95 does not have the ability to be aware of and contact a domain master browser.

Browsing across TCP/IP subnets is complicated and contains many subtle issues. It has taken several tries for Microsoft to get the system to its current mostly working state. Microsoft introduced the ability of browse lists to span multiple TCP/IP subnets with Windows NT 3.5. The implementation allows NT domains, but not workgroups, to span multiple TCP/IP subnets. According to Microsoft documentation, a workgroup spanning two subnets is really two completely separate workgroups sharing the same name. Unfortunately, with Samba (and even in a few cases involving Windows 95 and Windows NT machines in the same workgroup/NT domain) workgroups can appear to span more than one subnet from certain perspectives. These situations will be explained in detail, but for the sake of simplicity I will only refer to NT domains for the time being. To make cross subnet browsing possible we have to introduce the *domain master browser*.

Domain Master Browser

The domain master browser is responsible for maintaining the browse list for an NT domain spanning more than one TCP/IP subnet. Each subnet of the NT domain elects its own master browser. Each master browser is considered *authoritative* for the names of hosts contained in its own subnet. Once selected as a master browser a host queries the WINS server to see if a domain master browser exists for the NT domain. If one does the master browser contacts the domain master browser and schedules a browse list synchronization. These synchronizations take place at least every 15 minutes. The master browser running on the primary domain controller always acts as the domain master browser. If there are no hosts running NT Server, a Samba host can also act as a domain master browser.

An Example of Cross Subnet Browsing

The behavior of the protocol is easiest to explain with an example. Consider the following NT domain which spans three subnets.

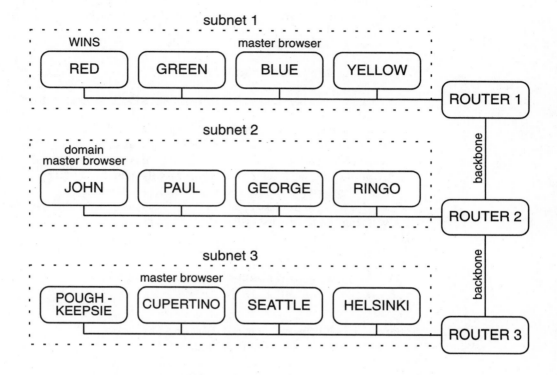

For simplicity, also assume the three subnets are connected via routers attached to a backbone. Also assume that each host is offering a network service and therefore should appear in the browse list. RED will be defined as the WINS server. JOHN is the primary domain controller for the network. Note that the WINS server doesn't need to be running on a host in the NT domain—it could be located on a host that is part of a different NT domain.

When the machines are booted an election for master browser takes place. Because JOHN is the primary domain controller it will win the election on its subnet and become the domain master browser. Assume that BLUE and CUPERTINO become the master browsers for their corresponding subnets. As each host makes a service available on the network it broadcasts an announcement on its local subnet and registers its name with the WINS server. The master browser on each subnet registers each of these hosts when it receives the broadcast announcement. Each master browser is considered "authoritative" for the name it learns of via a local broadcast. A record of a machine located on another subnet is considered "non-authoritative."

If these machines were all started at the same time, immediately after boot the browse lists in each domain will contain these hosts:

subnet 1: **RED, GREEN, BLUE, YELLOW**

subnet 2: **JOHN, PAUL, GEORGE, RINGO**

subnet 3: **POUGHKEEPSIE, CUPERTINO, SEATTLE, HELSINKI**

Now examine subnet 1. Once BLUE is elected as the master browser it will ask WINS for the location of the domain master browser. WINS will answer with the IP address of JOHN. At this point BLUE notifies JOHN that it is the local master browser for its subnet. JOHN then schedules a synchronization request with BLUE. After the synchronization has taken place in both directions between the network segments the browse lists will contain these hosts:

 Browser Synchronization Requires Anonymous Login

The browser synchronization request is performed by making an SMB connection to the \\SERVERNAME\IPC$ service using an anonymous login. This means that a server must support anonymous logins for browsing to work.

subnet 1: **RED, GREEN, BLUE, YELLOW**, JOHN, PAUL, GEORGE, RINGO

subnet 2: **JOHN, PAUL, GEORGE, RINGO**, RED, GREEN, BLUE, YELLOW

subnet 3: **POUGHKEEPSIE, CUPERTINO, SEATTLE, HELSINKI**

Note that hostnames in boldface are authoritative, hosts in regular type are non-authoritative.

The same sequence of events will take place between JOHN and CUPERTINO, of subnet 3. After the subsequent synchronization the browse lists will contain these values:

subnet 1: **RED, GREEN, BLUE, YELLOW**, JOHN, PAUL, GEORGE, RINGO, SEATTLE, POUGHKEEPSIE, CUPERTINO, HELSINKI subnet 2: **JOHN, PAUL, GEORGE, RINGO**, RED, GREEN, BLUE, YELLOW

subnet 3: **POUGHKEEPSIE, CUPERTINO, SEATTLE, HELSINKI,** RED, GREEN, BLUE, YELLOW, JOHN, PAUL, GEORGE, RINGO

The lists will finally all be consistent once BLUE and JOHN synchronize again.

subnet 1: **RED, GREEN, BLUE, YELLOW,** JOHN, PAUL, GEORGE, RINGO, SEATTLE, POUGHKEEPSIE, CUPERTINO, HELSINKI

subnet 2: **JOHN, PAUL, GEORGE, RINGO**, RED, GREEN, BLUE, YELLOW, SEATTLE, POUGHKEEPSIE, CUPERTINO, HELSINKI

subnet 3: **POUGHKEEPSIE, CUPERTINO, SEATTLE, HELSINKI,** RED, GREEN, BLUE, YELLOW, JOHN, PAUL, GEORGE, RINGO

If either router fails the following will occur:

1. Names of hosts on the opposite side of a broken router will continue to be maintained in the browse list for up to 36 minutes. Once the router is restored the browse list will not show all hosts until all master browsers have synchronized with the domain master browser.

2. Attempts to access a computer on the other side of a broken router will fail.

3. If a host is cut off from the WINS server by the broken router it will only be able to access hosts on its own subnet using NetBIOS broadcast name resolution. The host will be unable to resolve the IP address of hosts located on other subnets.

Unusual and Frustrating Situations

In a heterogeneous network consisting of multiple versions of Windows as well as UNIX hosts running Samba, there are many situations that can lead to unexpected and undesirable browser behavior.

Situation 1:

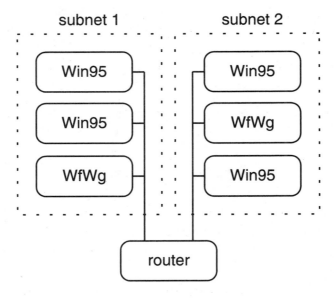

In this situation there will be two separate workgroups known by the same name. A master browser will be elected on each subnet. Neither master browser will be aware of the other, or any other workgroups or NT domains. The browse list will list only the hosts on the same subnet. If the hosts are configured to use WINS, it will be possible to access a host on the remote subnet if a user knows the remote host's name. One of the Windows 95 computers on each subnet will become the local master browser.

Situation 2:

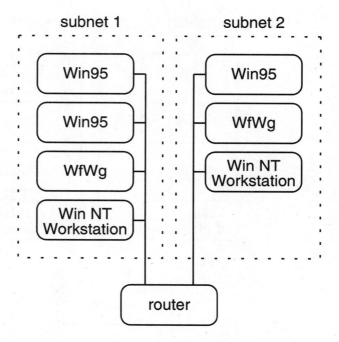

Since there is no Windows NT Server host acting as the primary domain controller, this situation will behave exactly the same as the first situation. Remember that Windows NT Workstation computers that are not part of an NT domain cannot browse across subnets. The NT Workstation computers on each side will become local master browsers.

Situation 3:

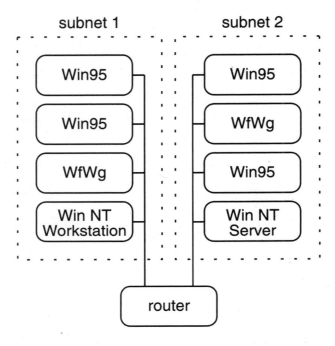

Assuming that the Windows NT Server host in subnet 2 is configured as a primary domain controller and the Windows NT host in subnet 1 is a member of the resulting NT domain, this situation will behave as a single NT domain. Browsing will work properly across both subnets. The NT Server on subnet 2 will be the domain master browser. The NT Server on subnet 1 will be a local master browser. Note that a Samba server could be included on either side with no change in behavior.

Situation 4:

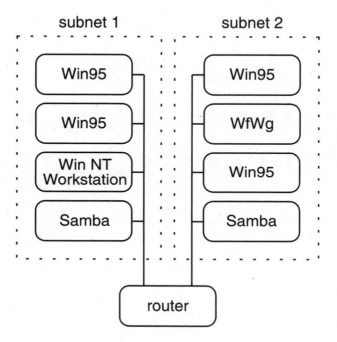

If Samba is properly configured, this situation has the same effect as Situation 3. Either of the Samba servers can be configured to become the domain master browser. The Samba server on the other subnet will become a local master browser. Note that if the Samba server on subnet 1 were eliminated the cross subnet browse list would not be properly maintained.

Chapter 3: Downloading and Building Samba

Enough background info—now its time to install Samba. This section covers downloading Samba, deciding if you should build Samba yourself, and then step-by-step instructions for performing the build. Most of this chapter was written to help you along if you are not familiar with compiling software on a UNIX machine.

If you are already comfortable with building software yourself, skip ahead to the description of the Makefile options, starting on page 63.

Where to Get Samba

The latest version of Samba will always be available from the Samba home page, located at `http://samba.anu.edu.au/pub/samba/`. The Samba web page also provides links to the latest incarnation of the Samba FAQ, notices about recent versions, and other useful reference information. The Samba archive is accessible via ftp at `ftp://samba.anu.edu.au/pub/samba`. Since Australia's access to the Internet is still limited (relatively speaking) you should be polite and download Samba from an archive located closer to your geographic location. The current "official" mirror sites are:

```
ftp://sunsite.auc.dk/pub/unix/networking/samba/
ftp://src.doc.ic.ac.uk/packages/samba/
ftp://ftp.uni-trier.de/pub/unix/network/samba/
ftp://sunsite.mff.cuni.cz/Net/Protocols/Samba/
ftp://ring.aist.go.jp/archives/net/samba/
ftp://ring.asahi-net.or.jp/archives/net/samba/
ftp://ftp.cs.ucr.edu/pub/software/samba
ftp://ftp.ua.pt/pub/misc/samba/
ftp://sunsite.unc.edu/pub/packages/samba/
```

One of these archives is Sunsite USA, which is in turn mirrored on many sites all over the world.

 The Sunsite Archive

If you don't already know about the Sunsite archive its high time you discovered it. Sunsite is an enormous software archive hosted by the University of North Carolina. The Sunsite web page is located at `http://www.sunsite.unc.edu` and the corresponding ftp archive is located at `ftp://sunsite.unc.edu`. Sunsite was started in 1992 to distribute software for Sun workstations, but quickly grew into a more general distribution site. The UNC Sunsite is now technically Sunsite USA as there are now Sunsites located all over the world. Snapshots of the Sunsite archive are available on inexpensive CD-ROMs from companies such as InfoMagic.

Obtaining Samba Via CVS

CAUTION!

A bug exists in Samba versions prior to 1.9.17p2 that allows an attacker to exploit a buffer overrun bug to obtain root access to your system. Since it is possible for an attacker to determine what version of Samba is running on your system and an exploit for this bug was widely disseminated on the Internet, you can expect somebody to try it on your system sooner or later.

People familiar with the GNU Concurrent Versions System (cvs) may wish to use cvs to maintain their Samba source code. Using cvs makes upgrading to new versions simpler and allows hackers to make local changes to Samba without having to reapply their patches with each new release. You can learn more about obtaining Samba this way at `http://samba.anu.edu.au/cvs.html`.

To Compile or Not to Compile?

Should you install a precompiled binary for your system or build Samba yourself? The answer to this question depends on several factors. A precompiled binary can save you a lot of time, especially if it is organized into an easily installed package. A Red Hat package is now distributed from the main Samba archive and a Debian package of the latest version is available from Debian archives. Packages are also available for Sun Solaris and AIX.

While I'm happy to be beyond the days when I had to compile practically every program on my system, I still prefer to build Samba myself. If you like playing with the latest bleeding edge alpha release, like to tune compile-time options to your system, or just like building software yourself, you should know that building Samba is not difficult.

International Traffic in Arms Regulations (ITAR)

The International Traffic in Arms Regulations are laws that govern the export of technology with potential military applications from the United States. Part of these regulations place restrictions on the ability of U.S. citizens to distribute cryptographic technology outside of the U.S. and Canada. Unfortunately (in the opinion of this author and many learned scholars) these rules are a holdover from the time when IBM ruled the computer industry and computers were the size of Volkswagens. Cryptographic technology has traditionally been considered a military secret, useful only to governments and a handful of huge corporations. Cheap computers and the spread of the global Internet have made strong cryptography accessible and useful to average people. Many argue that, with the increasing amount of sensitive information flowing over relatively open networks, such as the Internet, strong cryptography is a necessary part of normal computer use.

CAUTION!

Samba version 1.9.18 does not require `libdes` to support encrypted passwords

Unfortunately, the law has not kept pace with the technology. As a result, U.S. companies cannot export products containing strong cryptography, while corporations based in other countries face no such restrictions. The first amendment prevents the government from restricting the export of papers and books about cryptography, including the source code for cryptographic software printed on paper. As a result strong cryptography developed in the U.S. is already available everywhere in the world. The DES libraries used in Samba were developed, like Samba, in Australia. There is nothing illegal about `importing` them into the United States by downloading them from their ftp site located at `ftp://samba.anu.edu.au/pub/libdes/`. Unfortunately, if these libraries were placed on the CD-ROM included with this book, SSC would not be able to sell this book outside of North America legally.

You can learn more about ITAR and other electronic public policy issues on the Electronic Frontier Foundation web site, at `http://www.eff.org`. For a very frank discussion of encryption policies and algorithms, consult the Cypherpunks home page at `ftp://ftp.csua.berkeley.edu/pub/cypherpunks/Home.html`.

An excellent archive of ITAR related information can be found at `http://www.cypher.net/info/itar.html`. Another excellent source of information is the Voter's Telecommunications Watch, which can be found at `http://www.vtw.org`.

 Data Encryption Standard

DES (Data Encryption Standard) has been a world-wide encryption standard since it was approved by the National Bureau of Standards (now the National Institute of Standards and Technology) in 1976. In the 1970s little was known about the science of cryptography outside of military institutions, like the National Security Agency (NSA). Standardizing on a single public algorithm meant that the cipher could be tested and certified and encryption equipment produced by different manufacturers could interoperate.

The algorithm itself is derived from the `LUCIFER` cipher, developed by IBM in the early 1970s. The NSA was asked to review the algorithm and reduced the key size from 112 bits to 56 bits and made some modifications to the internal workings of the algorithm.

While once considered very secure, in the late 1990s DES is considered to be at the end of its useful lifetime. In fact, DES was recently broken by brute force (details available at `http://www.rsa.com/des/`). Unfortunately, no widely accepted publicly available algorithm is poised to replace it.

Further, there are at least two more significant reasons to build Samba yourself. First, due to ITAR restrictions, distributors will frequently not compile Samba with DES encryption enabled. DES encryption must be enabled to allow encrypted password authentication. As of service pack three, the default behavior of Windows NT 4.0 is to deny access to clients using plaintext password authentication. Encrypted password support is also required if you wish to authenticate users against the Security Account Manager (SAM) in a remote Windows NT Server. This is very useful if you are using Samba to integrate a UNIX system into an already established Windows NT domain. Secondly, some common modifications to systems, such as the use of shadow passwords, will require you to adjust Samba compile time options.

Luckily, as of Samba version 1.9.18 it is no longer necessary to compile libdes to support encrypted password authentication. Version 1.9.18 contains a modified version of the DES algorithm that can be used to support SMB authentication, but not for encryption in general. If you are using version 1.9.18 or later you can skip this section.

Compiling `libdes`

As discussed, if you choose to compile Samba with support for encrypted passwords you will need to build `libdes` for your platform. This is actually very easy.

Downloading `libdes`

The primary distribution site for the DES library used by Samba is located at:

```
ftp://ftp.psy.uq.oz.au/pub/Crypto/DES/
libdes-x.xx.tar.gz
```

You can also retrieve it from the same site Samba is distributed from:

```
ftp://samba.anu.edu.au/pub/libdes/
libdes-x.xx.tar.gz
```

This is the same DES library that the Kerberos bones distribution has to be linked against. Since it was developed entirely outside the United States there are no restrictions on importing it back into the United States. The latest version of libdes at the time this was written was 3.23.

Unpacking `libdes`

The latest release of libdes (annoyingly) does not unpack into its own directory. So create a directory to unpack libdes into, move into that directory, then unpack the libdes tarball.

```
$ mkdir libdes
$ cd libdes/
$ gzip -cd ../libdes-3.23.tar.gz | tar xf -
```

Configuring `libdes`

There are very few machine specific options. Unless you are compiling on a Digital Alpha, plan to use the command line `des` command included with libdes, or have an ancient system that doesn't include the `times()` function, you can skip this step. Note that not supporting `times()` is very rare—it is part of System V, BSD 4.3 and the POSIX spec.

Digital Alpha

If you are building the system on a Digital Alpha, edit the `des.h` file and change the line:

```
#define DES_LONG unsigned long
```

to:

```
#define DES_LONG unsigned int
```

This will produce a 20% speedup in DES calculation time.

times()

If you system does not support the `times()` function you'll need to open up the `speed.c` file and change the line:

```
#define TIMES
```

to

```
#undef TIMES
```

This line is located just after the comments at the top of the file.

Terminal Options

If you plan to use the command-line `des` command included with libdes, read the Makefile and choose the correct terminal I/O option.

Compiling `libdes`

Type `make`. There aren't many things that can go wrong—on all the various systems I've compiled it on I've never had a problem.

Once compilation is finished, run `./destest`. This will ensure that everything is working properly. If you plan to use the command-line des command, run `./rpw` to test the terminal code. If you are curious about how fast the des library is, run `./speed`. You can sometimes improve performance by tweaking compile time options, such as compiler optimizations. In general I wouldn't worry about it. A slow DES library will still be fast enough for Samba.

Building Samba

Before starting you need to make sure you have a C compiler installed on your system. In the past all UNIX systems came with a C compiler installed as part of the base system. However, it has become increasingly common to charge extra for "optional" development tools like `make` and `cc`. IBM and Sun are two companies which no longer include `cc` in the standard installation. If you don't have a C compiler on your system you can avoid purchasing one by downloading `gcc`, the GNU Project's C compiler. You will also need `make` to build Samba. If you make modifications to Samba you will also need `awk` to rebuild the prototypes, though you probably know this if you're modifying Samba.

 Downloading gcc

The GNU project's C compiler is a full-featured C, C++ and Objective C compiler. It is competitive with all commercial UNIX compilers and is arguably superior to many of them. It is freely available under the GNU public license. If possible you should find a binary distribution of the compiler for your platform. The alternative, compiling gcc yourself, is quite complex but not difficult if you carefully follow the instructions distributed with the source code. You can download gcc from the GNU distribution site at `ftp://prep.ai.mit.edu/pub/gnu`, or from a GNU mirror site. Here are some of the mirror sites located in the United States.

```
ftp.hawaii.edu/mirrors/gnu
f.ms.uky.edu/pub3/gnu
ftp.digex.net/pub/gnu
wuarchive.wustl.edu/systems/gnu
uiarchive.cso.uiuc.edu/pub/gnu
ftp.cs.columbia.edu/archives/gnu/prep
jaguar.utah.edu/gnustuff
gatekeeper.dec.com/pub/GNU
labrea.stanford.edu/pub/gnu
archive.cis.ohio-state.edu/pub/gnu/mirror
ftp.uu.net/archive/systems/gnu
```

Unpacking the Distribution

The Samba source distribution, like virtually all other free UNIX software, is packed in a gzipped tar archive (also called a *tarball*.), called something like `samba-1.9.17.tar.gz`. Once you've downloaded the archive, unpack it with a command like

```
gzip -cd samba-1.9.17.tar.gz | tar xf -
```

or, if you have GNU tar installed, the more succinct:

```
tar xzf samba-1.9.17.tar.gz
```

What's in the Source Distribution?

The latest version of Samba at the time I'm writing this is 1.9.17. Unpacked, it looks like this:

```
$ ls -l samba-1.9.18p1/
total 45
-rw-r--r-- 1  jdblair jdblair 17982 May   4  1996 COPYING
-rw-r--r-- 1  jdblair jdblair  2753 Aug 24 22:21 Manifest
-rw-r--r-- 1  jdblair jdblair  6579 Dec 20 18:00 README
-rw-r--r-- 1  jdblair jdblair     0 Aug 21 05:10 Read-Manifest-Now
-rw-r--r-- 1  jdblair jdblair  1310 Oct 27 05:11 Roadmap
-rw-r--r-- 1  jdblair jdblair  7014 Jan 12 12:45 WHATSNEW.txt
drwxr-xr-x 3  jdblair jdblair  2048 Jan 12 12:47 docs
drwxr-xr-x 12 jdblair jdblair  1024 Jan 12 12:45 examples
drwxr-xr-x 2  jdblair jdblair  1024 Jan 11 07:53 packaging
drwxr-xr-x 2  jdblair jdblair  3072 Jan 12 12:49 source
```

COPYING is a copy of the GNU Public License, which was explained in the first chapter. README and WHATSNEW.txt are pretty self-explanatory—if you have a source archive released after 1.9.17 you should read them to learn about changes since this book was written. The *source* archive contains the Samba source code. The *examples* archive contains numerous example config files. Chapters 5 and 10 augment the files in this directory with examples to solve specific problems. The *docs* directory contains copies of the Samba man pages, the Samba FAQ, and numerous files covering behavior of specific parts of Samba. As of release 1.9.18 the header of each of these files contains a status line describing how old the information is. You can use `grep` to display a summary of the status of the current documentation to help decide if there's anything that may have changed since this book was written.

```
$ grep ^Status: *
Application_Serving.txt:Status: Current
BROWSING.txt:Status: Current - For VERY Advanced Users ONLY
DOMAIN_CONTROL.txt:Status: Current - New Content
Faxing.txt:Status: Current
HINTS.txt:Status: May be useful information but NOT current
INSTALL.sambatar:Status: Current
NetBIOS.txt:Status: Current
Passwords.txt:Status: Current
Printing.txt:Status: Current
README.DCEDFS:Status: Current but needs updating
README.sambatar:Status: Obsoleted - smbtar has been a stable part of Samba
SCO.txt:Status: Obsolete - Dates to SCO Unix v3.2.4 approx.
SMBTAR.notes:Status: Mostly Current - refer man page
Speed.txt:Status: Current
Tracing.txt:Status: Questionable
UNIX_INSTALL.txt:Status: Current
WinNT.txt:Status: Current
grep: faq: Is a directory
security_level.txt:Status: Current
```

Non-OS Specific Compile-Time Configuration Options

Samba doesn't use the easy GNU autoconf process used to compile GNU tools, but it's not much more difficult. Compile time options are set by editing the Makefile. The Samba `Makefile` is quite well documented, but this chapter covers a few minor points that you might miss. You should just need to read through this entire section, then the notes for your operating system in the OS Specific Section. I've listed these options in what I think is a more logical order than they appear in the Makefile.

Keeping the Makefile Pristine

A trick you can use to keep the distributed Makefile pristine is to create a file called `makefile` (all lower case) that contains your `FLAGSM` and `LIBSM` lines, but the line "`include Makefile.`" For example:

```
FLAGSM = -DLINUX -DFAST_SHARE_MODES
LIBSM =
include Makefile
```

`make` will load the file called `makefile` instead of loading `Makefile`. This file defines `FLAGSM` and `LIBSM`, then includes the original Makefile.

Installation Options

The base directory for the Samba installation is set with the `BASEDIR` variable:

```
BASEDIR = /usr/local/samba
```

Depending on your local setup you may wish to store it someplace else, like `/opt/samba`. If you would rather store the components in the normal system directories, like `/usr/local/bin`, `/usr/local/sbin`, and the like, modify these more specific variables:

```
BINDIR = $(BASEDIR)/bin
SBINDIR = $(BASEDIR)/bin
LIBDIR = $(BASEDIR)/lib
```

Precompiled Samba packages frequently set these to

```
BINDIR = /usr/bin, SBINDIR = /usr/sbin, and LIBDIR = /usr/lib.
```

The base directory for man page installation is set with the `MANDIR` variable:

```
MANDIR = /usr/local/man
```

The permissions assigned to executables are set with the INSTALLPERMS variable. You shouldn't need to modify this.

```
INSTALLPERMS = 0755
```

Default Configuration Options

Each of these settings assigns a default for a value that can be set to some other value in the Samba configuration file, `smb.conf`. The only value I recommend changing is the CONFIGFILE variable if you want to store the `smb.conf` file in some other location. There is a chicken-and-the-egg problem of using the smb.conf file to set an alternate location for the smb.conf file. Samba supports doing so, but you'll end up with two smb.conf files on your system. If you're in a hurry you can skip this section and deal with these values when it comes time to write your `smb.conf` file.

```
CONFIGFILE = $(LIBDIR)/smb.conf
SMBLOGFILE = $(VARDIR)/log.smb
NMBLOGFILE = $(VARDIR)/log.nmb
LMHOSTSFILE = $(LIBDIR)/lmhosts
```

Unless you can compile Samba with the `-DFAST_SHARE_MODES` option set, Samba will need to store share mode information in files. The LOCKDIR variable sets the directory these files will be stored in. This directory should not be on an NFS drive. If your operating system will support it, you should use the `-DFAST_SHARE_MODES` option. The only really popular operating system that does not support FAST_SHARE_MODES is Linux version 1.2 and earlier. FAST_SHARE_MODES is described in more detail at the beginning of the OS Specific section.

```
LOCKDIR = $(VARDIR)/locks
```

You can set the default workgroup that your Samba server will participate in with the WORKGROUP option. If your network is split into NT Domains, not Workgroups, you can set your Domain name here. This is described in more detail on page 115 of chapter 5.

```
WORKGROUP = MYGROUP
```

The GUESTACCOUNT variable sets the user account used for guest shares, unauthenticated printing, and other services like browsing and receiving WinPopup messages. Using `nobody` can sometimes cause problems (on some systems it is unable to print). I suggest using `ftp` — if I trust randoms all over the Internet to log into my machine as `ftp` I should be able to trust local users. If you're in doubt, create a user with minimal privileges specifically for the Samba guest account.

```
.GUESTACCOUNT = nobody
```

Why A Guest Account of "nobody" Can Cause Problems

Never create a guest account with a user or group id of 65535 or -1. This will cause `setreuid()` to leave the real and effective userid unchanged. The result is to set the guest account to root. Obviously, this is a major security hole. Consult the `setreuid()` man page for details.

The `setreuid()` system call on some versions of UNIX fails when asked to set the real and effective userid of a process to a high (i.e., greater than 32K) userid, yet these systems set the `nobody` account to a high userid.

The location of the `smbrun` binary is set with the `SMBRUN` variable. The `smbrun` command is used whenever Samba has to execute a shell command. Samba needs to execute shell commands to support printing and password changing, among other services.

```
SMBRUN = $(BINDIR)/smbrun
```

Authentication Options

These compilation options control the way that Samba authenticates non-guest users.

LanManager Encrypted Password Support (Recommended!)

```
# DES_BASE=/usr/local/libdes
# DES_FLAGS= -I$(DES_BASE)
# DES_LIB= -L$(DES_BASE) -ldes
# PASSWD_FLAGS=-DUSE_LIBDES -DSMB_PASSWD=\"$(BINDIR)/smbpasswd\" \
        -DSMB_PASSWD_FILE=\"$(BASEDIR)/private/smbpasswd\"
```

These options enable support for LanManager encrypted passwords. You first need to download libdes to compile this option. If the `getpass()` on your system is limited to 8 characters you'll need to add `-DREPLACE_GETPASS` to the `PASSWD_FLAGS` option (this is pointed out in several of the OS Specific compilation notes).

PAM (Pluggable Authentication Module) Support

You need to uncomment these options if you use PAM authentication on your system. Red Hat Linux uses PAM authentication. Be aware that you also need to add a `samba` config file to `/etc/pam.d` for proper operation. The Samba Red Hat package does this automatically. For details about configuring PAM to support Samba, see page 67.

```
# PAM_FLAGS = -DUSE_PAM
# PAM_LIBS = -ldl -lpam
```

Pluggable Authentication Module for Linux

Linux-PAM (Pluggable Authentication Modules for Linux) is a suite of shared libraries that enable the local system administrator to choose how applications authenticate users.

In other words, without (rewriting and) recompiling a PAM-aware application, it is possible to switch between the authentication mechanism(s) it uses. Indeed, one may entirely upgrade the local authentication system without touching the applications themselves.

Alternate Authentication Options

Several people have modified Samba to authenticate passwords using the Andrew File System, DCE, or Kerberos. This can be useful if you use one of these authentication methods to maintain passwords. However, you may wish to think twice before doing this. Samba uses AFS, DCE and Kerberos by accepting a **plaintext** password from a client then checking this password against the authentication server. For example, if you enable Kerberos authentication, a plaintext password will be transmitted from the SMB client to the Samba server. Samba will then attempt to obtain a Kerberos ticket. Kerberos is not used between the SMB client and the server, potentially compromising a user's Kerberos password.

Note that none of the Samba team members use any of these three authentication systems and have never tested these authentication options.

Andrew File System Support

These options enable Andrew File System authentication. Set AFS_BASE according to your local filesystem setup. You may need to add -laudit to the AFS_LIBS option.

```
# AFS_BASE = /usr/afsws
# AFS_FLAGS = -DAFS_AUTH -I$(AFS_BASE)/include
# AFS_LIBDIR = $(AFS_BASE)/lib
# AFS_LIBS = -L$(AFS_LIBDIR) -L$(AFS_LIBDIR)/afs -lkauth -lprot -lubik
# -lauth -lrxkad -lsys -ldes -lrx -llwp -lcom_err
# $(AFS_LIBDIR)/afs/util.a
```

Distributed Computing Environment Support

If you use the Distributed Computing Environment, uncomment these lines so smbd can act as an authenticated user entity.

```
# DCE_BASE = /opt/dcelocal
# DCE_FLAGS = -I$(DCE_BASE)/include
# DCE_LIBDIR = -L$(DCE_BASE)/lib
# DCE_LIBS =
```

Kerberos 5 Support

Kerberos 5 authentication. Set KRB5_BASE to your Kerberos base installation directory. If you're using Kerberos 4 in your environment, its time to upgrade to 5! Until you get around to it, you can integrate Samba by compiling the Kerberos 5 libraries with Kerberos 4 compatibility enabled.

```
# KRB5_BASE = /usr/local/krb5
# KRB5_FLAGS = -DKRB5_AUTH -I$(KRB5_BASE)/include
# KRB5_LIBS = -L$(KRB5_BASE)/lib -ldes425 -lkrb5 -lcrypto -lcom_err
```

Support for Other Services

Support for specific services and behaviors are set with these options. Most of the examples for each operating system demonstrate how to use them when they are appropriate. If you want to enable a service that is not demonstrated in an example you may also need to set LIBSM to include an appropriate library.

-DNETGROUP: Supports NIS (Yellow Pages) netgroups.

-DAUTOMOUNT: To determine a user's home directory by asking for the yp auto.home value.

-DSHADOW_PWD: Enables support for shadow passwords.

-DGETPWANAM: To use the getpwanam() call to authenticate passwords. This option is mutually exclusive with the -DPWDAUTH option. Do not enable them both.

-DPWDAUTH: To use the pwdauth() call to authenticate passwords. This option is mutually exclusive with the -DGETPWANAM option. Do not enable them both.

-DUFC_CRYPT: Enables the fast crypt routine.

-DALLOW_CHANGE_PASSWORD: To allow users to be able to change their password though Samba. This works on only some systems.

-DQUOTAS: Enables disk quota support. Unfortunately, this option is badly broken in Samba version 1.9.17 and 1.9.18. The problem is that none of the Samba team uses disk quotas. Volunteers willing to fix the code will be very welcome!

Japanese Extension

To enable support for the Kanji character set, set -DKANJI to the appropriate code value. Note that only run-time configuration, using the client code page parameter, is necessary starting with Samba version 1.9.18. The client code page option is described on page 151.

```
-DKANJI=\"<code>\"
```

Where <code> is one of the following codes describing the Kanji character set on your system:

sjis: for SJIS
euc: for EUC
jis7:   for JIS7
jis8:   for JIS8
junet: for jis7 + junet rule
hex: stores the hexadecimal code for the Kanji file name on systems that only support 7 bit ascii file names.

You should also read the README.jis file in the docs directory. This section has been included for completeness, but if you're enabling Japanese Extensions you already know more about it than me.

Problems with the DAVE Macintosh SMB Client

Samba version 1.9.16, and less, contained several bugs that only manifested themselves when accessed by the DAVE SMB client for the Macintosh. If you plan to use Dave you need to use a recent (at least 1.9.17p2) version of Samba. Really, you should almost always use the latest stable version of Samba.

Configuration Options Not Documented in the Makefile

There are additional compile-time configuration options which are not documented in the Makefile but are explained in the `local.h` file.

The Most Useful Settings

The two most useful undocumented options are `GUEST_SESSSETUP` and `PASSWORD_LENGTH`. These values can be set in the `Makefile` by adding them to the `CFLAGS` option in the Makefile. For example, to set `GUEST_SESSSETUP` to 1 just add `-DGUEST_SESSSETUP=1` to the `CFLAGS` option.

CAUTION!

You need to set `GUEST_SESSETUP = 1` if you want to support traditional, non-authenticated guest logons.

GUEST_SESSSETUP

This macro controls Samba's response to attempts to access a service with no password or an invalid password when the server is using user level security. These settings are necessary because providing a traditional "guest" account is difficult when using user level security.

`GUEST_SESSSETUP` can be set to one of three possible values:

`GUEST_SESSSETUP = 0`

Session setups with an invalid password are denied access. This is the default setting.

`GUEST_SESSSETUP = 1`

Session setups with an existing username and an invalid password are rejected. Setups with an invalid password and a non-existent username are allowed guest access.

`GUEST_SESSSETUP = 2`

Session setups with an invalid password are granted guest access, even if the accompanying username exists on the system.

The default value of 0 requires that clients provide a correct username/password pair to access services which allow guest access. This is not the behavior most people think of as guest access. However, neither of the other two options is entirely satisfactory either. Setting `GUEST_SESSSETUP` to 1 is only useful if you never want users who have an account on your system to be able to connect to a guest account. Setting `GUEST_SESSSETUP` to 2 would seem to do the trick, but it too has problems. Suppose you grant guest access to a service, with minimal privileges, as well as granting additional privileges to authenticated users. This means that a user that enters an incorrect password will seem to connect normally, but will receive no indication that he or she has actually connected with only guest access rights. It won't be until the user tries something that the guest user is not allowed to do that he or she will notice something is up. Unless you have particularly enlightened users, it is unlikely that the user will realize what happened.

Under the SMB authentication model there are really only two good ways to provide guest access. The first is to create a guest username and password. This solution is common in large public computer labs where the public username and password are just posted on the wall.

The second solution is to use share level security, not user level security. Samba grants guest access to all tree connect requests presenting blank passwords. Unfortunately, you will probably also wish to provide other access privileges to specific users on the same server. The most convenient way to do this is to use user level security. Luckily, Samba provides you with a way out of this bind. You can use NetBIOS aliasing to provide one virtual server using share level security, from which you provide your guest services, and another virtual server using server level security. An example showing how to do this is on page 257.

PASSWORD_LENGTH

This macro sets the longest significant password on your system. The default value is 8. If your system supports a different number of significant characters in passwords you should adjust this value. This value is especially significant if you set the password level parameter to a value other than 0. The password level parameter is explained on page 135.

Other Settings

There are additional values that you can set in the `local.h` file. In nearly all cases you will want to leave these alone, but they are documented here for the sake of completeness and because there are some situations where they might be useful. There are even more settings, including settings that may not have been available when this book was printed. The comments in the `local.h` file will always be the definitive documentation.

GLOBAL_NAME, HOMES_NAME, PRINTERS_NAME

These three macros allow you to redefine the strings used to identify the [global], [homes], and [printers] sections in the smb.conf file. Normally you can't define a file or printer service with any of these names because it would conflict with one of these special sections. If for some reason you absolutely need to give a service one of these names you can redefine the string used to identify the special section. In general this shouldn't ever be necessary.

PRINTCAP_NAME

This macro allows you to set the location of the printcap file Samba uses to set up dynamic print services. It makes more sense to use the printcap name configuration option in smb.conf than to modify this macro.

MAX_CONNECTIONS, MAX_OPEN_FILES

These macros allow you to define the maximum number of simultaneous connections and open files from a single client. Neither of these macros limit the overall number of connections or open files, only the maximum from a single client. The default maximum number of connections from a single client is 127. The default maximum number of open files is 100. The MAX_OPEN_FILES value needs to be increased to use Samba with the PC source code management tool *ClearCase*.

MAXSTATUS

This macro sets the maximum number of connections stored in the smbstatus file, and therefore displayed by smbstatus. The default value is 1000.

MAXDIR

Sets the maximum number of directories that can be opened by a single client at one time. Note that a client can actually have as many directories open as it wishes. If the client opens more directories than this number Samba idles some of them to save memory. The default value is 64 by default.

PAGER

This macro sets the default pager used by the smbclient command. The default value is "more." It can be overridden by the PAGER environmental variable. There is probably never any need to set this macro.

OS Specific Compile-Time Configuration Options

This section describes settings required to build Samba on specific operating systems and specific configurations of these operating systems. The variables FLAGSM and LIBSM are intended to contain compiler settings specific to certain situations unique to an operating system.

Each of the suggested options in this section have been contributed by somebody who wanted Samba to run on their own equipment. In most cases all you will have to do is find the line for your OS in the Makefile and uncomment it. Sometimes there may not be a pre-written example for you specific situation—you may have to combine parts of a few examples, or do some research to come up with your own. If you write new compile-time options send them to samba-bugs@anu.edu.au so your discovery can be shared with others. If you run into problems you can seek help on comp.protocols.smb and the Samba mailing list.

A/UX 3.0

```
FLAGSM = -DAUX
LIBSM =
```

AIX

For version 3.2.5 with DCE/DFS support:

```
FLAGSM = -DAIX -DDFS_AUTH -DSIGCLD_IGNORE -DNO_SIGNAL_TEST
LIBSM = -lc_r -ldce -lpthreads
CC = cc_r
```

For version 4.x:

```
FLAGSM = -DAIX -DFAST_SHARE_MODES
LIBSM =
```

Add -DQUOTAS to FLAGSM for quota support.

Altos Series 386/1000

```
FLAGSM = -DALTOS -DHAS_RDCHK
LIBSM = -lsocket -lxenix
```

Amiga (using gcc and ixemul.library 43.0 or later)

```
FLAGSM = -DAMIGA -Dfork=vfork -mstackextend
LIBSM =
```

Smbd and nmbd must be run from inet.d, not as stand-alone
daemons.

Apollo Domain/OS sr10.3

```
FLAGSM = -DAPOLLO -D_INCLUDE_BSD_SOURCE -D_INCLUDE_XOPEN_SOURCE
LIBSM =
```

You may need to add -A ansi to the FLAGSM option to get cc to
compile in ANSI mode.

BSDI

```
FLAGSM = -DBSDI -DFAST_SHARE_MODES
LIBSM =
```

For versions of BSDI prior to 2.0 you may need to add
-DUSE_F_FSIZE for disk usage information to be correct.

Bull Operating System (B.O.S.)

```
FLAGSM = -DBOS -DNO_RESOURCEH -DUSE_WAITPID
LIBSM = -linet
```

Convex

```
FLAGSM= -DCONVEX -DSHADOW_PWD
LIBSM=
```

Cray Unicos 8.0

```
FLAGSM = -DCRAY -U__STDC__ -DQUOTAS
LIBSM =
```

DGUX

```
FLAGSM = -DDGUX
LIBSM =
```

If you are running DGUX on an Intel box, set LIBSM to the following
line:

```
LIBSM = -lsocket -lnsl -lresolv
```

DNIX

```
FLAGSM = -DDNIX -I/usr/include/bsd
LIBSM = -ln
```

You may need an updated `libc.a` from your vendor as older versions have broken mktime calls and do not support `initgroups()` call. Further, the DNIX libc contains no `seteuid()` (set effective userid) and `setegid()` (set effective group id). Samba has a workaround, but some things will never work properly without these commands. The file `docs/DNIX.txt` contains the assembly code needed to implement these commands, and thus create a fully functional Samba server.

If you want to enable shadow passwords, add `-lpasswd` to the `LIBSM` option.

FreeBSD

```
FLAGSM = -DFreeBSD -DFAST_SHARE_MODES
LIBSM = -lcrypt
```

You may need to add `-DBSD44` to `FLAGSM` if password authentication does not work correctly.

HP-UX

```
FLAGSM = -DHPUX -Aa -D_HPUX_SOURCE -D_POSIX_SOURCE
LIBSM =
```

Use the following lines to support the Distributed Computing Environment (DCE/DFS):

```
FLAGSM = -DHPUX -Aa -D_HPUX_SOURCE -D_POSIX_SOURCE -DDFS_AUTH \
        -D_REENTRANT -I/usr/include/reentrant
LIBSM = -ldce -lM -lc_r
```

In both cases if you have trouble compiling, try removing the `-Aa` flag. You need to add `-DREPLACE_GETPASS` if you compile Samba with encrypted passwords enabled.

Use the following lines for the HP-UX 10.x Trusted System:

```
FLAGSM = +O3 -Ae -DHPUX -DHPUX_10_TRUSTED
LIBSM = -lsec
```

Intergraph

```
FLAGSM = -DCLIX -D_INGR_EXTENSIONS=1
LIBSM = -lbsd -lc_s
```

Linux (Alpha)

Directions for Alpha Linux are identical to the following Intel Linux directions, with the addition of -DAXPROC in the FLAGSM line.

Linux (Intel)

You are probably not surprised to learn that there are multiple variations of configuration options for Linux.

For a basic installation without shadow passwords or quota support, use the following lines:

```
FLAGSM = -DLINUX -DFAST_SHARE_MODES
LIBSM =
```

For shadow password support, add -DSHADOW_PWD to FLAGSM and -lshadow to LIBSM. For quota support, add -DQUOTAS to the FLAGSM line. Thus, for shadow passwords and quota support, use these lines:

```
FLAGSM = -DLINUX -DSHADOW_PWD -DQUOTAS -DFAST_SHARE_MODES
LIBSM = -lshadow
```

If you're using glibc2, you'll need to use the following lines. Remember that you can add quota and shadow support as described above.

```
FLAGSM = -DLINUX -DNO_ASMSIGNALH -DGLIBC2 -DFAST_SHARE_MODES
LIBSM = -L/lib/libc5-compat -lcrypt
```

You may also want to add the -O2 optimization flag to FLAGSM. This will result in a slightly larger but faster binary. You can also add the appropriate gcc flag to optimize for your particular Intel processor; e.g. -m386, -m486, -m585 or even -m686.

Lynx 2.3.0

```
FLAGSM = -DLYNX -DUFC_CRYPT -mposix
LIBSM = -lbsd
```

MachTen

```
FLAGSM = -DMACHTEN
LIBSM =
```

Motorola 88xxx/9xx machines

```
FLAGSM = -DSVR4 -DSHADOW_PWD -DGETTIMEOFDAY1
LIBSM = -lsocket -lnsl -lc -L/usr/ucblib -lucb
```

NetBSD

```
FLAGSM = -DNETBSD -DSHADOW_PWD
LIBSM = -lcrypt
```

Add `-DNETBSD_1_0` to `FLAGSM` if you are running NetBSD 1.0.

NextStep

For release 2.x with no POSIX support, use:

```
FLAGSM = -DNEXT2
LIBSM =
```

For release 3.x:

```
FLAGSM = -DNEXT3_0
LIBSM =
```

To compile fat binaries, add the appropriate -arch flag to the `FLAGSM` option. Valid flags are:

```
-arch m68k
-arch i386
-arch hppa
-arch sparc
```

To compile 4-way fat binary, you would append:

```
-arch m68k -arch i386 -arch hppa -arch sparc
```

OS/2 using EMX 0.9b

```
FLAGSM = -DOS2
LIBSM = -Zexe -lsocket
```

OSF1 (Alpha)

```
FLAGSM = -DOSF1
LIBSM =
```

QNX 4.22

```
FLAGSM = -DQNX
LIBSM =
```

RiscIX

```
FLAGSM = -DRiscIX -DNOSTRDUP
LIBSM =
```

RISCOS 5.0B

```
FLAGSM = -systype svr4 -std -DSVR4
LIBSM = -lsocket -lnsl -lc -L/usr/ucblib -lucb
```

SCO

Before you start you need to install the libcrypt library to build Samba. You can download it from `ftp://ftp.sco.com:/SLS/lng225b.*` or `ftp://ftp.uu.net:/vendors/sco`.

Note that a bug in the TCP/IP code of SCO version 3.2.4 and older will cause files to be corrupted during transfer with a Samba server. The UOD385 Connection Drivers Support Level Supplement, from SCO, will correct the problem. Download `uod385a.Z` and `uod385a.ltr.Z` from `ftp://ftp.sco.com/SLS` and install them. Realistically, you should consider upgrading your installation to a more recent version.

For SCO Unix 3.2v2 (ODT 1.1) with TCB passwords use the following. You will also need to set `CC` = `gcc` for this one case.

```
FLAGSM = -DSCO -DSecureWare -DSCO3_2_2
LIBSM = -lprot -lcrypt_i -lsocket -lm -lintl
CC = gcc
```

In all of the rest of these cases you need to set `CC` = `cc`.

For SCO OpenServer 3.0 with the default TCB passwords:

```
FLAGSM = -DSCO -DSecureWare
LIBSM = -lprot_s -lcrypt -lsocket -lm -lc_s
CC = cc
```

To support SCO with shadow passwords, use:

```
FLAGSM = -DSCO -DSHADOW_PWD
LIBSM = -lsec -lsocket -lcrypt_i
CC = cc
```

To add support for NIS (Yellow Pages), append `-DNETGROUP` to `FLAGSM` and `-lrpc -lyp -lintl` to `LIBSM`. Thus, to support shadow passwords and NIS, use:

```
FLAGSM = -DSCO -DSHADOW_PWD -DNETGROUP
LIBSM = -lyp -lrpc -lyp -lsec -lsocket -lcrypt_i -lintl
CC = cc
```

For SCO OpenServer 5 with TCB passwords, use the following. Note that in this case, you need to append -Xc to CC:

```
FLAGSM = -DSCO -DSecureWare -DEVEREST -DUSE_MMAP
LIBSM = -lprot -lcurses -lcrypt -lsocket -lPW -lm -lx -lc_s -lc
CC = cc -Xc
```

For the European distribution of SCO, with shadow passwords, use the following:

```
FLAGSM = -DSCO -DSHADOW_PWD
LIBSM = -lsec -lsocket /usr/lib/libcrypt_i.a -lintl
CC = cc
```

Sequent

```
FLAGSM = -DSEQUENT -DSHADOW_PWD -DHAVE_TIMEZONE
LIBSM = -lrpc -lsocket -lPW -linet -lnsl -lseq -lsec
```

SGI Irix

IRIX 4.x.x, use:

```
FLAGSM = -DSGI -DHAVE_TIMEZONE
LIBSM = -lsun
```

For 5.x.x, use this instead:

```
FLAGSM = -DSGI5 -DSHADOW_PWD -DHAVE_TIMEZONE -DFAST_SHARE_MODES
LIBSM =
```

Solaris 2.2 and 2.3 (SunOS 5.2 and 5.3)

Solaris comes with a broken version of awk by default, and a version that works correctly called nawk, so you need to set the AWK option.

```
FLAGSM = -DSUNOS5 -DSHADOW_PWD -DNETGROUP -DNO_STRFTIME -DFAST_SHARE_MODES
LIBSM = -lsocket -lnsl
AWK = nawk
```

Solaris 2.4 and later (SunOS 5.4 and later)

Like Solaris 2.2 and 2.3, you need to set AWK for configuration to work properly.

```
FLAGSM = -DSUNOS5 -DSHADOW_PWD -DNETGROUP -DFAST_SHARE_MODES
LIBSM = -lsocket -lnsl
AWK = nawk
```

Sony NEWS-OS

For version 4.2.x, use the following:

```
FLAGSM = -DNEWS42 -DKANJI=\"sjis\"
LIBSM =
```

For version 6.1.x, use the following:

```
FLAGSM = -Xa -DSVR4 -DNEWS61 -DSHADOW_PWD -DNETGROUP -DGETTIMEOFDAY1 \
         -DKANJI=\"euc\"  -D_SONYILS_H
LIBSM = -lsocket -lnsl
```

-DKANJI enables support for Samba Japanese extensions. See the Japanese Extensions section and the README.jis file for details.

SunOS 4

Note that you cannot use Sun's cc compiler because it is not ANSI compliant. Use gcc or acc instead.

```
FLAGSM = -DSUNOS4
LIBSM =
AWK = nawk
CC = gcc
```

Sunsoft ISC (Sun Interactive)

```
FLAGSM = -posix -D_SYSV3 -DISC -DSHADOW_PWD
LIBSM = -lsec -lcrypt -linet
```

SVR4

```
FLAGSM = -DSVR4 -DSHADOW_PWD -DALLOW_CHANGE_PASSWORD
LIBSM = -lsocket -lnsl -lc -L/usr/ucblib -lucb
```

Ultrix

Add -DULTRIX_AUTH for Ultrix enhanced security.

```
FLAGSM = -DULTRIX
LIBSM =
```

UnixWare

For version 1.x:

```
FLAGSM = -Xa -DSVR4 -DSHADOW_PWD
LIBSM = -lsocket -lnsl -lc -L/usr/ucblib -lucb
```

For version 2.x with libdes support:

```
FLAGSM = -Xa -DSVR4
LIBSM = -lsocket -lnsl -lc -L/usr/ucblib -lucb
```

UXP/DS

```
FLAGSM = -DSVR4 -DSHADOW_PWD
LIBSM = -lsocket -lnsl
```

Compiling Samba

Once you've finished editing the Makefile, type make. This will create the binary files. If this operation is successful you can use the command make install to install the binaries and man pages. You will have to be root to perform this step. Alternately, you can use the commands make installbin or make installman to install the binaries and man pages in separate operations.

Note that if you are upgrading from a previous version of Samba installed in the same location your original binaries will be renamed with the ".old" extension. Should you decide that the new version is a disaster you can restore the original version with the make revert command. Remember that you can only revert back to the last install, so if you type make install twice you'll completely delete the old version. Once you're satisfied that the new installation is running correctly you may want to delete all the *.old files to cut down on clutter.

Completing the Installation

At this point you've nearly completed installing Samba, whether you compiled it yourself or unpacked a pre-built binary. This section describes the final steps of the installation procedure—choosing how you will start up smbd and nmbd and testing your installation.

How to Start smbd and nmbd?

The two Samba daemons—smbd and nmbd—can be started using two different methods. First, they can be run as stand-alone daemons, started from your system start-up script. Secondly, with the exception of the

Amiga OS noted above, `inetd.conf` can be configured to start `smbd` and `nmbd` when an appropriate request arrives.

inetd

`inetd` is the system "meta-daemon." It listens to certain TCP/IP ports and invokes the appropriate program to service requests on any of these ports. Before inetd was introduced every service on a UNIX system was handled by a separate stand-alone daemon process which would listen on a specific port and service requests. This design has the advantage of simplicity and speed, since each server process is already loaded and ready to service a request. Unfortunately, it can also strain a system's resources—each service will use up some memory and cpu time even when it is not servicing a request. If there are many services which are only requested occasionally considerable system resources can be wasted. `inetd` solves this problem at the expense of the extra overhead necessary to invoke the appropriate program to service an incoming request. As a result, it makes sense to use `inetd` for occasionally accessed services, like finger, but is not a good idea for something like a web server that can receive many requests in a short period of time. Using inetd also means that the `tcpwrapper` system can be used to provide uniform access control and logging of service requests.

tcpwrapper

`tcpwrapper`, by Weitse Venema, is an excellent mechanism for adding uniform logging and access controls to existing standard services. It is restricted to use with services that are invoked from inetd and functions by "wrapping" the invocation of the program responsible for each service. That is, rather than invoking a program directly, inetd uses `tcpd`, the tcp wrapper program, to invoke the process. `tcpd` logs the IP address of the host requesting the service and allows for sophisticated actions to be invoked in response to specific conditions. To sum up, tcpwrapper is a swiss army knife that should be in every sysadmin's bag of tools. You can download tcpwrapper from `ftp://ftp.win.tue.nl/pub/security/tcp_wrapper*`. Note that since Samba provides its own mechanism for logging and access filtering, tcpwrapper should not be used to invoke Samba.

There are advantages and drawbacks to each approach. Using `inetd` means that no system resources are wasted keeping the `smbd` and `nmbd` processes alive between requests. However, it does mean that there is an additional layer to be executed before a request can be serviced. Running `smbd` and `nmbd` as stand-alone daemon processes means that each request will be serviced in the minimum possible time, but also means that some system resources will continue to be used between requests. My recommendation? Use `inetd` if your Samba server will be accessed rarely, such as when it is used to provide interconnectivity between a personal UNIX workstation and Windows PCs. The overhead of using inetd will be negligible if smb sessions are set up only occasionally. If your Samba server is accessed frequently run `smbd` and `nmbd` as stand-alone processes.

Note that if you installed Samba using a pre-built package, the package installation script may have already configured one of these start up methods. Read the documentation that came with the package or do a little investigating to find out exactly what happened.

Starting smbd and nmbd with inetd

You first need to check your `/etc/services` file to see if the appropriate NetBIOS services have been defined. First, see if a service has been defined for `139/tcp`. If none exists, add the following line:

```
netbios-ssn 139/tcp
```

If one does exist, make sure the service it defines is `netbios-ssn`. Similarly, check to see if a service is defined for `137/udp`. If none exists, add the following line:

```
netbios-ns 137/udp
```

Next, you need to add the following lines to your `/etc/inetd.conf` file.

```
netbios-ssn stream tcp nowait root /usr/local/samba/bin/smbd smbd
netbios-ns dgram udp wait root /usr/local/samba/bin/nmbd nmbd
```

The exact syntax needed for your flavor of UNIX may differ from this. Check other lines in your `inetd.conf` file to see if it is correct and modify it if necessary. If you are using NIS, remember that you have to modify the `/etc/services` file on the NIS master, not the clients. Note that some systems define `netbios_ssn` instead of `netbios-ssn`. This error is easy to miss and can cause endless hours of frustration!

If you are using tcpwrapper to invoke other services listed in your `inetd.conf` file, you should not do the same for Samba. Samba has the logging and filtering features provided by tcpwrapper built into it. See the documentation for host-based access control on page 169.

Starting `smbd` and `nmbd` as Stand-alone Daemons

Invoking `smbd` and `nmbd` with the `-D` flag will cause them to detach themselves from the shell and run in the background as daemons. You should make the appropriate changes to cause both programs to be started automatically when your system is booted. Note that all of these examples assume that the Samba suite was installed under `/usr/local/samba`. If you installed Samba in some other location adjust these examples accordingly. If you use BSD style start-up scripts, add the following lines to your `rc.local` file, or to another appropriate script:

```
echo -n "starting smbd and nmbd..."
/usr/local/samba/bin/smbd -D
/usr/local/samba/bin/nmbd -D
echo "done"
```

If you use System V style start-up scripts, you can use something like the following example. This is taken from a Red Hat Linux system.

```
#!/bin/sh #
# start/stop script for Samba on a Redhat Linux system
#
#

# Source function library.
. /etc/rc.d/init.d/functions
# Source networking configuration.
. /etc/sysconfig/network

# Check that networking is up.
[ ${NETWORKING} = "no" ] && exit 0

# add /usr/local/samba/bin to path
PATH="/usr/local/samba/bin:$PATH"
```

```
# See how we were called.
case "$1" in
  start)
        echo -n "Starting SMB services: "
        daemon smbd -D
        daemon nmbd -D
        echo
        touch /var/lock/subsys/smb
        ;;
  stop)
        echo -n "Shutting down SMB services: "
        killproc smbd
        killproc nmbd rm -f /var/lock/subsys/smb
        echo ""
        ;;
  *)
        echo "Usage: smb {start|stop}"
        exit 1
esac
```

Before going on, start both `smbd` and `nmbd`. Remember that you must start both programs as root.

```
$ /usr/local/samba/bin/smbd -D
$ /usr/local/samba/bin/nmbd -D
```

Testing the Installation

This is a simple procedure to make sure Samba is working before you begin the larger task of writing your `smb.conf` file.

Install a Simple `smb.conf` file

Create the following `smb.conf` file using your favorite editor. By default `smb.conf` is stored at `/usr/local/samba/lib/smb.conf`. If you modified the Makefile to look for `smb.conf` someplace else you will need to adjust accordingly.

```
; if you have a workgroup already running, set YOURGROUP accordingly
workgroup = YOURGROUP

    [homes]
        guest ok = no
        read only = no
```

Test NetBIOS Name Lookup

See if nmbd responds to broadcast name queries:

```
$ nmblookup YOURHOSTNAME
```

Note that YOURHOSTNAME should be just your hostname, not the fully qualified domain name. An example response is:

```
$ nmblookup FRODO
138.26.25.10 FRODO
```

If the name query failed there are several things that could be wrong:

1. Make sure that nmbd is running or started properly by inetd.

2. Make sure that Samba autodetects your network interface properly. Try adding interfaces = IP address of primary interface to your smb.conf file. See page 123 for details.

3. Make sure that nmbd thinks your hostname is the same as what you think it is. You could check this by restarting nmbd using the -n option to set a hostname or by adding a netbios name option to your smb.conf file. This option is explained on page 115. After you have Samba running it is much better to use the netbios name configuration option since it keeps the NetBIOS name properly synchronized between all the components of the Samba suite.

```
$ nmbd -n YOURHOSTNAME -D
```

Test 4 of the Samba diagnosis procedure, located on page 270, has a much more detailed procedure for diagnosing problems with nmbd.

Try Connecting with smbclient

Use smbclient to connect to your home directory:

```
$ smbclient //YOURHOSTNAME/yourusername
```

 Older Versions of smbclient Require DOS Style Paths

Prior to Samba version 1.9.17 smbclient required that network paths be described using DOS style backslashes

("\"). This required that they be quoted or escaped when used in a UNIX shell. For example, instead of smbclient //HOSTNAME/SHARENAME you would have to write smbclient '\\HOSTNAME\SHARENAME' or smbclient \\\\HOSTNAME\\SHARENAME.

smbclient will prompt you for a password. If everything works properly you will be connected to your home directory and enter the smbclient command shell. For example:

```
$ smbclient //FRODO/jdblair
Password:
Domain=[UAB-TUCC] OS=[Unix] Server=[Samba 1.9.17alpha5]
smb: \>
```

If this doesn't work:

1. Make sure that smbd is running.

2. Make sure you entered your password correctly.

Test 3 of the Samba diagnosis procedure, located on page 267, has a much more detailed procedure for diagnosing problems with smbd.

Chapter 4: Components of the Samba Suite

The Samba Core: The Server Programs
Samba Utilities
SMB client tools
lib directory contents
var directory contents

By default Samba will install into the `/usr/local/samba` directory. Immediately after running make install, the samba directory will contain the following files:

```
samba/
      bin/
            addtosmbpass
            nmbd
            nmblookup
            smbclient
            smbd
            smbpasswd
            smbrun
            smbstatus
            smbtar
            testparm
            testprns
      lib/
      private/
      var/
```

The `bin` directory contains all the programs included in the samba suite. The `lib` directory is used to store configuration files, which you will create yourself shortly. The `private` directory should be only readable by root and is used to store the SMB encrypted password file for encrypted password support. The `var` directory is used for log files and share mode files if you did not compile samba with shared memory file lock support. Most of these commands are explained in man pages which were also installed. The following sections provide summaries of these man pages as well as descriptions of programs for which no man pages are written.

Samba Executables

The Samba Core: The Server Programs

```
smbd [ -D ] [ -a ] [ -d debuglevel ] [ -1 log file ] [ -p port number ]
     [ -O socket options ] [-s configuration file ]
```

The smbd program is responsible for the actual sharing of filesystems and printer services to Windows networking clients. When started smbd binds to port 139 and listens for SMB requests from clients. Each client session is serviced by its own copy of smbd. Once the client is authenticated smbd switches effective userid to the authenticated identity and thus assumes all accompanying user rights. This copy stays resident in memory until the client closes the connection or the session times out from inactivity.

In almost all cases it is much easier to use the configuration options in smb.conf instead of the corresponding command line options.

Important Options:

-D   Starts smbd as a daemon. If invoked with this switch, smbd will detach itself from the starting process and run in the background. By default smbd does not run as a daemon. This option is used if you do not start smbd from inetd or another metadaemon. This option cannot be specified in smb.conf.

-s   configuration file
Defines the location of smb.conf. This option is necessary if you store smb.conf in a location other than that specified at compile time.
This option can also be set using the config file parameter in smb.conf. Of course, this means you will have

to create a config file containing this parameter in the location that the `smbd` expects to find it. See page 85 for details.

Hacker Options:

-O   `socket options`
Defines special socket options to tune Samba's behavior to your specific hardware, OS, and network conditions.

This option corresponds to the `socket options` parameter in for details. This option cannot be specified in `smb.conf`.

-p   `port number`
Specifies a port number other than 139 to bind to. If you want to use this option you know what you're doing and probably don't need this book. It can be used to run a Samba server from a machine that you do not have root access to. This option cannot be specified in `smb.conf`.

Debugging Options:

-l   `log file`
Specifies a base file name into which debugging information will be written. This option can also be set using the `log file` parameter. See page page 146 for details.

-d   `debug level`
Sets the debug level. This option can also be set using the `debug level` parameter, explained on page 147.

-a   Overwrites the log file with each connection. Normally logging information is appended to the log file. I group this option with debugging options but it could also be used to avoid creating logs.

```
nmbd [ -D ] [ -H netbios hosts file ] [ -d debuglevel ] [-l log basename ]
     [ -n netbios name ] [ -p port number ] [-s configuration file ]
```

When started nmbd binds to port 137 and services incoming NetBIOS name server requests. It can also be configured to be a potential master browser, a domain master browser, and act as a WINS server.

Again note that in almost all cases it is easier to use the corresponding option in `smb.conf` rather than a command line option.

Important Options:

-D   Starts nmbd as a daemon. If invoked with this option, nmbd will detach itself from the starting process and run in the background. By default nmbd does not run as a daemon. This option is used if you do not start nmbd from inetd or another metadaemon. There is no parameter in smb.conf that corresponds to this option.

-H   netbios hosts file
Before Samba version 1.9.18, this parameter allowed nmbd to answer name queried on behalf of other hosts. As of Samba version 1.9.18, this file behaves the same as a Windows LMHOSTS file.

-s   configuration file
Defines the location of smb.conf. This option is necessary if you store smb.conf in a location other than that specified at compile time.This option can also be set using the config file parameter in smb.conf. Of course, this means you will have to create a config file containing this parameter in the location that the smbd expects to find it. See page 114 for details.

Hacker Options:

-n   netbios name
Allows you to override the NetBIOS name that Samba sets for itself. This option corresponds to the netbios name parameter in the smb.conf file.

-p   port number
Specifies a port number other than 137 to bind to. If you want to use this option you know what you're doing and probably don't need this book. There is no corresponding option in smb.conf

Debugging Options:

-l   log basename
Specifies a base file name into which debugging information will be written. This option corresponds to the log file parameter.

-d   debug level
Sets the debug level.

Obsolete Options (provided for backwards compatibility):

-I, -N, -B

These options have all been replaced by the `interfaces` option in the `smb.conf` file. They let you specify multiple network interfaces which Samba should listen on.

-C   comment string

Lets you specify the comment string that will appear in browse lists and the printer comment box. This option has been replaced by the `server string` option in the `smb.conf` file.

Samba Utilities

addtosmbpass

`addtosmbpass` is an awk script that will automate the process of adding users to `smbpasswd`, Samba's encrypted password file. Its usage is explained in more detail when setting up encrypted password support is explained on page 66.

Since this script does not properly lock the `smbpasswd` file you should only use it to set up your initial `smbpasswd` file. To add users after your server is running use `smbpasswd -add`.

nmblookup [-M] [-S] [-U] [-S] [-B broadcast address] [-d debuglevel] name

`nmblookup` lets you perform NetBIOS name lookups, usually for debugging purposes. It will also allow you to request the status of all available NetBIOS services on a given machine. If a name ends in `#xx` `nmblookup` will search for the name of hexadecimal type `xx`. For example,

`nmblookup UAB-TUCC#1E`

will return the potential master browsers on the local network segment in the UAB-TUCC workgroup. Common NetBIOS name types are listed on page 17.

-M   Causes `nmblookup` to search for a master browser.

-S   Looks up the node status of the remote NetBIOS host. Unfortunately, this doesn't work with most Microsoft clients due to a bug in the way they handle these requests. They always respond to port 137 rather than the source port of the request. Since nmbd is bound to port 137, the reply is not received. Proxying this reply through nmbd is planned as a workaround to be added soon.

-B   broadcast address
Specifies a broadcast address to use to resolve NetBIOS names. This can be useful if you are attempting to query a NetBIOS host on a different network segment.

-U   Causes nmblookup to use a unicast NetBIOS packet. Note that due to the oddities of NetBIOS, it is possible to broadcast a unicast packet and unicast a broadcast packet.

-R   Sets the recursion_desired flag on the name lookup packet, which causes a proper WINS query to take place.

-d   debug level Sets the debug level. This option can also be set using the debug level parameter, explained on page 147.

smbprint

smbprint is a shell script that makes it possible to print to a printer shared from an SMB server. It does so by acting as an input filter in the printer's entry in the printcap file, piping the data submitted to the print job into smbclient, which actually sends the data to the remote SMB server. This is very useful for UNIX machines running in a computing environment dominated by Windows machines. Setting up smbprint is explained in more detail on page 253.

smbrun

smbrun is a simple glue program that runs shell commands for smbd. smbrun first changes to the highest userid that it can, then runs the command using the system() call. Using smbrun to run commands provides a platform-independent method for executing commands as a non-root user.

smbstatus [-b] [-d] [-p] [-s configuration file]

smbstatus is a very simple program that displays status information about the current Samba connections. An example of the output is as follows:

```
Samba version 1.9.17p2
```

Service	uid	gid	pid	machine
accounting	tammi	staff	43963	192.192.195.114
				(192.192.195.114) Thu Sep 18
03:39:46	1997			
accounting	lyn	staff	19947	192.192.195.118
				(192.192.195.118) Thu Sep 18
00:25:55	1997			
lcshare	nobody	nobody	39439	192.192.195.103
				(192.192.195.103) Thu Sep 18
00:41:43	1997			
pan1	lyn	staff	19947	192.192.195.118
				(192.192.195.118) Tue Sep 16
01:02:43	1997			
lex1	nobody	nobody	39439	192.192.195.103
				(192.192.195.103) Thu Sep 18
00:53:31	1997			
hpcolor	tammi	staff	43963	192.192.195.114
				(192.192.195.114) Thu Sep 18
03:43:47	1997			
hpcolor	lyn	staff	19947	192.192.195.118
				(192.192.195.118) Mon Sep 15
01:57:12	1997			
accounting	mark	staff	23570	192.192.195.117
				(192.192.195.117) Thu Sep 18
07:10:56	1997			

```
No locked files

Share mode memory usage (bytes): 101888(99%) free + 456(0%) used + 56(0%)
overhead = 102400(100%) total
```

Important Options:

-b   Brief output. Here's an example of brief output:

```
Samba version 1.9.17p2
```

PID	Username	Machine	Time logged in
23570	mark	192.192.195.117	Thu Sep 18 07:10:56
39439	nobody	192.192.195.103	Thu Sep 18 00:41:43
19947	lyn	192.192.195.118	Mon Sep 15 01:57:12
32461	nobody	192.192.195.102	Wed Sep 10 00:32:15
24299	nobody	192.192.195.202	Wed Sep 17 00:07:08
43963	tammi	192.192.195.114	Thu Sep 18 03:39:46

-d   Verbose output. This includes more detailed information about config and lock files.

```
using configfile = /usr/local/samba/lib/smb.conf
lockdir = /usr/local/samba/var/locks
Opened status file /usr/local/samba/var/locks/STATUS..LCK
Samba version 1.9.17p2


Service    uid       gid        pid          machine


No locked   files



Share mode memory usage (bytes):
      101888(99%) free + 456(0%) used + 56(0%) overhead = 102400(100%)
      total
```

-p   Prints a list of running smbd processes and exits.

-s   Lets you specify an alternate config file.

SMB Client Tools

```
smbclient servicename [ password ] [ -A ] [ -E ] [ -L host ] [ -M host ]
      [ -I IP number ] [ -N ] [ -P ] [ -U username ] [ -d debuglevel ]
      [ -l log basename ] [ -n netbios name ] [ -W workgroup ]
      [ -O socket options ] [ -p port number ] [ -c command string ]
      [ -T tar options ] [ -D initial directory ]
```

smbclient is a command line SMB client. It can be used to access remotely shared volumes in an ftp-like command line shell, pipe jobs to printers shared on SMB servers, query remote machines for browse lists, send WinPopup messages, and more. Note that smbclient does not let you mount remote SMB shares as a local filesystem. The only free tool that can do that currently is the SMB filesystem that is included as part of the Linux kernel. See Part IV for more information about the SMB filesystem under Linux. Also note that all file transfers will be made in binary mode unless the translate option, which translates between DOS and UNIX style line endings, is toggled to true.

Parameters:

servicename The complete UNC (Universal Network Convention) name of the remote resource. A UNC name takes the form \\server\servicename. Remember that from the command line you will need to quote

('\\server\servicename') or escape
(\\\\server\\servicename) the backslashes when
using smbclient from a UNIX shell. Samba version 1.9.17
and greater allows you to replace the backslashes in the UNC
name with forwardslashes (//server/servicename),
which makes using smbclient simpler. Also remember that
the server name is the NetBIOS name, which is not
necessarily the DNS name. In the annoying case that the
NetBIOS name is different from the DNS name you should
either take steps to make the NetBIOS and the DNS names
the same, or use the -I option to specify the IP address or
DNS name of the server.

password If the remote resource requires a password for access you
can include it on the command line. If you do supply a
password the -N option, which suppresses asking for a
password, is assumed. The password can also be supplied as
part of the username argument following the -U flag. This
option is useful for including a password in a scripted task,
though be very cautious about doing so since it will be
visible in the process table.

Optional Parameters:

-I   ip address/hostname
The IP address or DNS hostname of the remote host. This is
useful if the client is unable to resolve the NetBIOS
hostname of the server.

-L   host
Allows you to view the list of services available from a
server. This option will also show the browse list and domain
browse list if they are available. The -I option will again be
useful if your NetBIOS name doesn't match the DNS name
of the server. The -W option is often also needed if the
remote host is not in the same workgroup as that specified in
your smb.conf file.

-M   host
This option lets you transmit a "WinPopup" message to
another host. The command will then allow you to enter the
message, terminating with a control-D. If the receiving
computer is running WinPopup (Windows for Workgroups
and Windows 95), or the remote computer is a Windows NT
machine with Windows Messaging enabled, the message

will be displayed on the remote computer's screen. If the remote computer is not able to receive WinPopup messages the command will silently fail.

You can pipe messages into smbclient thusly:

```
cat message | smbclient -M FRODO
```

The -U and -I options are useful for controlling the FROM and TO line in the WinPopup message. This command is especially useful for notifying Windows users of events via scripts on the UNIX host.

-E   Causes the client to write errors to standard error rather than to standard out. This can be useful in a scripting context.

-N   Suppresses the password prompt. This option is useful when accessing a server that does not require a password. A client will always prompt for a password unless a password is supplied or this flag is invoked. This occurs because the SMB client must present a name/password pair when attempting to access the server—it cannot determine ahead of time if no password is required.

-P   Causes the requested service to be treated as a printer service rather than a filesystem. This flag is used by the smbprint script.

-U   username Sets the username used to open a session. This is useful in a scripting context, if you must connect to a server with a different username than your UNIX login name, or if the server requires usernames to be sent in all uppercase. You may specify a username/password pair in the format username%password. This value can also be set with the USER environmental variable.

-n   netbios name Allows you to specify the NetBIOS name of the client that will be presented to the server. By default the NetBIOS name is the hostname in all uppercase.

-W   workgroup Allows you to override the workgroup setting in the smb.conf file.

-T   tar options This option allows you to write remotely shared files to a tar file or extract information from a local tar file and write it to a remotely shared directory. It is frequently easier to use the `smbtar` command, described on page 250, than to mess with this option on its own. The `-T` options are complex enough they deserve their own syntax description.

-D
    `initial directory` Changes the working directory to `initial directory` before starting. This option is probably only useful with the `-T` option, though it is legal to use it what any other option.

-c
    `command string` Executes commands from a semicolon separated command string rather than from standard input. The `-N` flag is implied by using this option. This is useful for scripting smbclient's actions.

```
smbclient \\server\share -TcxIXbgNa [ blocksize ] [ newer-file ] tarfile
     [ file names.... ]
```

c
    Creates a tar file on UNIX. This option must be followed by the file name of a tar file, a tape device, or the "–" option for standard output.

x
    Restores (extracts) a local tar file back onto the remote filesystem. The `-D` option can be used to restore the file to a location other than the top level of the remote shared filesystem. This option must be followed by the file name of a tar file, a tape device, or the "–" option for standard output.

I
    Allows a list of files to be included in the tar file creation or extraction. Any files not in the include list are implicitly excluded. The X option behaves in an opposite manner.

X
    Allows a list of files to be excluded from the tar file creation or extraction. Any files not in the exclude list are implicitly included. The I option behaves in an opposite manner.

b
    Causes tar file to be written out in `blocksize * TBLOCK` blocks. `TBLOCK` is a compile-time option normally set to 512.

g
    Causes only files with the archive bit set to be written to the tar file.

N
    Causes only files newer than the specified file to be written to the tar file.

a
    Causes the archive bit to be reset when a file is written to a tar file.

Debugging Options:

-d   `debug level` Sets the debug level. This option can also be set using the `debug level` parameter, explained on page 147.

-1   `log basename` Allows you to set the logging basename for logs of this client session.

Hacker Options:

-O   Defines special socket options to tune Samba's behavior to your specific hardware, OS, and network conditions.

-p   `port number` Specifies a port number other than 137 to bind to. If you want to use this option you know what you're doing and probably don't need this book.

General Command Shell Commands:

?   [command] Displays a summary of command usage if a command is specified. If no command is specified a list of available commands is displayed.

exit   Terminates the connection and exits the `smbclient` command shell.

help   A synonym for "?".

q   A synonym for `exit`.

quit   A synonym for `exit`.

!   [shell command] Runs the specified command in a local shell. If you would like to escape to a shell, use ! sh.

File Related Command Shell Commands:

archive <level>

Changes the behavior of `mget` with respect to the archive bit of files on the remote system. Level 0, the default, causes `mget` to ignore the archive bit. Level 1 only retrieves files with the archive bit set. Level 2 only retrieves files with the archive bit set but resets the archive bit after transferring the file. Level 3 causes `mget` to ignore the archive bit, but resets the archive bit on all transferred files.

`blocksize <blocksize>`
> Specifies the blocksize for tar files.

`cd [directory name]`
> Displays the current working directory if no directory is specified. Otherwise it changes the working directory to the specified location.

`del [glob pattern]`
> Deletes files matching the specified glob pattern.

`dir [glob pattern]`
> Behaves like the UNIX `ls` command, but displays output similar to the DOS `dir` command. If the glob pattern is specified only files or directories matching the pattern are displayed. Otherwise all files in the current working directory are listed. If `recurse` is toggled ON this command will recursively descend all matched directories.

`get <file name> [local file name]`
> Copies a remote file to the local system. If `local file name` is specified the file is renamed after transfer. The remote file name cannot be specified as a glob pattern. Use `mget` to retrieve multiple files using a glob pattern.

`lcd [directory name]` Displays the current working directory if no directory name is specified. Otherwise changes the current local working directory to the specified location.

`lowercase` Toggles the lowercasing of file names. Lowercasing is toggled ON by default, meaning the file name of retrieved files is converted to the UNIX norm of all lowercase.

`ls [glob pattern]` A synonym for `dir`.

`mask <glob pattern>` Sets the default glob pattern to be used during recursive operation of the `mget` and `mput` command. Only files matching the specified glob pattern will be transferred.

`md <directory name>` A synonym for `mkdir`.

`mget <glob pattern>` Copies all files matching the glob pattern to the local system from the remote system. If `recurse` is toggled ON all matching directories are recursively descended.

mkdir <directory name> Creates a directory in the current
working directory on the remote machine.

mput <glob pattern> Copies all files matching the glob pattern
on the local system to the remote system. If recurse is
toggled ON all matching directories are recursively
descended.

newer <file name> Causes mget to retrieve only files that are
newer than the local file.

prompt Toggles prompting for confirmation of file transfer during
mget and mput operations. Prompt is toggled ON by
default, meaning that mget and mput always prompt for
confirmation.

put <local file name> [remote file name] Copies a
local file to the remote system. If remote file name is
specified the file is renamed after transfer.

recurse Toggles the recursive behavior. When ON all mput, mget,
and dir commands recursively descend any matched
directories. get and put are unaffected.

rename <old file name> <new file name> Renames a file
on the remote system.

rm   A synonym for del.

rmdir   Removes the specified directory from the remote system.

setmode <file name> <perm=[+|-]rsha> Allows the
attributes of the remote file to be set in the same manner as
the DOS attrib command.

tar c|x[IXbgNa] Performs a tar operation. See the explanation of
the -T command for more details. Note that using the "-"
option with the x command won't work inside the command
shell. Behavior is affected by the blocksize and
tarmode commands.

tarmode full|inc|reset|noreset Changes the behavior of
tar with respect to archive bits on the remote system. full,
which is the default setting, causes all files to be written to
the tar file regardless of the state of the archive bit. If inc is
specified only files with the archive bit set will be written to
the tar file. reset mode clears the archive bit of all files
written to the tar file. noreset mode prevents this behavior.

Printer Related Command Shell Commands:

You must be connected to a remote print service using the -P option for these commands to work.

cancel <jobid> Cancels a job in the print queue.

print <file name> Submit the specified file into the print device on the remote machine. You must be connected to a print service, not a filesystem service, to use this command. Note that you can also use put to print to most SMB servers. It's often faster than using print.

printmode graphics | text Sets the print mode for all subsequent print commands.

qinfo Displays information about the remote print queue.

queue Displays the print queue on the remote system.

translate Toggles text translation for printing.

```
smbtar -s server [ -p password ] [ -x service ] [ -X ] [ -d directory ]
        [ -u user ] [ -t tape ] [ -b blocksize ] [ -N file name ] [ -i ]
        [ -r ] [ -l log level ] [ -v ] file names...
```

smbtar is a shell script that makes it easy to dump a remotely shared volume directly to a tape drive. It can be used to cobble together a UNIX-based backup system for any networked PC. Examples of using this command to backup a Windows share are on page 250.

-s   server The NetBIOS name of the PC that is serving the share that will be written to tape.

-x   service The name of the share that will be written to tape. -X excludes file names (listed at the end of the option list) from files restored from or written to a tar file.

-d   directory Changes to this directory before running the backup or restore.

-v   Runs in verbose mode.

-p   password Used to specify a password used to access the remote machine.

-u   user The user id used to access the remote share. This defaults to the UNIX login id. This parameter can also be used to specify the username and password at the same time using the username%password syntax.

-t   tape The tape device. This may specify a regular file or a tape device. Normally smbtar uses the TAPE environment variable to set this value. If neither are set, smbtar defaults to a file called tar.out.

-b   blocksize The default blocksize. Normally defaults to 20.

-N   file name Only backs up files if they are older than the timestamp on file name. This could be used to implement incremental backups by specifying the backup log file.

-i   Specifies incremental mode. A file is only backed up if it has the DOS archive bit set. The archive bit is reset after each file is read.

-r   Causes files to be restored to the share from the tar file or tape.

-l   log level Specifies the logging level. This value is used to set the -d value on the smbclient command.

The TAPE environment variable is used to set the default tape device.

lib **Directory Contents**

Config files are placed by default into the /usr/local/samba/ lib/ directory, though they could potentially be placed anywhere on the filesystem. There are two important configurations files: smb.conf, and username map files, if they are needed. If a NetBIOS hosts file is specified it will usually also be placed in this directory. The smb.conf file contains all of Samba configuration options that describe all aspects of its behavior. Shared filesystems, printers, and other services are all specified in this file. The smb.conf file is explained in chapters 5, and 10. It is common for pre-built Samba packages to place the smb.conf file inside the /etc directory rather than /usr/local/samba/lib/.

CAUTION!

It is essential that smb.conf and any other Samba configuration files be writeable only by root.

The username map file is an optional file whose location is set in the smb.conf file. It is used to map UNIX usernames to usernames which may already be present in an NT domain. This allows the process of authenticating an SMB session to be simplified by mapping an existing UNIX account to an existing Windows user. There is no predefined location for the username map file, though it is convenient to place it in the same directory as the `smb.conf` file.

`var` **Directory Contents**

Samba's log files are normally stored in the `/usr/local/samba/var/` directory.

 Alternate `log file` Location

Note that putting the Samba log files in `/usr/local/samba/var` violates the Linux file system standard, which specifies that the contents of the `/usr` directory be read-only. It is common to change the log file location to `/var/log/samba` using the `VARDIR` compile-time option or the `log file` configuration parameter to correct this discrepancy.

By default Samba generates two log files: `log.smb`, which contains file access logs, and `log.nmb`, which contains logs from the browser and WINS service. You will need to make your own arrangements to clear or archive these log files periodically. If a debugging level is set, other files will be generated and also written to this directory by default. The `log.nmb` file typically does not grow very quickly, but the `log.smb` file can become very large if your server is active. The `max log size` configuration option allows you to specify a maximum log file size. See page 147 for details.

The `var` directory will also, by default, contain a `lock/` directory. This directory contains lock files for any files Samba currently has open. If Samba is functioning as a master browser, the list of all machines in the workgroup will be stored here in the `browse.dat` file. If Samba is functioning as a WINS server, all currently registered names will be stored here in the `wins.dat` file. If you are using `FAST_SHARE_MODES` and mmap-based shared memory, then this directory must not be located on an NFS mounted drive.

Chapter 5: Global Configuration Options

Index of Global Configuration Parameters

This chapter covers the structure of the smb.conf file and Samba's global configuration options. The next chapter covers the configuration options specific to each network service Samba provides. Rather than organize the options alphabetically the options are grouped by the goal they exist to accomplish. This is intended to help you avoid sifting through a large number of options to find the parameter you are looking for to accomplish a particular task. It also makes explaining many options easier by minimizing the need for cross references.

smb.conf **Structure**

The smb.conf file is the configuration file for both smbd and nmbd, and is large and complex enough to warrant its own chapter. This is a result of the complexity of Samba and the fact that virtually every aspect of Samba is open to configuration. As of version 1.9.17, there are at least 165 possible configuration values. While some of these are synonyms for the same option, a large number of them will appear once for every service that is defined. The bottom line? While there are a large number of options, most of them can be left alone until you learn more about Samba and exactly how you want it to behave in your situation.

smb.conf is structured similarly to a Windows .INI file, consisting of sections and parameters. Every section corresponds to a network service, or the special [global] section used to set global configuration options. Each line must be terminated with a new-line character and is either a section name, a parameter, or a comment. Each section is started with the section name in square brackets on a line of its own. Each parameter is in the form "name = value". No quotation marks are used to delimit a parameter name or value. Instead, all whitespace on either side of the first equal sign in a line is dropped. All leading and trailing whitespace is also ignored. The remaining text, including any whitespace internal to a parameter name or value, is significant. In contrast, neither the parameter name or the section names are case sensitive.

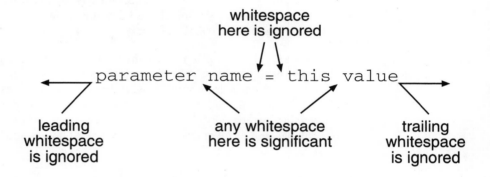

Lines that begin with a semicolon or contain only whitespace are ignored. A line ending with a "\" is considered to continue to the next line in the customary UNIX shell fashion.

The parameter value is parsed as a string, boolean, integer or enumerated value, depending on the parameter. From a user's point of view, its simplest to think of the parameters as either accepting boolean values or a string. A true boolean value can be specified with true, yes, or 1; false is specified with false, no, or 0. While case is not significant in a boolean value or enumerated value, case is preserved in string values. Remember that no quotation marks are ever needed. However, for convenience, if leading and/or trailing quotation marks are found, they will be dropped.

There are two main types of parameters: global and service. The global parameters control the overall behavior of the Samba server and will usually only appear once in a configuration file. Examples of this sort of parameter are those which set the NetBIOS name of the server, the security policy of the server, and network tuning options. Service parameters configure the behavior of specific services, such as the path of the shared directory, the name of the share, access controls, authentication options and browsing behavior.

Substitution Macros

Each of the string parameter values can include any of the following string substitutions. There are two classes of substitution macros: those that are always used and those that can be used in a "share context." To illustrate the difference, consider %U, which is the username a client gives Samba at session setup, and %u, which is the username that Samba actually uses for the session. Since %u is only known in a share context (after a client has authenticated), it won't work in all places.

There are only a few places where these are obviously relevant, such as using the %u variable to describe the pathname of a home directory. However, there are many unexpected and creative uses for these variables. The parameter definitions will suggest some as they are relevant. Many of the things Samba can do that Windows-based servers only wish they could do are a result of the flexibility these substitutions provide.

 Examining the Values of the Substitution Macros

You can examine the value of all substitution macros by setting the preexec parameter to execute this perl script. This script is stored in the scripts/ directory on the CD-ROM included with this book, as show-macros.

```perl
#!/usr/bin/perl

# change the following to the full path of smbclient on your system
$smbclient = "/usr/local/samba/bin/smbclient";

($S, $P, $u, $g, $U, $G, $N, $H, $v, $h, $m, $L, $M, $d, $a, $R, $I, $T) =
@ARGV;

open SMBCLIENT, "|$smbclient -M $m -U $L -I $I";
print SMBCLIENT "\%S Current Service Name: $S\n";
print SMBCLIENT "\%u User Name: $u\n";
print SMBCLIENT "\%P Service Root Dir: $P\n";
print SMBCLIENT "\%g Primary Group of $u: $g\n";
print SMBCLIENT "\%U Session User Name: $U\n";
print SMBCLIENT "\%G Primary Group of $U: $G\n";
print SMBCLIENT "\%H Home Dir of $u: $H\n";
print SMBCLIENT "\%N NIS Home Directory Server: $N\n";
```

```
print SMBCLIENT "\%v Samba Version: $v\n";
print SMBCLIENT "\%h Hostname: $h\n";
print SMBCLIENT "\%m Client's NetBIOS Name: $m\n";
print SMBCLIENT "\%L Server's NetBIOS Name: $L\n";
print SMBCLIENT "\%M Client's Internet Name: $M\n";
print SMBCLIENT "\%d Server's Process ID: $d\n";
print SMBCLIENT "\%a Client's Architecture: $a\n";
print SMBCLIENT "\%R Protocol Level: $R\n";
print SMBCLIENT "\%I Client's IP Address: $I\n";
print SMBCLIENT "\%T Current Date: $T\n";
close SMBCLIENT;
```

Macros That Are Always Available

%U   The session user name. This is the user name that the client
      passed to the server, not necessarily the UNIX user name that was
      eventually used. Since it is always defined, it is a good idea to use
      this macro instead of %u unless absolutely necessary. Guest
      logins, as well as users affected by a username map, will cause
      this value to differ from %u.

%G   The primary group of the user described by %U.

%M   The DNS name of the client machine, all in lowercase.

%I   The IP address of the client machine.

%m   The NetBIOS name of the client machine.

%h   The hostname of the system that Samba is running on.

%L   The NetBIOS name of the server, in all lowercase. This allows
      you to change your config based on what the client calls you,
      giving your server a "dual personality" much like a multi-homed
      web server.

%a   The architecture of the remote machine. Only some are
      recognized, and those may not be 100% reliable. It currently
      recognizes Samba, WfWg, WinNT and Win95. Anything else
      will be known as "UNKNOWN". If this value gets an architecture
      wrong, send a level three log to the Samba Team so they can fix
      the problem.

%R   The protocol level selected by protocol negotiation. It can be one
      of CORE, COREPLUS, LANMAN1, LANMAN2 or NT1.

%N   The name of the NIS home directory server, obtained from your
      amd.conf file.

%T   The current date and time.

%d   The process id of the current server process.

%v   The Samba version.

Macros Available Only in a Share Context

%H   The home directory of the user given by %u.

%P   The root directory of the current service, if defined.

%S   The name of the current service, if defined.

%g   The name of the primary group of the user described by %u.

%u   The user name of the current service, if defined.

Special Sections

Every section except for one corresponds to a network service. The one exception is the [global] special section that is used for setting global configuration values and defaults for the other sections. There are three special sections: the [global] section already mentioned, the [homes] section, and the [printers] section. These are described in detail below.

Each service description describes either a filespace service, which describes a shared directory, or a printer service, which describes a print spooler service. Each service description contains a filesystem pathname, access controls, and housekeeping parameters. Technically every parameter is optional—leaving a service description blank would create a filespace service which gave every user who has access to your system read-only access to the /tmp directory.

The [global] Section

This section is for parameters which apply to the server as a whole, rather than to a specific service. It can also be used to specify default values for service-specific parameters which are then inherited by other services. A service parameter in the global section can always be overridden by specifying the parameter again in a specific service.

The [homes] Section

The [homes] section is designed to easily grant access to all users' home directories. Each client that connects to the Samba server requests access to a particular service. If the requested service is not already defined, Samba scans the password file, or the local equivalent, for matches. If the requested service refers to an existing username, and the correct password is supplied, a temporary virtual service is created and given all the parameter settings which appear in the [homes] section. The name of this temporary service will be the same as the connecting username.

A home directory can also be mounted by requesting the "homes" service. The username that is subsequently supplied will be used to determine the home directory to mount. This allows a single client computer to service multiple users with a pre-set configuration. For example, a start-up script can be defined to map the "homes" service to a drive letter where users can always expect to find their UNIX home directory. However, be careful if you choose to do this! Some clients, like Windows 95, cache network connections and assume they are userid-independent. This means that after a user "logs off" of the network, his or her home directory can remain mounted. The next user of the machine can then access that home directory.

If no path parameter appears in the section, the path is set to the user's home directory. If you decide to set the path parameter yourself, you will find the variable substitution macros useful. For example, you could create a separate Samba home directory with the definition "path = /pchome/%S". The %S and %U macros are identical in this context.

Note that granting guest access in the [homes] section by using the setting "guest ok = yes" or "public = yes" is **perfectly legal** but **almost always undesirable.** This setting would allow anybody to access any home directory.

With some clients, like Windows 95, the HOMES share can remain mounted after a user logs off of the network. This share can then be accessed by the next user of the machine.

Samba will let you grant guest access to users' home directories! This is almost certainly not a good idea to actually do.

Using Macros to Create the [homes] Section

This is a cute use of macros to create your own [homes] section.

```
[%U]
path = %H
```

The [printers] Section

If a [printers] section exists in the smb.conf file clients are allowed to use any printer specified in the local /etc/printcap file. If a client requests a service that isn't explicitly defined in the smb.conf file, and a [homes] section exists, Samba checks to see if the request is a valid username. If it is not a username or no [homes] section exists, and a [printers] section does exist Samba will check to see if the service name is a valid printer name. Any printer name or alias appearing in the printcap file will be assumed to be a legal printer name. If this isn't true, or your system, like AIX, doesn't use a printcap file you'll need to create a pseudo printcap file listing all the valid printer names on your system. All the various printer-specific parameters are described in more detail on page 202. Examples of printer configurations are explained starting on page 157.

Some patches that may be incorporated into Samba by the time you read this allow Samba to determine printer names properly on systems without printcap files.

Configuration File Options

config file

Default: none, meaning use the default configuration file

Example: config file = /usr/local/samba/lib/
        smb.conf.%m

**include **

Default: none, meaning no other files are included

Example: include = /usr/local/samba/lib/
        smb.conf.%L

The config file option allows you to specify a pathname for the smb.conf file other than the default location. Obviously, there is a chicken in the egg problem here—the setting must appear in a file at the default config file location to be of any use. As a result, this parameter is actually much more useful to create conditional config files. Macro substitutions can be used to load special config files for specific client hostname or architectures. If a specified file does not exist, then the default config file will continue to be loaded normally. This behavior allows you to define just the default configuration and the special cases.

Generally, the `include` parameter is a better choice for creating conditional config files. Rather than replacing the current config file with a completely new file, `include` just causes the referenced file to be inserted verbatim into the current file. More than one `include` parameter can appear in the same config file.

None of the "share context" substitution macros will work with either the `config file` or the `include` parameter. If the referenced file does not exist the parameter is ignored. This allows you create a conditional configuration file. For example, `include = /usr/local/samba/ lib/smb.conf.%a` lets you tweak some configuration settings depending on the architecture of the client machine.

You could avoid the need to create two `smb.conf` files by using the `-s` option for each Samba tool. However, this is usually more inconvenient than just creating the two `smb.conf` files.

Browser Options

These options control how the Samba server appears in browse lists, as well as its interaction with other network browsers.

Naming

Setting the NetBIOS Name

`netbios name`

Default: the first component of the server's DNS name

Example: `netbios name = FRODO`

The `netbios name` parameter sets the NetBIOS name which `nmbd` will advertise the Samba server as on the network. By default this will be set to the first part of the host's DNS name. If Samba is acting as a browse or logon server these services will be advertised under this name. There is no reason other than convenience and administrative sanity to set the NetBIOS name to be the same as the first component of the server's DNS name.

netbios aliases

Default: none

Example: netbios aliases = ABBOTT COSTELLO

The netbios aliases parameter specifies a space-separated list of additional names nmbd will advertise the Samba server as on the network. This allows a single machine to appear as multiple hosts in the network browse list. Combining this option with the config file parameter and the %m macro allows you to create multiple "virtual servers," each with their own services. Examples of doing this can be found on page 257.

Note that if Samba is acting as a browse or logon server these services will be advertised under the primary NetBIOS name (set by the netbios name parameter), not any of the names listed in this parameter.

Setting the Workgroup

workgroup

Default: WORKGROUP (can be set at compile time)

Example: workgroup = UAB-TUCC

The workgroup parameter specifies the name of the workgroup the Samba server will appear to be a part of in browse lists. If this value is not set correctly browsing will not work properly.

Setting the Server Comment String

server string

Default: server string = Samba %v

Example: server string = Pathology Dept. File
            Server

The server string parameter defines the server's comment string. This comment string will appear next to the machine name in browse lists, such as the network neighborhood. This string will also appear in the comment box in the print manager.

Manually Adding Services to the Browse List

auto services

Default: none

Example: `auto services = jdblair lp laser-printer`

Synonym: `preload`

The `auto services` or `preload` parameter defines a space-separated list of services that will be automatically added to the browse lists. This is most useful for `homes` and `printers` services that would otherwise not be visible. Remember that adding a service to this list only adds it to the browse list. If you do not add a corresponding service, clients will receive an error when they attempt to access it.

Note that if you just want all printers in your printcap file loaded then the `load printers` option is easier.

Setting a Default Service

default service

Default: none

Example: `default service = Public`

Synonym: `default`

The default service parameter specifies the name of a service that a client will be connected to if the service actually requested does not exist. Typically the default service is some sort of public, read-only service. Note that the specified service name is not surrounded in square brackets, as the service name appears in service definitions in the `smb.conf` file.

As of Samba version 1.9.14 the apparent service name will be changed to the requested, but non-existent, service name. This means that `%S` will be substituted with the name of the non-existent service the client requested. Since any "_" characters in the name of the service are mapped to "/", the `default service` option can be used to describe a wildcard service. For example, suppose `default service = wildcard` and `path = /%S` for the wildcard service. This would mean that if you accessed `\\SERVERNAME\usr_local` you would be granted access to the `/usr/local` directory. Obvisouly this is a potentially dangerous feature and should only be carefully used.

Influencing Browser Elections

The browser election protocol establishes the master and backup browsers for a workgroup or NT domain. The protocol is explained in detail on page 42.

Influencing Samba's Chance to Become a Master Browser

local master

Default: `local master = yes`

Example: `local master = no`

If `local master` is set to true nmbd will attempt to become a local master browser. If set to false nmbd will not attempt to become a master browser, losing all browse elections by default. Setting this value to true doesn't mean nmbd will become a master browser, only that it will participate in browse elections.

preferred master

Default: `preferred master = no`

Example: `preferred master = yes`

If set to true this parameter causes nmbd to advertise itself as a "preferred master" during browse elections. This will cause Samba to force an election when it first comes on-line, and will have a slight advantage to win this election.

A good policy only is to set this value to true if Samba is set to be a domain master (by setting `domain master = true`). If you have a Windows NT Server host on your network you will probably be best off leaving this value alone and letting the NT machine be the master browser.

os level

Default: os level = 0

Example: os level = 33

The os level parameter specifies the operating system level which Samba advertises itself as during browse elections. By default the os level is set to zero, which causes Samba to lose all browse elections. If you want Samba to have a chance at winning browse elections you need to set its os level to equal that of any other potential browsers in the workgroup or NT domain. If you want Samba to win all browser elections set this value to greater than any other browser. The meaning of the OS level is described in detail on page 42.

Implementing Cross Subnet Browsing

Cross-subnet browsing allows a Workgroup or NT domain to span multiple network segments. The protocol is explained in detail on page 46.

wins server

Default: none

Example: wins server = cccadmin.ccc.uab.edu

Cross-subnet browsing requires that there exist a WINS server responsible for registering all NetBIOS names on the extended network. The wins server parameter specifies the DNS name or IP address of the WINS server that Samba should register its name with. Setting this parameter at the same time that the wins support option is set to true will generate an error.

Note that this parameter is not included with the other WINS related options in the "Using Samba as a WINS Server" section since it is used to support cross-subnet browsing, not to implement a WINS server.

domain master

Default: domain master = no

Example: domain master = yes

nmbd has the ability to function as a domain master browser (DMB), which acts as the central master browser for workgroup or NT domain spanning multiple network segments. If domain master is set to true nmbd will attempt to do so. This means that master browsers on broadcast isolated subnets will contact this server to receive the browse list for the entire NT domain. If you have a Windows NT Server host on your network you should probably let it act as the domain master browser. More detail can be found on page page 46.

Note that if you set this option to true you must also either specify a WINS server using the wins server parameter, or set up Samba as the only WINS server on your network. The domain master browser uses the WINS server to notify other master browsers of its existence.

remote announce

Default: none

Example: remote announce = 138.26.25.255/UAB-TUCC

The remote announce option provides a technique for solving some cross-subnet browsing problems by allowing Samba to announce itself to an arbitrary IP address with an arbitrary workgroup name.

In most cases it makes more sense to set up a WINS server and a domain master browser to enable cross-subnet browsing. However, there are some situations described on page 216 where this will be the simplest solution.

Normally this value would be the broadcast address of a remote network, though it can be the specific address of a known master browser if your network is that stable.

Using Samba as a WINS Server

wins support

Default: wins support = no

Example: wins support = yes

The wins support option controls whether or not Samba will function as a WINS server. Note that Samba does not have the ability to replicate its WINS database with Microsoft WINS servers, since Microsoft will not publish the protocol they use for WINS replication. If you have a computer running Windows NT Server on your network you will probably be better off configuring it to act as your WINS server.

remote browse sync

Default: none

Example: remote browse sync = 192.168.2.255
192.168.4.255

This parameter allows you to configure nmbd to periodically request a browser synchronization with the browse master on a remote network segment. This feature allows the local and remote browse lists to be synchronized across routed networks in situations where the normal browser synchronization rules do not work. The remote browse master must be a Samba server. This feature does not work with other servers.

The above example synchronizes the browse lists with the browse masters present in the two remote subnets. Normally one would specify the broadcast address on the remote network. However, you can specify a specific machine if your network is stable enough. Remember if you specify a specific IP address, Samba makes no attempt to verify that the machine is available, listening, or is actually the browse master. If you specify a broadcast address, no attempt is made to determine if Samba actually contacts a browse master.

Using Samba to Proxy WINS Requests from Older Clients

wins proxy

Default: wins proxy = no

Example: wins proxy = yes

Samba can function as a proxy WINS server, responding to broadcast name queries on behalf of other hosts by consulting the WINS server. This can provide a correct response to clients that are unable to consult the WINS server or have an incorrect WINS server setting. Setting the wins proxy option to true enables this proxy support.

Using DNS to Resolve WINS Queries

dns proxy

Default: dns proxy = yes

Example: dns proxy = no

If dns proxy is true, then when nmbd, acting as a WINS server, finds that a queried NetBIOS name has not been registered, it will attempt to resolve the requested NetBIOS name using DNS.

Note that the maximum length for a NetBIOS name is 15 characters, so the DNS name must be equally limited. Also note that nmbd will block until the DNS query is finished. This will result in a temporary loss of browsing and WINS services. Leave this option set to true only if your DNS resolution is fast, or you can live with periodic pauses in nmbd's service.

Changing the Announced Browser Type and Version

announce as

Default: announce as = NT

Example: announce as = Win95

The announce as parameter allows you to set the type of browser that nmbd announces itself as. The valid options are NT, Win95 or WfW meaning Windows NT, Windows 95 and Windows for Workgroups respectively. The default value is Windows NT. Do not change this value unless you know what you are doing and you have a specific need to stop Samba from appearing to be an NT server. Changing this value will interfere with Samba's ability to act as a master or backup browser.

announce version

Default: announce version = 4.2

Example: announce version = 2.0

The announce version parameter specifies the major and minor version numbers that nmbd will use when announcing itself as a server. The default is 4.2. Do not change this parameter unless you have a specific need to set a Samba server to be a down-level server.

Network Options

Network Interface Configuration

Dealing with Multiple Network Interfaces

`interfaces`

Default: the primary network interface and netmask

Example: `interfaces = 138.26.25.10/24`
            `138.26.25.39/24`

Many computers have more than one network interface. The `interfaces` option allows you to inform Samba of each interface you wish it to provide services on by defining a list of ip/netmask pairs. The netmask may be described as either a netmask or a bitlength, describing the number of leading ones in the netmask. Samba will answer requests on all listed network interfaces.

For example, the following two lines both describe the same values:

```
interfaces = 138.26.25.10/24 138.26.25.39/24
interfaces = 138.26.25.10/255.255.255.0 138.26.25.39/255.255.255.0
```

If this option isn't set Samba will attempt to determine the primary network interface and netmask on its own. It will never attempt to find more than one interface. You should always set this parameter if you have more than one network interface, even if you only want Samba to provide services on one interface—Samba may guess the wrong "primary" interface.

`bind interfaces only`

Default: `bind interfaces only = no`

Example: `bind interfaces only = yes`

This parameter, which is available starting with Samba version 1.9.18, affects the name service server (nmbd) and the file-sharing server (smbd) in slightly different ways.

For name service, this parameter causes nmbd to bind to port 137 and

138 on the interfaces listed in the `interfaces` parameter. To receive broadcast name registration announcements, nmbd normally also binds to the "all addresses" interface on each of these ports. Any received packets not addressed for interfaces listed in the `interfaces` parameter are discarded. For file-sharing service, this parameter causes smbd to bind only to the interfaces listed in the `interfaces` parameter.

Note that you should not use this parameter if Samba serves clients connected using PPP or other intermittent or non-broadcast network interfaces. This is a dangerous option and should only be used if you know what you are doing.

socket address

Default: will respond to connections on any port

Example: `socket address = 138.26.25.39`

On systems with multiple network interfaces, the `socket address` option specifies the socket on which smbd and nmbd will listen for connections. If you wish Samba to listen to every interface on a system setting this option is not necessary. This option is necessary if you would like Samba to listen on only one network interface.

Only use this option if you understand Samba very well. It will cause Samba to stop listening to broadcast packets. If you don't know what you're doing, this can be a disaster.

Note that the `socket address` option will only have an effect if you run smbd and nmbd as daemons, not if you start them from inetd.

Setting Low Level Socket Options

socket options

Default: none

Example: `socket options = SO_KEEPALIVE`

This parameter allows you to tune the low-level network interface by setting socket options. Samba recognizes ten socket options, though it is possible that your version of UNIX does not support them all. Unless you have done some socket programming they will probably not be familiar to you. The setsockopt() man page will provide some explanation of these options. The detailed meanings and effects of these options is outside the scope of this book—a good book about socket programming will explain them in detail. The exact behavior of these options will vary some between flavors of UNIX.

Briefly, these options have the following meanings. The four options followed by "*" accept an argument of the form OPTION=number. No spaces may appear on either side of the equal sign.

SO_KEEPALIVE

Causes the TCP/IP stack to monitor the status of the connection by transmitting periodic ACKs. This allows a lost connection, caused by a network problem or a down client, to be detected. This conserves resources on the server by closing connections when a client is not longer available.

The same effect can be achieved by specifying a value for the keepalive parameter. In general the SO_KEEPALIVE option will be more efficient, but will not allow you to specify how frequently keep-alive packets are sent. Also note that the keepalive option sends NetBIOS keepalives. The SO_KEEPALIVE socket option sends TCP keepalives.

SO_REUSEADDR

Allows the reusing of local socket addresses.

SO_BROADCAST

Enables the transmission of broadcast messages.

TCP_NODELAY

Normally the TCP/IP stack will use a technique known as Nagle's algorithm to minimize the individual number of packets needed to transmit information when the size of the transmitted data unit is significantly smaller than the minimum payload size of a TCP packet. This option disables the use of this algorithm, causing each data unit to be transmitted immediately, regardless of the amount of wasted space in the TCP payload.

Usually this option can improve performance slightly at the expense of a potentially significantly larger network load. However, in some situations it seems to make a tremendous performance difference. If you are having performance problems this is one of the first things you should try. Note that this option should rarely be used if your Samba server is accessed from other network segments and never if it is accessed across the Internet.

IPTOS_LOWDELAY, IPTOS_THROUGHPUT

These options set the "type of service" field in the IP datagram packet. The `IPTOS_LOWDELAY` option requests that the packet be delivered on a path with low delay, and the `IPTOS_THROUGHPUT` option requests it be delivered on a path with high throughput. In theory, a router connected to a leased line (with low delay but low bandwidth) and a satellite link (with high delay but high bandwidth) could use this field to decide which route to use for each packet. Unfortunately, most hosts and routers ignore the type of service field.

`SO_SNDBUF` *

Sets the size of the send buffer.

`SO_RCVBUF` *

Sets the size of the receive buffer.

`SO_SNDLOWAT` *

Sets the size of the send "low water mark." This is the minimum amount of data that must be available before the socket interface processes a non-blocking output operation. The default size is usually 1024 bytes.

`SO_RCVLOWAT` *

Sets the size of the receive "low water mark." A receive call will block until it has received the smaller of the requested amount or the low water mark. The default size of the low water mark is usually 1 byte.

The only options I've ever felt the need to use are `SO_KEEPALIVE` and `TCP_NODELAY`. The other options will be useful to socket hackers looking to push the performance of their server. Note that it is possible to describe a set of options which will cause your Samba server to fail.

If an option is not available on your system you will receive an "Unknown socket option" error.

Defining the Maximum SMB Protocol Extension

`protocol`

Default: `protocol = NT1`

Example: `protocol = COREPLUS`

Specifies the maximum protocol extension that will be negotiated for use with a client. Normally Samba should be left to negotiate an appropriate protocol with a client, though there are situations where you may wish to override this value. An example of using this option to deal with Windows for Workgroups clients is presented on page 264.

Possible values are CORE, COREPLUS, LANMAN1, LANMAN2 and NT1.

Setting the Maximum SMB Packet Size

`max xmit`

Default: `max xmit = 65535`

Example: `max xmit = 8192`

Sets the maximum packet size which Samba can negotiate with a client. This is the maximum packet size that smbd will ever accept from a client, setting an upper limit on the packet size that will be negotiated with a client at session setup. There are some cases, such as with Windows for Workgroups clients, where a smaller packet size may increase performance.

Improving Network Performance

Supporting Raw Reads and Writes

`read raw`

Default: `read raw = yes`

Example: `read raw = no`

`write raw`

Default: `write raw = yes`

Example: `write raw = no`

Raw reads and writes allow 65535 bytes to be sent in each packet and can provide a significant performance boost. Samba supports raw reads and writes by default.

Determining when a Client is Not Responding

keep alive

Default: keep alive = 0 (meaning no keepalive packets are sent)

Example: keep alive = 60

This parameter describes the number of seconds between NetBIOS "keepalive" packets. These packets allow a server to determine if a client is alive and responding.

This parameter has pretty much the same effect as the SO_KEEPALIVE socket option, except that NetBIOS keepalives are sent instead of TCP keepalives, and the time between keepalives is configurable. The socket options parameter is explained on page 124.

Kicking Off Idle Clients

dead time

Default: dead time = 0

Example: dead time = 15

An inactive client will consume server resources even though it is not doing anything. Each client has a corresponding server process that will consume memory and cpu time, even if idle. The dead time parameter accepts an integer value describing the number of minutes of inactivity before a session is automatically disconnected. The "dead time" is considered to begin when a client has no open files. This option stops the server from being bogged down by inactive connections. Since most clients have an auto-reconnect feature, this behavior is transparent to users.

The default dead time of zero indicates that no client should ever be dropped because of inactivity. A time of five minutes is appropriate for most systems and will rarely be noticed by users.

User Authentication

Providing both seamless and secure access to services is one of Samba's trickier problems. The problem stems from the concept of "username" on Windows systems. UNIX has been a multi-user operating system from the beginning. As a result, its concept of user rights is pervasive throughout the system. Every process and every file is owned by a user and a group, and has no rights or access privileges beyond those granted to that user or group. Until Windows NT, Windows and OS/2 had only a vague concept of username and its accompanying rights and privileges. Since a personal computer was a simple, single-user machine that was rarely remotely accessible, no username was necessary. It wasn't until SMB introduced the ability to share files and printers on a LAN that Windows even dealt with access rights.

The Process of Username/Password Validation

=The process of user authentication depends on whether or not Samba is running in share level or user level authentication. Remember that the `security = server` is just a variation on user level authentication. In each step a password is considered correct if it is validated for the supplied username using whatever password authentication technique Samba is currently configured to use. Access rights after a user is authenticated are enforced by switching the effective userid of the server process associated with this client to the authenticated userid.

It may be useful at this point to review the example SMB exchange that appeared on page 25. When connecting to a service using user level security, the client sends a `sesssetupX` (session setup) SMB that includes the user's name and password, which may be encrypted. If the client provides the correct password, the server returns a session identifier. The client then uses this identifier to connect to the share using a `tcon` or `tconX` (tree connect) SMB.

In contrast, no SMB session setup step is necessary when a client connects to a service using share level security. A `sesssetupX` SMB may still be transmitted to supply an optional username, but this step is not necessary. Instead, each tree connect operation authenticates separately by including a password, but no username.

Each mode treats the concept of guest login differently. Under share mode security, guest access will be granted to clients that issue a tree connect operation with a blank password. Under user level security, guest access will be granted to clients which supply a blank username and password in the session setup SMB. This is the way that browse lists are distributed. Unfortunately, due to the design of Microsoft clients, it is difficult to supply a blank username and password when connecting to a server. As a result, guest access is difficult to provide when using user level security. The GUEST_SESSSETUP compile time option allows you to adjust the algorithm used to grant guest access. The GUEST_SESSSETUP option, as well as a more detailed discussion of guest access, is located on page 70.

Share Level Authentication

This is the process for granting access under share level security. Note that the public and revalidate service options affect this process.

1. If a service is marked as guest only (not guest ok or public) then access is granted with the rights of the username given in the guest account parameter for the service.

2. If a client passed a username/password pair to Samba, and that username and password are validated, the client is granted access with the rights of that username. This applies even if the client passes the username as part of the requested service using the syntax \\servername\service%username.

3. If the client registered a username with Samba during a previous connection (such as an initial session setup request) and now supplies the correct password for that username, access is granted.

4. The NetBIOS name of the client is taken as a username. If the supplied password is correct for this username, then access is granted.

5. If the client validated a username/password pair with the Samba server during a previous connection, and now passes the correct corresponding access token, access is granted. This step will be skipped if the revalidate service parameter is true for this service.

6. If a user parameter exists for the service, the supplied password is checked against each user in the user parameter's list. If the supplied password is correct for any of these users, then access is granted.

7. If the service is marked guest ok or public and all of these

other attempts have failed then the client is granted access with the rights of the username given in the `guest account` parameter for the service.

User Level Authentication

User level authentication is much simpler than share level authentication. The only way a client can use a service is if the client supplies a correct username and password. The only exception is if the `GUEST_SESSSETUP` compile time option is set to something other than 0. Also note that the username may be passed using the syntax `\\server\nameservice%username` when attaching to a share.

If successfully authenticated, a client is normally granted the access privileges of the authenticated username. Exceptions to this are controlled by service level configuration parameters, such as `guest only`, `force user`, and `admin user`, which grant access privileges belonging to a username other than the authenticated username.

security

Default: `security = share`

Example: `security = server`

If the `security` parameter is set to `share`, Samba will tell clients it is granting access under share mode security. If `security` is instead set to `user` or `server`, Samba will tell clients it grants access under user level security. The `server` option is a variation on user level security using a remote SMB server to validate passwords. It is explained in detail below. Under both Windows and OS/2 share mode security means that access is granted to resources by assigning certain passwords to certain access privileges (i.e., one password for read-only access and another for read/write access). User mode security allows the granting of access rights by associating certain rights to certain users.

Internally, a Samba server can really only assign access privileges using the equivalent of user level security. Access privileges to any resource under UNIX are bound to a specific username or group of users. If correctly configured, Samba grants no access privileges not already granted to the username Samba authenticates for a client. Samba enforces this by running the server process associated with the client under the effective userid authenticated for the client.

However, Windows clients behave differently towards a server in share level security than they will towards a server in user level security. When a Windows client encounters a server in share mode security it assumes that the user will need to enter a password to access the service. When encountering a server in user mode security a Windows client will first try to access the server using the username and password that the client has already authenticated for the local user. Recall that user level security authenticates during the SMB session setup using a username and password. Share level security authenticates with a password, but no username, with each tree connect operation. This is explained more on page 25.

Having said all of that, setting this parameter is easy. If your usernames on your Samba server are usually the same as the usernames of users on the client machines, set this parameter to user. Further, if you use clients running Windows for Workgroups, you need to set this parameter to share if your Windows usernames differ from your UNIX usernames. A bug in Windows for Workgroups causes it to completely ignore the password you enter into the "connect as" dialog box if the server is in user level security mode. This makes it virtually impossible to connect to a resource using a username different from the one entered into the "network logon" dialog box.

Using share level security is also the easiest way to provide guest access to a share. This technique is explained on page 172.

User Authentication Techniques

Samba provides three techniques for validating the username and password a client supplies. The first is to use the standard user authentication technique for your UNIX system—usually by checking against the hashed password in the passwd file, though it could use NIS, DCE, Kerberos, or some other UNIX authentication method. The second method is to use encrypted password authentication against a special locally stored Samba password file containing plaintext passwords. The third is to use another SMB server, such as a Windows NT machine, to check the validity of username/password pairs. The technique you choose will depend on the security needs of your situation.

Enabling Encrypted Passwords

`encrypt passwords`

Default: `encrypt passwords = no`

Example: `encrypt passwords = yes`

The `encrypt passwords` options controls whether or not Samba uses encrypted passwords to validate the identity of users. Encrypted passwords provide an additional level of security since a malicious user cannot use a packet sniffer to capture a plaintext password. If you are using a Samba version prior to 1.9.18 and you haven't compiled the DES library into your server, this parameter will have no effect.

The situations where you will want to enable plaintext passwords and the effects that doing so will have are explained in detail in the following sections.

Using Native UNIX User Authentication

The simplest user authentication technique is to use native UNIX user authentication. To do so, set `encrypt passwords = no` in your `smb.conf` file. The `server` parameter must be set to either `share` or `user`. By definition, `server` level security is not native UNIX authentication, and is explained shortly.

CAUTION!

Using native UNIX authentication means that passwords will be transmitted across the network in plaintext.

This authentication mode is by far the easiest access control technique, using the native UNIX password checking method to authenticate client access. On most systems this means checking the supplied password against the hashed password stored in the `/etc/passwd` file. Other techniques, such as checking against a NIS database, are possible but currently must be set at compile time (see page 66 for details). To grant a new user access to your Samba server, you add a new account to your UNIX system and make sure that this user has access to appropriate resources in the `smb.conf` file. Using native authentication avoids the need to compile Samba yourself, since most precompiled binaries do not contain the DES encryption library needed for encrypted logins.

The main disadvantage of this technique is that plaintext passwords are passed over the network. If you already allow plaintext passwords to use ftp and telnet on your UNIX system with plaintext passwords, also allowing Windows clients to authenticate with plaintext passwords is not going to make your security situation any worse. However, if you have implemented a non-plaintext authentication technique, such as

Kerberos, on your UNIX system you should probably use the encrypted password technique. Further, its my opinion that you should avoid plaintext password authentication whenever it is possible to do so. Since it is relatively easy to avoid doing so with Samba, you probably should.

Enabling Plaintext Authentication on Windows NT

Service Pack 3 disables the ability of Windows NT to use plaintext authentication to connect to a server. You can reenable this ability using the registry editor (REGEDT32.exe). To do so, find this hive key entry:

HKEY_LOCAL_MACHINE\system\CurrentControlSet\Services\rdr\parameters\

Add the key EnablePlainTextPassword. When asked to enter its value, select type DWORD and set its value to 1.

A quicker, less error prone method to accomplish this is to copy the file NT4_PlainPassword.reg from the /samba/docs directory of the accompnaying CD-ROM to the NT machine or share it from a server, then double-click on it when logged in as Administrator.

Enabling Plaintext Authentication on Windows 95

One of the recent updates to Windows 95 (specifically VRDRUPD.EXE) disables the ability of Windows 95 to use plaintext authentication to connect to a server. You can re-enable this ability using the registry editor (REGEDT.EXE). Start the registry editor and find this hive key entry:

HKEY_LOCAL_MACHINE\System\Current\ControlSet\Services\VxD\VNETSUP\

Select Edit->New->DWORD Value from the menu bar. Rename the entry "New Value #1" to EnablePlainTextPass-word. Set its value to 1.

A quicker, less error-prone method to accomplish this is to copy the file Win95_PlainPassword.reg from the /samba/docs directory of the accompanying CD-ROM onto your Windows 95 machine or share it from a server, then click on it. The necessary update will automatically be performed.

Finally, as of Service Pack 3 for Windows NT 4.0, and the latest update for Windows 95 (at the time of publication) the ability to log onto servers using plaintext authentication is disabled. It is possible to override this setting by editing the registry, but doing so on a large number of client machines is tedious and potentially prone to error. It makes more sense just to add the ability to do encrypted authentication on the server side.

Dealing with Clients Which Pass Only Single Case Passwords

`password level`

Default: `password level = 0`

Example: `password level = 2`

Some clients insist on converting all passwords to uppercase before sending them to a server for authentication. One such client is Windows for Workgroups, which forces passwords to uppercase when connecting to a server using any protocol extension greater than COREPLUS.

Obviously, this can be very annoying if a user has a mixed-case UNIX password but attempts to connect from an offending client. This option defines how Samba may twiddle a password to attempt to get a match.

A value of zero causes only two passwords to be attempted: all uppercase and all lowercase. If non-zero this option defines the number of characters which may be uppercase.

For example, if `password level = 1` and both 'taul' and 'TAUL' failed as a password, then 'Taul,' 'tAul,' 'taUl,' and 'tauL' will be tried. If `password level = 2` then 'TAul,' 'TaUl,' 'TauL,' 'tAUl,' 'tAuL,' and 'taUL' would also be tried in addition to those tried in level 1. You get the picture. A larger value increases the likelihood that a user will be properly authenticated, but at the cost of some security and potentially increased time to authenticate a user.

As a result, it's probably more sensible to have users use numbers or punctuation, rather than mixed case, to increase password security. Note that using encrypted passwords gets rid of this problem completely.

Dealing with Mixed Case UNIX Usernames

`username level`

Default: `username level = 0`

Example: `username level = 2`

Many SMB clients send usernames only in uppercase. This parameter, available starting with Samba version 1.9.18, allows Samba to authenticate mixed case UNIX usernames properly, in the same way that password level deals with mixed case passwords. The higher this value, the more possible mixed case usernames Samba will try to authenticate as a username passed from the client.

Note that it may make more sense to use the `username map` option, explained on page 141, to map an uppercase version of a username to the corresponding mixed-case UNIX username.

Using Encrypted Local Password Authentication

To use encrypted password authentication against a password database stored on the Samba server, set `encrypted passwords = yes` and set the `server` parameter to either `user` or `share`. To complete the setup of this authentication method you must create a Samba password file. The format of the file is explained shortly. The complete step-by-step process for setting up encrypted password support is explained in detail on page 66.

There are several very big advantages to using encrypted passwords. Most of these advantages address problems with using plaintext passwords and native UNIX authentication that were discussed in the last section. To review, plaintext passwords will not be sent over the network, Windows NT will not ask for a password for every connection, and you will not need to edit the registry to force Windows NT or Windows 95 to negotiate access using a plaintext password.

Of course, there are disadvantages. Both LAN Manager and Windows NT style encrypted password authentication are incompatible with the standard UNIX password authentication method. This leads to the unfortunate situation that two password files must be maintained if users are to access the server machine using both Samba and an interactive shell, ftp, or other standard UNIX service. Keeping these two password files in sync is a not impossible. On a well run system it is not even that difficult. However, it is an additional level of complexity that can go wrong.

Secondly, while a plaintext version of the password is not stored in Samba's password file, the hashed passwords that are stored there are "password equivalents." This means that, while the original passwords are not stored, it is possible for a relatively sophisticated intruder to use this information with a modified SMB client to gain access to the shares on your system. Of course, if an intruder has gained access to Samba's password file, the intruder has probably gained access to root. In this case the jig is up—the intruder already has access to all the Samba resources. Unfortunately, since users usually use the same password on multiple systems, the information in Samba's password file will probably allow the intruder to gain access to other systems as well.

The bottom line? Zealously protect root. You should already, but this should give you added incentive. Some other pointers to improving the security of your system can be found on page 261. If you are especially paranoid you may wish to ask your users to select passwords for your Samba server that are different from passwords on other systems. However, in my experience, asking most users to cut off their left hand will be only slightly more difficult.

How Do SMB Encrypted Passwords Work?

There are two styles of SMB encrypted password authentication: LanManager and Windows NT. Both techniques use a file which contains hashed values of a user's password, just as the standard UNIX authentication method does. Unfortunately, neither technique is as secure as the hash algorithm used in the UNIX password database.

LanManager encryption uses this algorithm to generate the hash:

1. Convert the password entered by a user to all capitals.

2. Either truncate the resulting password to 14 characters if it is longer, or pad the password with null bytes if it is shorter than 14 characters.

3. Use this 14 byte value as two 56 bit DES keys to encrypt a "magic" 8 byte value twice, creating a 16 byte value. This value is the "hashed password" which is stored in the password file.

The Secret Magic Value

Microsoft has finally given legal authorization to release the magic value used by the LanManager hashing algorithm. The magic value is the string consisting of "KGS!@#$%". I think the shift-1,2,3,4,5 sequence is particularly amusing. This string had previously been determined by reverse engineering the algorithm.

> An unfortunate side-effect of this algorithm is that an intruder can avoid trying mixed case passwords when engaging in a brute-force password guessing attack.

> The Windows NT hashing algorithm consists of computing an MD4 hash of a Unicode version of the user's password. Since the password is not truncated or converted to uppercase the potential keyspace is significantly larger. Both techniques create a hash that cannot be reversed into the original password other than by using a brute-force attack.

Cracking the Windows NT Password Database

The hashed NT password database can be cracked by brute force in a relatively short length of time. Because the LanManager hashing algorithm converts the password to uppercase before computing the hash, the keyspace that needs to be searched for a brute force attack is significantly reduced.

However, we wouldn't be out of the woods even if LanManager backward compatibility were dropped. Neither algorithm uses any salt, a technique of attaching random data to the plaintext before encrypting it. The salt is not kept secret—the algorithm used by the UNIX crypt() command stores the salt in the first two characters of the hashed password. The salt is used to prevent the same password from always hashing to the same value. Because neither the NT nor the LanManager algorithm use any salt it is possible to precompute a dictionary of all possible hashes. There is even some talk of creating a web-accessible CGI interface to such a database.

The L0phtCrack tool, from L0pht Heavy Industries, will crack the NT password database for you. You can retrieve it from `http://www.l0pht.com/advisories.html`.

Remember that, while it may be convenient, it isn't even necessary to crack the password hashes to use them. The hashes are "password equivalents" and can be used by a custom SMB client, like a modified version of `smbclient`.

When a client indicates that it can support encrypted password authentication during the protocol negotiation stage, the server will respond with a random 8 byte value. This value is known as the *challenge*. The challenge will be different for each client request. The server stores the challenge until the client is authenticated or denied access.

After the client obtains the password from the user, it computes the hash value using one of the previously defined algorithms. The resulting 16 byte value is appended with 5 null bytes. This 21 byte value is used as three 56 bit DES keys to encrypt the 8 byte challenge value three times. The resulting 24 byte value is known as the *response*.

The server also executes the same algorithm, using the stored hashed password. If the value the server computes matches the value returned by the client, then the client had to have known the password, or at least the 16 byte hash value generated from the password. As a result access will be granted as the authenticated user. Otherwise, access is denied. A cleartext password was never passed over the network.

Note that, as mentioned previously, an intruder can use the hashed password value and a custom client program to gain access to a service. Since the source code to `smbclient`, part of the Samba suite, is obviously widely available, creating this custom client is not very difficult.

The Samba Password File

`smb passwd file`

Default: `smb passwd file = /usr/local/samba/ private/smbpasswd` (but can be changed at compile time)

Example: `smb passwd file = /etc/smbpasswd`

The Samba password file stores both the LanManager and the Windows NT style 16 bit hashed versions of the user's password. By default the Samba password file is stored at `/usr/local/samba/private/`

smbpasswd. This value can be changed at compile time, or by setting the smb passwd file parameter. Wherever you end up putting the private directory, make sure it has only owner read and execute permissions (mode 500). Make sure the smbpasswd file has only owner read and write permissions (mode 600). Last, make sure both files are owned by root.

The format of a record in the smbpasswd file is:

```
username:uid:XXXXXXXXXXXXXXXXXXXXXXXXXXXXXXXX:XXXXXXXXXXXXXXXXXXXXXXXXXXXXXXXX
XX:Long name:user home dir:user shell
```

It is essential that there be exactly 32 characters between the two colons in the hashed password fields. The Samba password code and the smbpasswd program will fail to validate any entry without exactly 32 characters in the hash fields.

A hash value consisting of 32 X characters is considered by Samba to be a null password. When a password has been set the X characters are replaced with 32 hexadecimal digits (0-9 and A-F) which represent the 16 bytes of the hashed password. For example, my record might appear as:

```
jdblair:500:F6D1A9C0D56014DFAAD3B435B51404EE:513DD6CB4015097C752397085365FC
99:John Blair:/home/jdblair:/bin/bash
```

A null password is not the same as no password. Unless the null passwords parameter is true, Samba will not grant access to a service with a null password. However, Samba will grant access to a service with no password. To set a user to have no password replace the hash value with this value:

```
NO PASSWORDXXXXXXXXXXXXXXXXXXXXXXX
```

For example, if I have the following record, I will not be required to enter a password when connecting to a service.

```
jdblair:100:NO PASSWORDXXXXXXXXXXXXXXXXXXXXXXX:XXXXXXXXXXXXXXXXXXXXXXXXXXXXXXXX
XX:John Blair:/home/jdblair:/bin/bash
```

The mksmbpasswd.sh awk script, included with the Samba distribution, will generate a Samba password file containing null passwords for every user in the UNIX password file. You can also use the smbpasswd -add option to add a single user at a time to the password file.

Step-by-step instructions for setting up the encrypted password file are explained on page 66.

Using Another SMB Server to Validate Passwords

password server

Default: none

Example: password server = TUCCSTER

The third technique Samba provides for checking passwords is almost as simple as using native UNIX authentication. Rather than checking passwords against a locally stored database, Samba can ask a remote SMB server, such as your Windows NT Primary Domain Controller. This option makes the most sense if you are integrating a UNIX system into an already existing Windows NT domain. If configured properly your UNIX host will behave almost like it is actually a part of the Windows NT domain security structure. Users' Samba passwords will automatically be the same as they are in your NT domain. If a user changes a password there is no synchronization delay. To enable this mode of password validation, set security = server and encrypt passwords = yes. You also need to set the password server parameter to the DNS name of a trusted SMB server, which will be used to check passwords for validity. In most cases it makes the most sense to set your NT primary or backup domain controller as your password server. There are cases where it may make more sense to use a different computer.

Note that for server mode security to work your Windows usernames must also exist on your UNIX host. This is because, while Samba implements its own logon procedure, it enforces access rights by running under the effective username of the authenticated user. This is obviously impossible if the user does not exist on the UNIX host.

Mapping Windows Usernames to UNIX Usernames

username map

Default: no username map

Example: username map = /usr/local/samba/lib/
username.map

If your users already have accounts on your UNIX host, and their usernames there are different from their Windows usernames, you will need to specify a username map file. This file maps Windows usernames to UNIX usernames, allowing users to login with a different name than their effective userid on the UNIX host. You specify the location of your username map file with the `username map` parameter. I use:

```
username map = /usr/local/samba/lib/username.map
```

The syntax of the username map file is simple. Each line consists of a UNIX username and a list of possible Windows username equivalents, separated by an equal sign. The list of names may also contain references to UNIX groups in the form `@group`. Any username in that group is added to the list. Like `smb.conf`, lines that begin with "#" or ";" are ignored. For example, this smb.conf file will map the Windows Administrator account to the UNIX root account:

```
# A simple username map file
root = Administrator admin
```

Note that the user mapping occurs before any other steps in the connect process. As a result, if you connect to `\\server\john` and "john" is remapped to "laura" then you will really be connecting to `\\server\laura` and you will have to supply the correct corresponding password.

Also note that no reverse name mapping is ever applied. This can be a problem in certain situations, such as when a user tries to delete a job from a print queue. The print manager will not believe the user has a job in the print queue, since none of the jobs will appear in the user's name.

Remember to make this file writeable only by root! Anybody that can modify this file can gain root access to your system.

Supporting Windows 95 Network Logins

Making the Samba Server the Windows 95 Domain Controller

`domain logons`

Default: `domain logons = no`

Example: `domain logons = yes`

This activates support for Windows 95 domain logins. If set to true

Samba will process Windows 95 domain logins, authenticating users and supplying a list of users for "user level" security of resources. The option is described in detail on page 229. If you have a Windows NT Server machine on your network you probably don't want to use this option.

Supporting Windows 95 Roving Profiles

`logon path`

Default: `logon path = \\%N\%U\profile`

Example: `logon path =`
`\\PROFILE_SERVER\HOME_DIR\%U\PROFILE`

The `logon path` parameter specifies the network path to the directory containing roaming profiles for Windows 95 logins. This directory will be passed to the Windows 95 client during the logon process. Windows 95 creates a file called USER.DAT in this directory to store the user's profile. This directory also stores the user's own "start menu," "network neighborhood," and "programs" directories.

The user must have write access to the share containing the profile. The USER.DAT file and all the directories will be created the first time the user logs in. If you don't want these directories to be modified by the user you can then make them read only. However, you should not make the USER.DAT file read-only—doing so can cause problems for Windows 95. Instead rename it USER.MAN, for MANdatory profile.

An example of using Samba to support roving profiles can be found on page 232.

Providing a Logon Script to Windows 95 Clients

`logon script`

Default: none

Example: `logon script = %U.bat`

Describes the location of a batch file which will be executed on the client machine when a user successfully logs in. The specified path must be relative to the root directory of the [netlogon] service. In other words, if your the root directory of your [netlogon] service is

143

`/usr/local/samba/netlogon` and `logon script = STARTUP.BAT` then the logon script is stored at `/usr/local/samba/netlogon/STARTUP.BAT`.

The logon script behaves similarly to a Novell Netware logon script. The script can contain whatever commands you feel necessary. You could use it to map commonly used services or the user's home directory to a drive letter with `NET USE G: \\SERVER\GAMES` or `H: \\SERVER\HOMES`. You could use it to synchronize the client's clock with the server's clock, using `NET TIME \\SERVER /SET /YES`.

You can use macro substitutions to create different logon scripts for specific users or client machines. You could get really creative and use the `preexec` parameter to generate a logon script on the fly for each connection. An example of a script that does this is on page 231.

Note that this file must use DOS-style cr/lf line endings. UNIX-style line endings will cause the client to choke on the script. Be very careful granting write access to this file since it could be used by an intruder to execute arbitrary commands on a client machine.

Other Password Related Parameters

Allowing Clients to Connect Without Passwords

`hosts equiv`

Default: none (no host equivalences)

CAUTION!

Be very careful if you use the `hosts equiv` parameter! No password will be required to connect from any host listed in the file specified by `hosts equiv`.

Example: `hosts equiv = /usr/local/samba/lib/hosts.equiv`

This parameter defines the location of a file containing a list of DNS hostnames. Users connecting from any of these hosts will not require a password to authenticate their connection.

Obviously, this is an extremely dangerous option. It is only useful for situations where you completely trust the client host. This might be the case if the client were an NT or UNIX machine administrated by yourself or someone you trust. Don't use this option unless you really know what you're doing or you're on an isolated network.

Don't mix up this parameter with the `hosts allow` service option, which describes which hosts are allowed to connect to a service. The hosts allow parameter is explained on page 169.

null passwords

CAUTION!

Setting `null passwords` to true can have unexpected side-effects, like granting access under users like `daemon` and `bin` under some systems. Be very careful!

Default: `null passwords = no`

Example: `null passwords = yes`

If the null passwords parameter is true, Samba will allow access to accounts which have null passwords. Set this to true only if you know exactly what you are doing.

Setting the Local Password Changing Program

passwd program

Default: `passwd program = /bin/passwd`

Example: `passwd program = /bin/passwd %u`

Defines the program which will be used to set user passwords. This option will only be necessary if you enable password changing at compile time.

Remember that many password programs require "good" passwords, which are often required to be a minimum length, mixed case and include numbers or punctuation marks. This can cause problems with some clients, like Windows for Workgroups, which insist on changing passwords to all uppercase before sending them.

Note that the password program will be executed with the effective userid of the owner of the password, not as root.

passwd chat

Default: `passwd chat = *old*password* %o\n`
`*new*password* %n\n *new*password* %n\n`
`*changed*`

Example: `passwd chat = "*Enter OLD password*" %o\n`
`"*Enter NEW password*" %n\n "*Reenter NEW`
`password*" %n\n "*Password changed*"`

This parameter controls the "chat" conversation which takes place between Samba and the local password changing program. It is only necessary if Samba has been configured as a logon server and to allow users to change their passwords. The string is a set of response-receive pairs which describes what Samba should send to the password change program and what it can expect back. If this expected response is not received Samba assumes the password was not changed.

In addition to all the standard macros, the password chat string can contain %o and %n, which will be replaced with the old and new passwords. The string can also contain the escape values \n, \r, \t, and \s, which stand for line feed, carriage return, tab, and space. Double quotes can be used to delimit a string to preserve space characters. The string can also contain a "*", which stands for a string of zero or more of any character.

The dot (".") character defines a null string. If used to describe a send string then no string will be sent. If used to describe a response string then no string will be expected.

Remember that, in general, this password changing technique does not work very well. Now that the encrypted password changing technique used by Windows 95 is publicly documented you can expect Samba to implement it soon. This password changing technique is likely to be much more reliable.

Setting Logging Behavior

Setting the Location of the Log File

`log file`

Default: set at compile time

Example: `log file = /usr/local/samba/var/log.%m`

The `log file` parameter allows you to override the compiled-in log file location. This option is most useful in combination with macro substitutions to create log files for specific users, clients, or architectures. An example of using this technique to solve problems with specific hosts is found on page 232.

Setting the Maximum Size of the Log File

`max log size`

Default: `max log size = 5000`

Example: `max log size = 10000`

The `max log size` option specifies the maximum size, in kilobytes, to which log files can grow. If the file exceeds the specified size it is renamed by adding the `.old` extension.

Note that it is usually more useful to set up a script to roll Samba's log files daily or weekly. This allows more than just the last log file to be archived.

Setting the Debug Level

`debug level`

Default: Zero, unless a debug level is specified from the command line.

Example: `debug level = 3`

Synonym: `log level`

The debug level parameter allows the debug logging level to be set in the `smb.conf` file, rather than from the command line. Adjusting the debug level in the `smb.conf` file is usually more convenient than doing so from the command line. Combining the `config file` or `include` parameter along with substitution macros allows you to increase the debug level for particular situations, such as specific clients or client architectures.

The debug level can range (as of Samba version 1.9.17) from 0 to 10. Larger values cause more detailed information to be logged. Log level 100 also exists, which logs passwords passed by a client to authenticate a connection. Most of these debug levels exist to help programmers debug the Samba server. Level 0 only logs error messages. I've found log levels 1 to 3 are useful for debugging configuration problems. Anything larger than that logs information rarely useful for anything other than debugging Samba itself.

The following example illustrates the differences between log levels 0 through 3. Each example shows the log generated when the smbclient tool is used to connect to a Samba filespace service called NT on a server named FRODO. Server level security is used to validate passwords against a Windows NT server. Note that log level three logs very nearly every phase of connect, authentication, and disconnect.

level 0:

```
Nothing is logged.
```

level 1:

```
negprot w/password server as 13270frodo
Client requested max send size of 65535
10/07/97 14:53:03 frodo (138.26.25.10) connect to service NT as user jdblair
(uid=500,gid=500)
(pid 13270)
10/07/97 14:53:12 frodo (138.26.25.10) closed connection to service NT
```

level 2:

```
10/07/97 14:54:53 changed root to /
netbios connect: name1=FRODO name2=FRODO
negprot w/password server as 13313frodo
Client requested max send size of 65535
Allowed connection from frodo (138.26.25.10) to NT
10/07/97 14:54:57 frodo (138.26.25.10) connect to service NT as user jdblair
(uid=500,gid=500) (pid 13313)
10/07/97 14:55:03 frodo (138.26.25.10) closed connection to service NT
Closing connections
```

level 3:

```
10/07/97 14:55:53 changed root to /
priming nmbd
sending a packet of len 1 to (127.0.0.1) on port 137 of type DGRAM
10/07/97 14:55:54 Transaction 0 of length 76 netbios connect: name1=FRODO
name2=FRODO
10/07/97 14:55:54 Transaction 1 of length 168
switch message SMBnegprot (pid 13346)
Requested protocol [PC NETWORK PROGRAM 1.0]
Requested protocol [MICROSOFT NETWORKS 1.03]
Requested protocol [MICROSOFT NETWORKS 3.0]
Requested protocol [LANMAN1.0]
Requested protocol [LM1.2X002]
Requested protocol [Samba]
Connecting to 138.26.25.25 at port 139
connected to password server TUCCSTER
negprot w/password server as 13346frodo
got session
password server OK
```

```
using password server validation
Selected protocol NT LANMAN 1.0
10/07/97 14:56:00 Transaction 2 of length 117
switch message SMBsesssetupX (pid 13346)
Domain=[UAB-TUCC] NativeOS=[Unix] NativeLanMan=[Samba]
sesssetupX:name=[JDBLAIR]
password server TUCCSTER accepted the password
adding home directory jdblair at /home/jdblair
jdblair is in 3 groups
19 100 500
uid 500 registered to name jdblair
Clearing default real name
Client requested max send size of 65535
10/07/97 14:56:00 Transaction 3 of length 62
switch message SMBtconX (pid 13346)
Allowed connection from frodo (138.26.25.10) to NT
ACCEPTED: validated uid ok as non-guest
found free connection number 12
Connect path is /home/jdblair/NT
jdblair is in 3 groups
19 100 500
chdir to /home/jdblair/NT
chdir to /usr/local/samba/lib
10/07/97 14:56:00 frodo (138.26.25.10) connect to service NT as user jdblair
(uid=500,gid=500)
(pid 13346)
10/07/97 14:56:00 tconX service=nt user=jdblair cnum=12
10/07/97 14:56:20 Transaction 4 of length 44
switch message SMBchkpth (pid 13346)
chdir to /home/jdblair/NT
unix_clean_name [./]
unix_clean_name [.]
10/07/97 14:56:20 chkpth . cnum=12 mode=5
10/07/97 14:56:26 Transaction 5 of length 39
switch message SMBtdis (pid 13346)
chdir to /usr/local/samba/lib
10/07/97 14:56:26 frodo (138.26.25.10) closed connection to service NT
Yielding connection to 12 NT
Yielding connection to 12 STATUS.
Yield successful
10/07/97 14:56:26 tdis cnum=12
end of file from client
Closing connections
10/07/97 14:56:26 Server exit (normal exit)
```

Logging Messages to Syslog

syslog

Default: `syslog = 1`

Example: `syslog = 3`

The `syslog` parameter controls which and with what priority Samba debug messages are logged by syslog. Samba assigns the syslog priority according to the chart below:

log level	syslog priority	loglevel from syslog.h
0	error	LOG_ERROR
1	warning	LOG_WARNING
2	notice	LOG_NOTICE
3	info	LOG_INFO

The `syslog` parameter specifies which messages are important enough to be sent to the system log facility. For example, if `syslog = 2` and `log level = 5` then messages with a debug level of 0 or 1 would be sent to the system log daemon as well as the Samba log files, and messages with a debug level of 2, 3, 4 and 5 would be sent only to the Samba log files. Messages with a debug level above 5 would not be logged at all.

When messages are sent to the syslog log daemon they are assigned a system log level according to their debug level. Messages with a debug level of 0 are assigned `LOG_ERR`. Messages with a debug level of 1 are assigned `LOG_WARNING`. Messages with a debug level of 2 are assigned `LOG_NOTICE`. Messages with a debug level of 3 are assigned `LOG_INFO`. Messages with a debug level above 3 are assigned `LOG_DEBUG`.

syslog only

Default: `syslog only = no`

Example: `syslog only = yes`

If `syslog only` is true Samba will forgo its own log files and send log messages only to syslog.

Disk and Filesystem Related Options

Global Name Mangling Options

All of these options affect the behavior of the name mangling related service options.

Improving the Likelihood of Correct Reverse Name Mangling

`mangled stack`

Default: `mangled stack = 50`

Example: `mangled stack = 100`

The mangled stack is a list of recently mangled long file names cached on the Samba server. This option controls the length of this list.

The longer this list, the more likely a mangled name will be converted back to the correct original file name. Unfortunately a large stack size slows file access and wastes memory—each name in the stack costs 256 bytes.

If a client requests a mangled file name that is no longer in the mangled stack Samba may not be able to determine the correct long file name. Be prepared for some surprises!

Working with Alternate Client Character Sets

`client code page`

Default: `client code page = 850`

Example: `client code page = 437`

This specifies the base DOS code page that is used by clients accessing Samba. The information is used to learn how to map lower case to uppercase letters for the character set in use by the client. To learn what code page you are using open up a DOS prompt and type chcp. Samba can currently recognize two codepages: 437 and 850. 437 is the default for MS-DOS, Windows 95, and Windows NT in the United States. 850 is the default for all Western European releases of those operating systems.

Starting with version 1.9.18, this command causes a code page definition file to be loaded. Prior to this version the code pages were hard-coded into the server. The make_smbcodepage tool is provided to allow people to create their own code page files.

This option has been added as a convenience to European users by avoiding the need for a complex valid chars string. If you wish to define a client code page and a valid chars string, the valid chars service parameter must appear after your client code page parameter. Otherwise the client code page parameter will override the valid chars string rather than augmenting it. The valid chars parameter is explained on page 163.

Prior to version 1.9.18, setting the client code page to a number other than 437 or 850 would cause it to default to 850. For 1.9.18 and later, setting this parameter to a number for which no code page file exists will cause it to default to 437.

character set

Default: none

Example: character set = iso8859-2

This setting allows a smbd to map characters in file names from a DOS code page to either a Western European (ISO8859-1) or Eastern European (ISO8859-2) code page before writing or fetching the file name to or from the disk. Normally no character translation is done.

Using NIS to Set a User's Home Directory

homedir map

Default: homedir map = auto.home

Example: homedir map = nis.map

The homedir map file specifies the location of the NIS (Network

Information System, formerly Sun Yellow Pages) map file used to determine a user's home directory if the `nis homedir` parameter is set to true. Currently only the Sun `auto.home` map file syntax is understood. This syntax is:

```
username server:/path/to/homedir
```

Note that NIS service must be compiled into the Samba server, and the `nis homedir` parameter must be true for this option to have any effect. There is some discussion about supporting other map file formats, such as the syntax used by the Berkeley Automounter. This is something which may be provided in future version of Samba.

nis homedir

Default: `nis homedir = no`

Example: `nis homedir = yes`

Without this option, if the Samba logon server is not the same machine that stores a user's home directory, two network hops are required for a client to access the directory: one SMB network hop to the Samba server, then one NFS network hop to the home directory server. The host running the Samba server would consult the NIS map and NFS automount the user's home directory from the remote server. File accesses can be very slow in this situation, especially when writing through Samba to an NFS mounted filesystem.

Normally when a client asks for a user's home directory during the login process, Samba returns `\\SERVER\USERNAME`, where SERVER is the NetBIOS name of the Samba server. Setting the `nis homedir` option to true causes SERVER to be replaced with the name of the server specified for the user in the NIS map file. As long as Samba is running on this server, this allows the client to contact this server directly rather than using two network hops.

CIFS introduces the ability to do drive redirection (called DFS). This allows an SMB server to redirect a connection to a different server. Samba does not (yet) implement this feature.

Improving Disk Access Time

Caching `getwd()` calls

getwd cache

Default: `getwd cache = no`

Example: `getwd cache = yes`

If set to true this option causes Samba to use a caching algorithm to reduce the time spent calling `getwd()` (get working directory). Setting this value to true can result in a significant increase in performance, especially when `wide links` is false. See `wide links`, on page 180, for more details.

Overlapping Network and Disk I/O Operations

read size

Default: `read size = 2048`

Example: `read size = 4096`

It is possible for Samba to provide greater performance by overlapping network read/writes and disk read/writes for certain SMB commands. When an SMB packet is greater than the value of this parameter, in the case of `SMBwrite` and `SMBwriteX` Samba begins transmitting before all the data has been read into memory. In the case of `SMBreadbraw` Samba will begin writing to disk after this much data has been received by the incoming packet.

This technique provides noticeable gains when the network speed and the disk access speed are very similar. If one is significantly slower than the other the size of this value will have little effect.

The optimum value for this parameter will vary between operating systems and specific hardware setup. A value over 65536 is pointless since it exceeds the maximum size of an SMB packet.

Reading Ahead to Prepare for the Next SMB Operation

`read prediction`

Default: `read prediction = no`

Example: `read prediction = yes`

If set to true then Samba will attempt to speed up client reads by pre-reading data from a file if it was last opened in read-only mode. This lets Samba guess at the next client request and potentially provide a quicker response. In most situations it makes sense to set this to true.

Unfortunately, as of Samba version 1.9.18, this code had been disabled due to bugs. Hopefully it will be fixed by the time you read this.

Miscellaneous Other Options

Setting the Maximum Size of a Disk

`max disk size`

Default: `max disk size = 0`

Example: `max disk size = 1000`

This parameter allows you to set an artificial upper limit on the apparent size of a disk, in megabytes. Shares will not appear to be larger than the value of this parameter. This parameter does not limit the amount of data a client can actually store on the server—it only affects the result a client will receive if it asks the server for the amount of free disk space.

A value of zero means there is no limit on the apparent disk size other than the actual size of the disk.

This option was added to work around bugs in some software that break when accessing large (usually greater than 1 gigabyte) disk drives.

Supplying a User's Real Name to the Client

unix realname

Default: unix realname = no

Example: unix realname = yes

If the unix realname parameter is true, then Samba will supply the real name field from the UNIX password file to the SMB client. This is often useful for semi-automating the setup of mail clients and web browsers on systems used by more than one person.

Setting an Alternative Free Disk Space Command

dfree command

Default: none, meaning the system will use internal routines to determine available disk space

Example: dfree command = /usr/local/samba/bin/ dfree

The dfree command only needs to be set on systems which incorrectly calculate available disk space. The bug has been confirmed under Ultrix, but may occur on other systems as well. The result of the bug was the error "Abort Retry Fail" at the end of each directory listing.

This setting replaces the internal disk space calculation routines with an external command that will return a correct value. The external command will be passed a directory path and should return two ASCII values: 1) the total disk space in block, and 2) the number of available blocks. An optional third value should return the block size in bytes if blocks on your system are not 1024 bytes.

The dfree script could be:

```
#!/bin/sh
df $1 | tail -1 | awk '{print $2" "$4}'
```

Note that the System V df command requires the -k flag in this context.

Setting an Alternate Lock File Directory

`lock directory`

Default: `lock directory = /usr/local/samba/var/`
          `locks` (can be set to a different directory at compile time)

Example: `lock directory = /usr/local/samba/locks`

This parameter specifies the directory which will contain lock files. This is useful of you wish to store lock files in a directory different from the one specified at compile time. These lock files are used to store the SMB deny modes open on files and to implement the `max connections` option. This option is unnecessary if you are using shared memory locks.

Be sure not to set this directory to an NFS drive unless you are using the newer SystemV-based fast share modes. Setting this to an NFS drive will cause problems if you are using the original mmap-based fast share modes.

Global Printer Service Options

Automatically Configuring Printer Services

`load printers`

Default: `load printers = no`

Example: `load printers = yes`

If the `load printers` parameter is set to true all printers defined in the `printcap` file will be shared by Samba.

Specifying the Location of the printcap File

`printcap name`

Default: `/etc/printcap`

Example: `/usr/local/samba/lib/printcap`

The `printcap` name option specifies the location of the `printcap` file. Samba uses the `printcap` file to determine all printers available on the system if the general [printers] service is used instead of defining each printer in its own service.

You might want to define a different `printcap` file if you use a system, like AIX, which doesn't use a conventional `printcap` file. You can also define a custom printcap file to make only a portion of the printers in the real printcap file available for use through Samba. In either of these cases you don't need a full-fledged `printcap` file. Samba only parses out the name of the printer from the beginning of each `printcap` stanza. You only need to create a file of one or more lines with this syntax:

`printername|printername|printername|printername`

Each printer name must be the name of a valid printer on your system.

Setting the Print Queue Cache Time

`lpq cache time`

Default: `lpq cache time = 10`

Example: `lpq cache time = 45`

Samba caches the output of the `lpq` command, by default every 10 seconds, to prevent it from being called too frequently. A separate cache is used for each variation of the `lpq` command—this allows you to create different queues for different users.

This is necessary because a Windows client polls the print queue every 15 seconds while the print manager is open. A hundred PCs with the print manager open can bring a system with a slow lpq command to its knees!

A value of 0 disables caching. A large value is a good idea if your `lpq` command is very slow.

Setting the Location of the Windows 95 Printer Definition File

printer driver file

Default: `printer driver file = /usr/local/lib/
printers.def`

Example: `printer driver file = /usr/local/samba/
printers/drivers.def`

This parameter specifies the location of the printer driver definition file. This file, along with some other configuration, allows you to support the automatic installation of printer drivers onto Windows 95 machines.

Miscellaneous Other Options

Disabling the Connection Status File

status

Default: `status = yes`

Example: `status = no`

Normally Samba logs all active connections to a status file. The `smbstatus` utility uses this file to report on active connections. If you never use the `smbstatus` command you may wish to set `status` to false. This may result in a marginal speed increase.

Setting a Root Directory other than /

root directory

Default: `root directory = /`

Example: `root directory = /usr/local/samba`

Synonym: `root`, `root dir`

The `root directory`, `root`, or `root dir` parameters specifies a directory that Samba will `chroot()` to on start-up. This provides an added level of security by making it impossible to access any files not under this directory. This security does come at a price—you will have to mirror any needed files not under this directory so they are accessible. In particular, you will probably have to mirror `/etc/passwd`, `/etc/group`, and `/etc/hosts`, as well as any printer commands and configuration files. You will also need to describe all pathnames relative to this new pseudo-root rather than the actual root. Symbolic links which link to files not directly under the `root directory` will be inaccessible.

This option is provided as a paranoid security check against bugs in Samba or mistakes in configuration. In most cases it is unnecessary.

Setting the WinPopup Message Handler

message command

Default: none

Example: `message command = csh -c 'xedit %s;rm %s' &`

This specifies a shell command to run to process incoming WinPopup messages. How you actually deliver the WinPopup message to the user is up to your imagination.

This command takes all the standard macro substitutions, as well as three substitutions unique to this option:

`%s`	The path of the file containing the WinPopup message.
`%t`	The destination of the message (usually the server's NetBIOS name)

`%f`   The user the message is from.

The Samba documentation suggests the solution shown in the example above. This is a nice simple solution, but unfortunately doesn't always work. First, it depends on having the X window system running. Second, since the command will be executed under the ownership of the guest user, your X server will refuse the connection if you are running X authentication (which you should be). I have written a Tcl/Tk script called TkPopup which works properly with X authentication and will also deliver messages to the console. This script is included in the `scripts/`directory of the CD-ROM included with this book. Examples of different ways to deal with WinPopup messages are explained on page 260.

It is very important that whatever command you set exits immediately. The sender of the message may hang until this command exits, leading to unpredictable behavior on many Windows machines. This is why the example above uses the "`&`" shell option to spawn a background process.

Setting the Location of the `smbrun` binary

`smbrun`

Default: `smbrun = /usr/local/samba/bin/smbrun` (but can be changed at compile time)

Example: `smbrun = /usr/sbin/smbrun`

The `smbrun` parameter sets the pathname to the `smbrun` binary. If you install smbrun in a different location than that specified at compile time you will have to set this option.

The `smbrun` command is used as a wrapper to run shell commands, such as printer commands, scripts, and the message command. It is necessary because the UNIX `system()` call on most systems does not provide a facility to run a command-line command with a different real userid than the current process. `smbrun` works around this problem by switching its own userid to the appropriate user (usually the guest user) and executing the shell script.

Using Samba as a Time Server

time server

Default: time server = no

Example: time server = yes

If true nmbd will advertise itself, and function as, a time server. This allows all your Windows networking clients to synchronize their local system time with your Samba server. Examples can be found on page 252.

time offset

Default: time offset = 0

Example: time offset = 1

The time offset option specifies a number of minutes to add to the normal GMT to local time conversion value. This lets Samba correctly synchronize the time on clients which may have trouble correcting for daylight savings time on their own.

Hacker Options

These parameters should only be set if you have a thorough understanding of Samba's internals.

browse list

Default: browse list = yes

The browse list parameter controls whether smbd will respond to a NetServerEnum by serving a browse list. This is set to true by default and normally should not be modified.

max mux

Default: max mux = 50

The max mux parameter defines the maximum number of simultaneous SMB operations that Samba informs a client it will allow.

max ttl

Default: max ttl = 14400

Describes the maximum "time to live," in seconds, for NetBIOS names registered with Samba.

shared mem size

Default: shared mem size = 102400

Defines the amount of memory, in bytes, used to implement shared memory file locking.

shared file entries

Default: shared file entries = 113

The options describes the number of hash buckets used to store file locks when Samba has been compiled to use shared memory file locking (the FAST_SHARE_MODES compile-time option).

Deprecated Options

Dealing with Special Characters

valid chars

Default: none

Example: valid chars = 0345:0305 0366:0326
0344:0304

This option is deprecated starting with Samba version 1.9.18, which introduced the client code page parameter. This parameter is explained on page 151.

These two parameters are kept for backwards compatibility with older configuration files, but are now considered deprecated.

strip dot

Default: strip dot = no

Example: strip dot = yes

If the strip dot parameter is true Samba will strip trailing dots off of a file name. Normally these trailing dots can result in undesirable name mangling behavior. This option is now considered deprecated because you can accomplish the same thing with the mangled map service parameter.

packet size

Synonym: max packet

This option has been deprecated since Samba version 1.7.00. It is kept only so old configuration files are not invalid. It once set the maximum packet size during a rawread.

Chapter 6: Service Configuration Options

Index of Service Configuration Parameters

The whole reason you're interested in the Samba server is to provide SMB networking services. The properties of each service are controlled by a section in the smb.conf file. This chapter organizes these options by the goals they accomplish. While this isn't the most efficient way to present all of the configuration options, it presents them in the order you are likely to need to encounter them. It also keeps related options, as well as configuration options outside the scope of the smb.conf file, close together where you will encounter them.

This chapter is split into three sections: options common to both filespace services and printer services, options specific to filespace services and options specific to printer services. Samba purists may note that every service option can appear legally in a definition for either type of service. However, in practice this doesn't really make sense. Presenting the options this way should follow your train of thought if you build a service definition from scratch.

Options Common to Filespace and Printer Services

These settings are important to both filespace and printer services.

Setting the Shared Directory

path

Default: `path = /tmp`

Example: `path = /home/ftp/pub`

Synonym: `directory`

The `path` parameter specifies the pathname of the shared directory. Any directory visible to the Samba server may be shared. Typically this includes the entire UNIX filesystem, but may be limited by the `root directory` global option.

For printer services this parameter describes the directory used to temporarily spool files sent from clients for printing before they are spooled to the local UNIX printer spool (i.e., the lp printer spool). The default setting of `/tmp` is usually adequate. If you decide to use a different directory it should typically be set to be world-writeable with the sticky bit set (mode 1777). This means any user will have permission to store a file in the spool directory, but not to delete files owned by others.

Controlling Appearance in the Network Browser

browseable

Default: browseable = yes

Example: browseable = no

This option controls whether or not the service appears in the browse list. Note that the service will still be accessible, just not visible in the network browser.

comment

Default: none

Example: comment = Publicly Available Files

The comment string will be seen listed next to the service in the output from the NET VIEW command. It is also visible in the Windows Explorer in the Properties box or if Details are selected to be shown.

Access Controls

Controlling Access by Client IP Address

allow hosts

Default: none, meaning all hosts are permitted access

Example: allow hosts = 138.26.,
holychao.cas.muohio.edu

Synonym: hosts allow

deny hosts

Default: none, meaning no hosts are explicitly denied access

Example: deny hosts = mordor.tucc.uab.edu

These parameters allow one to define a set of hosts which will be

CAUTION!

It is a good idea to use `allow hosts` in your `[global]` section to restrict access to hosts in your organization.

granted access to a service. Hosts are defined using patterns with a syntax similar to that used for tcpwrappers.[12]

If an `allow hosts` pattern is present, only hosts matching the pattern are allowed to access the service. If a `deny hosts` pattern exists only hosts not matching the pattern will be granted access. Both options can be used at the same time to define a range of valid hosts with exception. If the patterns in both `allow hosts` and `deny hosts` match a host, the host will be granted access.

Valid hosts can be specified using any of four patterns:

hostname: A string that starts with a '.' matches a host if the last components of the hostname match the string. For example, `.uab.edu` matches `frodo.tucc.uab.edu`. A single valid hostname can be described using a pattern that doesn't start with a '.', such as `borg.dpo.uab.edu`.

IP address: A string that ends with a '.' matches a host if the first components of its IP address match the string. For example, '138.26.' describes every computer on the academic network at the University of Alabama at Birmingham.

netgroup: A string that starts with an "@" refers to an NIS (formally YP) netgroup. A host matches if it is a member of the group.

network/mask: An expression of the form `n.n.n.n/m.m.m.m` is parsed as a network/mask pair. This allows for finer grained control than simply specifying whole class A, B, or C networks as ranges. For example, the pattern `138.26.25.0/255.255.255.128` describes the range of hosts from 138.26.25.0 to 138.26.25.63.

Exceptions can be included in a pattern by appending `EXCEPT` and a second expression to the end of the allowed pattern. For example, `.tucc.uab.edu EXCEPT morder.tucc.uab.edu` allows all computers whose hostname ends in "tucc.uab.edu" except for the single host `morder.tucc.uab.edu`. Ranges of hosts are also valid as exceptions. Patterns can be grouped into lists separated by commas. Very complex access rules can be constructed. An alternative to using the `EXCEPT` syntax is to use an appropriate combination of patterns in both `allow hosts` and `deny hosts`.

You can test your access controls by calling `testparm` with an IP

---

12. Actually, the code which implements the host allow and deny controls is derived directly from the tcpwrapper code written by Wietse Venema. Look at the access.c file for more info.

address or hostname as an argument. `testparm` will report whether or not the IP address is able to access each service.

Using a Conditional Configuration File to Implement Host-Based Access

You can use the `include` or the config file parameters, in combination with any of the substitution macros, to implement a conditional configuration file. While this is not an efficient way to block access to ranges of IP addresses, it is a good way to setup unique configuration files for specific clients or specific client architectures. This can, for example, cause a service to simply not appear in the browse list, rather than just denying access when a client attempts to access the service.

Granting Access to Users

These options grant or revoke the right to access a service. They do not affect a user's ability to access files shared by that service.

valid users

Default: none, meaning anybody can log in

Example: `valid users = jdblair, @coders`

invalid users

Default: none, also meaning anybody can log in

Example: `invalid users = root, @blacklist`

If neither of these parameters are set then any authenticated user will be granted access to the service. The `valid users` parameter may contain a comma-delimited list of users who will be allowed to access the service. The `invalid users` parameter may contain a similar comma-delimited list of users who will never be granted access to the service. This second option provides a convenient means for blocking specific users, especially as a last line of defense protecting against mistakes in other parameters. It is also useful in the `[homes]` service to deny remote home directory access to a subset of users. Note that invalid users take precedence over valid users. A user appearing in both lists will be denied access. In both cases a name starting with an "@" will be interpreted as a UNIX group, causing all users who are members of the group to be included in the list.

Granting Guest Access

Two types of guest access are allowed by Samba.

public

Default: `public = no`

Example: `public = yes`

Synonym: `guest ok`

guest only

Default: `guest only = no`

Example: `guest only = yes`

Synonym: `only guest`

If `public` or `guest ok` is true then guest access will be allowed. The access rights of a client connecting as guest will be those of the username set in the `guest user` parameter.

If either is false no password will be required to access this service. The access rights will be those of the account set by the `guest user` parameter. Note that then no password will be required to access this service. The access rights will be those of the account set by the `guest user` parameter. Note that the `public` or `guest ok` option does not force all users to connect as the guest user. A user will connect normally, assuming the rights of the authenticated username, if a valid password is supplied. Guest access rights are used if a user attempts a guest login, or if the password authentication fails and the `GUEST_SESSSETUP` compile-time option is non-zero. If `guest only` is true then non-guest authentication will not be allowed.

Note that just what a guest login is depends on whether the server is using user or share level security. See the User Authentication section on page for details. Also see page 70 for details on the `GUEST_SESSSETUP` option.

guest account

Default: `guest account = nobody` (can be set at compile time)

Example: `guest account = ftp`

CAUTION!

Don't grant your guest account user any more than the bare minimum of user rights. You might want to set the login shell of your guest account to `/bin/false`.

This sets the UNIX account used for connections to public services (services with `guest ok` or `guest only` set to true). Set this value with care! Any privileges granted to this user will be assigned to all guest accesses to the server.

Printer commands are executed with the user rights of the connected user. It is common in many situations to grant printing access to guest logins. On many systems `nobody` is not allowed to print. If this is the case then you will need to create an account with minimal user rights to use as a guest account. I like to set `guest account` to `ftp` with the reasoning that the account that I already use to grant anonymous ftp access is benign (or it better be!), and it is already created.

Limiting the Number of Simultaneous Users of a Service

`max connections`

Default: `max connections = 0`

Example: `max connections = 15`

This option allows you to set the maximum number of simultaneous connections which will be allowed to access a service from a single client. This is almost never what you actually want to do. As a result, this parameter is mostly useless and frequently misunderstood. If `max connections = 0`, an unlimited number of clients are allowed to access the service.

Kludging Usernames for Older Clients

`username`

Default: The name of the service will be used.

Example: `username = jdblair, @smbusers`

Synonym: `user`

The `username` parameter allows one to define a comma-delimited list of users against which Samba will test the client supplied password. This allows Samba to provide an approximation of user level security to clients that understand only share level security. Put another way, Samba doesn't provide a way to directly specify a password to associate with access rights, as user level security does. However, the username parameter allows you to accomplish the same thing by granting access to anyone using the same password as a particular username. This is especially useful for older clients that implement only the CORE or COREPLUS protocol extensions. It also allows you to serve Windows for Workgroups clients when the user's WfWg name is different from their UNIX name. (WfWg does not allow the user to supply a different name.)

If the username parameter is not present for a service, Samba will attempt to use the name of the service as a username. This allows users to connect to their home directories from clients which do not pass a username to the server.

In general, using a username list is not an excellent solution. Authentication will be slower, an intruder will automatically have guesses checked against multiple usernames, and a user can be logged in with the wrong access permissions if his or her password happens to be the same as another user.

All the members of a UNIX group can be specified by starting an entry with an "@". If a group is very large, searching through all the users can take quite a long time.

`only user`

Default: `only user = no`

Example: `only user = yes`

If the `only user` option is true then only users listed in the `username` list will be granted access to the share.

Forcing Revalidation of Passwords

`revalidate`

Default: `revalidate = no`

Example: `revalidate = yes`

When Samba successfully validates a client's password it passes back a token that the client can use to connect to other shares in the near future. This token is used to execute SMB operations on behalf of the client without reauthorizing until the client completely disconnects from the server. If `revalidate` is true then Samba will require that the client again present a valid username/password pair rather than just relying on

the token. For example, if you successfully connect to
`\\FRODO\Public` and then attempt to attach to `\\FRODO\CDROM`
Samba would validate your password a second time.

The default behavior is to accept the token as proof of identity. This
provides a minor performance boost, especially if `security =
server`.

Creating Multiple Services with Similar Options

`copy`

Default: none

Example: `copy = otherservice`

This option allows you to copy all parameters from a previously defined
service into the current service. This simplifies the structure of the
`smb.conf` file by allowing you to derive a service from a previously
defined service. Any additional parameters in the new service will
override the parameters copied from the other service, allowing you to
set options unique to the new service. The service being copied must
appear earlier in the configuration file.

Executing Scripts when a Service is Accessed

`preexec`

Default: none

Example: `preexec = echo '%T: %u connected to %S
           from %m' >> usagelog`

Synonym: `exec`

postexec

Default: none

Example: `postexec = echo '%T: %u disconnected from`
`%S from %m' >> usagelog`

root preexec

Default: none

Example: `root preexec = mount /cdrom`

root postexec

Default: none

Example: `root postexec = umount /cdrom`

These four parameters allow you to set a shell command that will be executed when a user connects to or disconnects from a service. This shell command is useful for mounting and unmounting filesystems, generating logging information, displaying announcements for a service using WinPopup messages, or anything else you can think of.

`preexec` executes a command when a user connects to a service. `postexec` executes a command when a user disconnects from a service. In both cases the command will be run with the effective username of the connected user. `root preexec` and `root postexec` are identical except that they run the script as root rather than the guest account. Note that the root options can be extremely dangerous. In most cases there is a better way to accomplish the same task. For example, if you wish to mount and unmount a cdrom on demand it makes more sense to add the user option to your `fstab` file, if your system supports it.

Filespace Services

Sharing the UNIX Filesystem

A filespace service shares a directory from the UNIX filesystem. These options control what directory is shared and what files and directories within it are visible.

Setting the Volume Name

`volume`

Default: the name of the share

Example: `volume = Office97`

SMB has a field which returns the "volume name" of a share. Samba normally returns the name of a share as the volume name. This parameter allows you to override this value. This is useful for installation programs which insist on the installation media having a particular name and you wish to set the name of the share to a different name.

Pruning the Shared Directory Tree

The shared directory tree can be "pruned." Files and directories within the shared directory can be effectively un-shared by making them invisible to clients.

`dont descend`

Default: none (meaning all directories will be descended)

Example: `dont descend = /proc,/dev`

The `dont descend` parameter specifies a comma-delimited list of directories which will appear, from the perspective of a client, to be empty. This is especially useful if you share the entire filesystem, since some directories like the `/dev` or `/proc` directory are not traditional filesystems and may cause undesirable behavior when accessed by a SMB client. The option is also useful to block recursive (and thus infinitely deep) directories caused by symbolic links. Note the parameters specific to symbolic links in the next section.

A significant but non-intuitive side effect of `dont descend` is that the directory itself will appear in the listing of its parent directory. Samba simply blocks attempts to enter the specified directory. If an SMB user attempts to delete this directory, the operation will succeed if the user has the appropriate UNIX permissions to delete the entire contents of the directory and the directory is empty.

Never use this parameter for security purposes! It is intended only to block access to inconvenient directories. There is no guarantee that an inventive user will not be able to circumvent this setting.

veto files

Default: none

Example: `veto files = /.AppleDouble/.bin/`
`.AppleDesktop/Network Trash Folder/`

delete veto files

Default: `delete veto files = no`

Example: `delete veto files = yes`

CAUTION!

Don't use `veto files` or `delete veto files` to enforce a security policy.

`veto files` specifies a list of patterns describing files and directories which will neither be visible to nor accessible by client machines. Each entry in the list is separated by a "/", allowing spaces to appear in a pattern. The "*" character can be used to specify one or more of any character, and the "?" character specifies exactly one of any character. The example above prevents Macintosh-specific directories created by the Netatalk AppleShare server from being visible to SMB clients. This parameter will slow down file accesses since Samba must consult this list before resolving every file access.

This parameter is affected by the `case sensitive` parameter, explained in the name mangling section. If `case sensitive = no` then the patterns listed in `veto files` will also not be case sensitive. You should use the hide files option if you want files to be hidden but still be accessible.

CAUTION!

A vetoed file or directory can still be deleted if the directory containing it is deleted.

Samba version 1.9.18 introduced the `delete veto files` parameter, which allows you to control this behavior. As of version 1.9.18, by default Samba will not delete any vetoed files when an entire directory is deleted. This will cause the directory to remain, but appear to be empty to the SMB client. If `delete veto files` is true then Samba will delete any vetoed files contained within the deleted directory, as long as this operation is permitted by the UNIX file permissions.

Setting the `delete veto files` parameter to true is especially useful when Samba is integrated with a Macintosh file sharing system like CAP or Netatalk. Both of these systems create hidden directories containing the Finder information and resource fork of files created by Macintosh clients. It is useful to hide these directories from SMB clients using the veto files option, but also useful to cause them to be deleted if an SMB client deletes an entire directory.

Just as with the `dont descend` parameter, do not use this feature to implement a security policy. It is just provided for convenience.

Dealing with Symbolic Links

With the exception of some extensions in CIFS 1.0, SMB doesn't have a way to deal with symbolic links. This is because, with the exception of POSIX compatibility mode under Windows NT, the Windows world doesn't have anything like a symbolic link (or a custom hard link, for that matter). Don't confuse the Windows shortcut with a UNIX symbolic link. While the two are similar on the surface, they are totally different.

The Windows shortcut is a user interface feature, allowing you to encapsulate a local or network pathname and/or command-line command within a file. This file appears in the Windows Explorer as an icon that, when clicked on, behaves like the file it references, and may pass command-line options if it references an executable file. However, it is the job of each individual program, not the operating system, to resolve shortcuts. Not all programs are able to transparently resolve shortcuts in the manner of Windows Explorer. In contrast, UNIX symbolic links are transparent to applications unless the application purposely provides exceptions for symbolic links.

By default Samba resolves symbolic links and makes them appear to an SMB client as if they are normal directories. Several options allow you to modify this behavior.

Note that since CIFS 1.0 is being pushed as an Internet standard, it has to be useful for sharing files between all operating systems, not just Microsoft operating systems. As a result, CIFS 1.0 contains support for symbolic links for when it is used to share files between UNIX machines. Samba does not yet support this option, but neither do any of Microsoft's SMB clients.

follow symlinks

Default: `follow symlinks = yes`

Example: `follow symlinks = no`

CAUTION!

Don't use `follow symlinks` to enforce a security policy.

This option controls whether or not the Samba server will follow symbolic links, presenting them to the client as normal files and directories. If this parameter is false a client will receive an error if it attempts to traverse a symbolic link.

This option is provided as an administrative convenience only. It looks like it could provide an additional layer of security (i.e., it stops users from putting a symbolic link to `/etc/password` in their home directory). Unfortunately, there is an inherent race condition when trying to do this sort of check that a clever attacker will be able to exploit.

wide links

Default: `wide links = yes`

Example: `wide links = no`

Don't use `wide links` to enforce a security policy.

If this parameter is false, Samba will not traverse a symbolic link that links outside the area directly under the shared directory tree. If true Samba will traverse symbolic links that link outside this directory tree. This option provides a very useful compromise between ignoring symbolic links and following all symbolic links.

Never use this option to enforce a security policy. Like `symbolic links`, it would appear that this option could be used to enforce a security policy. Unfortunately, this too suffers from an inherent race condition that an attacker could exploit.

Controlling Access to a Service

The right to access filespace resources are controlled by a combination of Samba configuration parameters and the UNIX file ownerships and permissions of the shared directory and its contents. The Samba configuration options allow you to control which users are allowed to access a share and what type of access that user will be granted. Users can be granted read/write access, read-only access, guest access, and of course, no access to a share. Samba enforces UNIX file access permissions by changing the effective userid of the server process to the authenticated user, or another user such as the guest user.

To sum up, a user's access rights will consist of the most restrictive of either the rights set in the `smb.conf` file or the UNIX file permission. For example, Samba may allow a user to access a filespace service. However, if the files in the shared directory are owned by a different user and read access is not granted to the connected user, the files will be visible in the directory but not accessible. Similarly, Samba can grant a user write access, but unless the UNIX file permissions grant write access, the user will not be able to create or modify files. The same problem applies in reverse. If the UNIX file permissions grant write access to a user, but Samba's configuration options for the service do not, the user will similarly not be able to create or modify files.

Disabling a Service

`available`

Default: `available = yes`

Example: `available = no`

This parameter lets you remove a service from availability. If `available = no` all attempts to connect to the service will fail. Such failures are logged. Using this option preserves the service's settings, and is usually much more convenient than commenting out the service. This parameter is also useful to create an inaccessible template service that is used to set defaults for subsequent services using the `copy` command. If you do this, don't forget to use `available = yes` in the actual service definition.

Controlling Read/Write/Administrative Access

These options control whether or not Samba will grant read-only or read/write access to a client. Remember that a user will not be allowed to do anything that the UNIX file permissions wouldn't otherwise allow.

`read only`

Default: `read only = yes`

Example: `read only = no`

`writeable`

Default: `writeable = no`

Example: `writeable = yes`

Synonym: `write ok`

These two options are negative synonyms for each other. In other words, `read only = yes` is identical to `writeable = no`. The options mean what they appear to mean. If `writeable` is true, clients will be granted read/write access to a share. The same effect can be achieved by setting `read only` to false.

Note that having both `read only = yes` and `writeable = yes` (or the opposite impossible case) will not produce an error. Since the `smb.conf` file is parsed line-by-line, a service will have the read-write privileges granted by the last occurrence of either option. For example, the following excerpt from a service definition will define a read-only service and not generate an error.

```
; impossible case
read only = no
writeable = no
```

write list

Default: none

Example: `write list = jdblair,@coders`

read list

Default: none

Example: `read list = atporter,@students`

Both of these options accept a comma-delimited list of users or UNIX groups, allowing you to grant or deny write access privileges to specific users or groups of users. In the case of `write list`, the users in the list will be granted write access to a service, even if the read only parameter is true. Users appearing in the read only list will be granted read only access to a service, even if writeable is true for the service. Note that `write list` takes precedence over `read list`. A user appearing in both will be granted write access.

In both cases if a name starts with "@" it will be interpreted as a UNIX group and implicitly include all the members of the group.

admin users

Default: none

Example: `admin users = administrator`

This is a list of users who will be granted administrative privileges on the share. This means that they will do all file operations as the super-user (root). The upshot is that a user in this list can do anything he or she wants to do to the files in the share, regardless of the actual file permissions or connected username. Any new files the user creates will be owned by root. This is obviously potentially very dangerous and there are few actual good reasons for using it. If you do use it, you

CAUTION!

Users specified in the admin users parameter have *root* access to the share!

should probably also restrict access to the service using host-based access controls.

Setting the UNIX Effective Userid

`force user`

Default: none, meaning connections are set to the authenticated userid

Example: `force user = someuser`

`force group`

Default: none, meaning connections are assigned the primary group of the authenticated user

Example: `force group = team1`

Synonym: `group`

These options specify effective user or group ids that will be assigned to all accesses to a service. Note that both the userid and the groupid, if provided, are assigned after a client has authenticated. A client must be an authenticated user, or guest access must be allowed, to access the service.

The `force user` option is useful for sharing files between multiple users, but is a potential security risk. It probably makes more sense to create a group containing all the users with access to a share and use the `force group` option to force the effective group ownership of the server to this group. If you then set the `force create mode` for a share to 660, all users will be able to edit all files created on the share, regardless of who actually created a given file. More info about the `force create mode` option is on page 184 .

Controlling File Permissions

These options control the way Samba sets UNIX file permissions when creating files. These parameters are considered distinct from those that appear in the Setting File Permission Mapping Behavior section because they affect file permissions on the UNIX side before or after they are mapped from the Windows file permissions.

create mask

Default: create mask = 0744

Example: create mask = 0775

Synonym: create mode

directory mask

Default: directory mask = 0744

Example: directory mask = 0775

Synonym: directory mode

This option behaves the same as the UNIX umask command, setting an octal value representing the "maximum" file permissions available to a file or directory created by Samba. When a file is created the DOS file attributes are mapped to UNIX file permissions. A bit-wise AND is then performed between these equivalent UNIX permissions and the value of the create mask. The default value of 0744 causes the group and other write and execute bits to be removed from files created by Samba. You can further refine the possible access permissions for files using the force create mode parameter.

Starting with Samba version 1.9.17 the create mask parameter no longer affects directory modes, as it did in earlier versions. This is significant if you are moving a configuration file from an earlier version of Samba.

force create mode

Default: force create mode = 0000

Example: force create mode = 0755

force directory mode

Default: force directory mode = 0000

Example: force directory mode = 1000

Both parameters describe a set of "minimum" UNIX file permissions that will always be set on files in the case of force create mode, or on directories, in the case of force directory mode, created by Samba. Both parameters are the semantic opposites of the create mask and `create directory` parameters. The file permissions for any file or directory created by Samba are assigned by first converting the DOS file permissions to UNIX file permissions. The resulting value is bitwise ANDed with the value of the `create mask` parameter, then ORed with the value of the `force create mode` parameter.

For example, if the value of this parameter is 0700 all files will, at minimum, have read/write/execute permission for the creator of the file, and read/execute permission for all other users. If a client requests the DOS equivalent of 0444 (just read permission for all users), the access permissions will actually be set to 0744 (read/write/execute for the creator of the file and read for all other users).

Translating Between UNIX and DOS

Samba uses various tricks and techniques to translate the UNIX filesystem structure into something that DOS, Windows and OS/2 machines can understand. If you've spent any time working on both types of systems you know it is an understatement to say they are different. While both use a hierarchical file structure where every file can be accessed using a unique pathname, the similarities pretty much end there. In order to make the UNIX filesystem accessible from Windows clients, Samba must translate the UNIX way of dealing with files into the various Windows ways of dealing with files. To accomplish this translation Samba needs to mangle long UNIX file names into valid DOS file names. It also needs to map UNIX permissions to DOS permissions, and vice versa. As you probably expect there are numerous configuration options to control the way Samba solves both problems.

Mangling UNIX File Names into DOS File Names

To make the UNIX filesystem compatible with the various DOS, Windows, and OS/2 filesystems, Samba must deal with two problems: 8.3 file names, and case-insensitive file name references.

During the protocol negotiation phase a client will tell Samba if it can handle long file names, or if it can understand only DOS 8.3 file names. Samba has to generate 8.3 equivalents of long file names for these feeble clients. This 8.3 equivalent is the "mangled" version of the UNIX file name. Note that the name-mangling algorithm used by Samba is different from the one used by Windows 95 and Windows NT. Samba's default algorithm for files which do not start with a dot is:

1. Up to the first five alphanumeric characters before the rightmost dot in the file name become the beginning of the mangled name. Non-alphanumeric characters are ignored.

2. The "mangling char," which is a tilde (~) by default, is appended to these first five characters. An additional two uppercase alphanumeric characters are generated by applying a hash function to the original file name without its extension, if any. See `mangling char` on page 187.

3. The extension is generated by forcing the first three alphanumeric characters to the right of the rightmost dot to uppercase. If the file name does not contain a dot then the file will not have an extension.

If the file starts with a dot:

1. The file will have the DOS "hidden" attribute set, unless the `map hidden` parameter is false or the `hide dot files` parameter is true. See page 191 for details on `map hidden` and page 192 for details on `hide dot files`.

2. The file name will be generated by removing the leading dot then applying the same process as step 2 above.

3. The extension "_ _ _" (three underscores) is assigned to the file regardless of its original extension.

The case of alphabetic characters must sometimes also be "mangled," that is, forced to uppercase. Several configuration options handle how this is performed. Unlike the algorithm used by Windows 95 and Windows NT, the same long file name will always be mapped to the same mangled name. Also unlike the Windows algorithm, it is possible for two different files to map to the same mangled name if they share the same first five alphanumeric characters. The chance of this occurring is 1 in 1296—possible but unlikely.

mangled names

Default: `mangled names = yes`

Example: `mangled names = no`

If this option is true then Samba will mangle long file names into 8.3 file names for clients that are unable to use long file names. If false, long file names will be invisible to 8.3 directory listings on these clients, but visible through some other actions.

`mangling char`

Default: `mangling char = ~`

Example: `mangling char = ^`

By default a tilde (~) is used to separate the first five characters of the original long file name from the hash characters. This parameter allows you to choose a different character.

`mangled map`

Default: none

Example: `mangled map = (*.html *.htm) (*;1 *)`

This parameter allows you to describe specific ways to map UNIX file names to DOS file names, rather than relying on the automatic name mangling. It consists of a list of pattern pairs, which describe the difference between certain UNIX files and DOS files. For example, the extension `.html` is used to describe HTML files under UNIX, while `.htm` is used under DOS. Thus, to map `html` to `htm`, use `(*.html *.htm)`. Another example would be to remove the `;1` from the end of file names on some CD-ROMs. To do so, use `(*;1 *)`.

This mapping does not (yet) work in reverse.

Name Mangling Reverse Mapping

CAUTION!

Samba may not always map a mangled name back to its correct long file name.

Under some circumstances an application will create a file (using rename or create) using a mangled name from a different file with a different extension. This happens quite frequently. For example, word processors often rename a file to `*.bak`, create a new temporary file, then rename the temporary file to the original file name. Samba maintains a cache of recently used mangled names to cope with this situation. Without this cache this series of operations would result in the same file name from the client's point of view, but would have renamed the file to the mangled name on the UNIX system.

Adjusting the size of this cache can affect Samba's speed of execution. Some weird situations may require a larger cache. This code is rarely used now that Windows 95 supports long file names.

Controlling Letter Case Mangling

DOS historically stores file names in all uppercase, but allows files to be referenced using upper or lower case characters. Later filesystems, like VFAT, NTFS, and HPFS allow mixed case names, but still ignore case when resolving file names. These options control how case is treated when resolving file names, and what case is used when passing file names back to SMB clients.

case sensitive

Default: case sensitive = no

Example: case sensitive = yes

Synonym: case sig names

This option controls whether or not references to file names are case sensitive. The default value is no, which is normal DOS behavior. Samba must search directories to perform a case-insensitive match. Setting this value to yes causes all file references to be case sensitive. Unfortunately, this can cause problems with all Microsoft clients. Even NT messes this up.

default case

Default: default case = lower

Example: default case = upper

This option sets the preferred case of file names for the mangle case, preserve case, and short preserve case options.

Setting Up Samba to Treat Case the Same as an NT Server

To have Samba treat case the same way that an NT server using NTFS would behave, use these settings:

```
preserve case = yes
short preserve case = yes
case sensitive = no
```

preserve case

Default: `preserve case = no`

Example: `preserve case = yes`

short preserve case

Default: `short preserve case = no`

Example: `short preserve case = yes`

Both of these options control whether or not new files are created exactly as the SMB client passes them to Samba. If `preserve case` is false file names will always be converted to the default case before being created. The `short preserve case` option controls whether or not file names which conform to the 8.3 syntax are created using the case supplied by the client. Oddly enough, the case of this file name often bears little relation to what the user entered!

A useful combination of settings is to set `preserve case = yes` and `short preserve case = no`. This causes the case to be preserved for long file names, but converts all 8.3 file names to the default case before storing them. The reason this option exists is because applications that can handle long file names seem less likely to mess with the case the user enters.

mangle case

Default: `mangle case = no`

Example: `mangle case = yes`

This option controls whether or not file names which do not consist of all "default case" characters are mangled before passing them to the client. This avoids passing mixed case file names to clients that might choke on them.

Mapping Between DOS Attributes and UNIX Permissions

Every DOS file can have four possible attributes: Read-Only, Archive, Hidden, and System. None of these attributes have direct mappings to UNIX permissions. However, Samba does have a way to simulate each of these attributes.

Mapping the DOS Read-Only Attribute

The easiest attribute to translate is the DOS Read-Only attribute. Even though this attribute lacks a direct mapping to UNIX file permissions, translation is relatively simple: lack of UNIX write permission sets the DOS Read-Only attribute. To elaborate, Samba sets the Read-Only attribute when the current SMB client doesn't have sufficient permission to modify the file. This could be because the file is owned by somebody in a different UNIX group and has the world write bit turned off (which is usually the case). It could also be because the file is owned by the current user and the user write bit is turned off.

If the current SMB client owns the file in question, the user will be allowed to modify the Read-Only attribute. If the user turns off the Read-Only attribute, the UNIX user write bit will be turned on, and vice versa.

Two options allow exceptions to Samba's rule for setting the Read-Only attribute.

delete readonly

Default: delete readonly = no

Example: delete readonly = yes

Samba maps a lack of write permission on the UNIX system to the Read-Only DOS attribute. It is not normal DOS behavior to allow users to delete files with the Read-Only attribute set. However, it is normal UNIX behavior to delete a file if the user has write permission to the directory containing the file, regardless of the permission the user has to modify the file itself. The default value of false causes Samba to behave like an NT server and prevent users from deleting a file if the user does not have write permission. Setting this parameter to true provides normal UNIX semantics.

alternate permissions

Default: alternate permissions = no

Example: alternate permissions = yes

This option selects one of two possible translations of UNIX file permissions to the DOS Read-Only attribute. If this option is false then the Read-Only DOS attribute is set for files on a writeable share which cannot be modified by the current user. If true, the Read-Only attribute is set for files that do not have the user write bit set, regardless of whether or not a user can actually write to the file.

For example, suppose we are connected as a non-root user to a shared directory we have write access to. This file exists in the shared directory:

```
-rw-r--r-- 1 root root 46 Aug 26 16:45 infile
```

From the view of a Windows machine, if `alternate permission = no` then the Read-Only attribute will be set for this file because it cannot be modified by non-root users. If alternate `permission = yes` then the Read-Only attribute will not be set because the user write bit is set, even though the file is not actually writeable.

This latter option is useful when users frequently copy files out of each other's directories. Many file managers (including the Windows Explorer) preserve a file's attributes when the file is copied, which means the user must unset the Read-Only attribute before a file can be modified.

Retaining the DOS Hidden, Archive, and System Attributes

map archive

Default: `map archive = yes`

Example: `map archive = no`

map hidden

Default: `map hidden = no`

Example: `map hidden = yes`

map system

Default: `map system = no`

Example: `map system = yes`

The DOS Archive, Hidden, and System attributes have no meaning in the context of UNIX file permissions. However, discarding these attributes can sometimes cause inconsistencies in Windows programs. These inconsistencies can manifest themselves when a Windows program writes to a Samba share, then reads back from it later. Note that the UNIX shell causes all files that start with a dot (.) to be hidden in normal directory listings. See the `hide dot files` option, described in the next subsection, for details about setting the DOS Hidden attribute on these files.

These three parameters take advantage of the fact that there is no DOS execute attribute. DOS execute permission is denoted by the EXE extension, not an attribute. If the files in a share are accessed only by SMB clients through Samba, the three UNIX execute bits can be used to store these three attributes. The `map archive` option maps the Archive attribute to the UNIX user execute bit, the `map hidden` option maps the Hidden attribute to the UNIX group execute bit, and the `map system` option maps the System attribute to the UNIX world execute bit. Note that these options will fail if `create mask` and `directory mask` do not allow the execute bits to be set.

The `map archive` parameter is set to true by default because there are a large number of PC applications that fail if the archive bit does not work as expected. However, setting these options to true can cause problems if the files in a Samba share are also accessed by UNIX applications other than Samba. If you notice that files in a directory shared by Samba suddenly have their user execute bit manipulated in strange ways, set `map archive` to false.

Setting the Hidden Attribute

hide dot files

Default: `hide dot files = yes`

Example: `hide dot files = no`

Though the UNIX permissions have nothing like the DOS Hidden attribute, the UNIX shell does cause all files which start with a dot (.) to be hidden from the user in normal directory listings. As a result, it is useful to set the Hidden attribute on any UNIX file that starts with a dot. Doing so can significantly reduce clutter in Samba shares, especially when sharing a user's home directory.

The `map hidden` option is still necessary if you want to preserve the hidden attribute on files created by SMB clients. Renaming UNIX files to start with a dot every time a user sets the hidden attribute would generate significant undesirable side effects.

hide files

Default: no files are hidden

Example: `hide files = /.*/DesktopFolderDB/`
`TrashFor%m/resource.frk/`

This parameter specifies a list of glob patterns describing files that will be visible to the client but have the Hidden DOS attribute set. It is frequently useful to reduce clutter by hiding files while still leaving them accessible to clients. This list takes the same syntax as the `veto files` parameter. Each entry in the list must be separated by a "/". "*" and "?" can be used to specify multiple directories in the usual fashion.

Setting this parameter will affect the performance of Samba, since it has to check each directory and file it accesses to see if it should have the Hidden attribute set.

One situation is with the DAVE Macintosh SMB client, which creates directories for the Macintosh Desktop Folder, Trash, and resource forks. The example above causes all of these files to be hidden.

Supporting DOS-Style Timestamp Semantics

`dos filetimes`

Default: `dos filetimes = no`

Example: `dos filetimes = yes`

POSIX semantics require that only root or the owner of a file can modify the timestamp on a file. DOS and Windows semantics allow any user that can write to a file to modify the timestamp on the file. By default Samba adheres to the POSIX semantics.

This parameter is very important in a software development environment. A PC-based make program will expect to be able to update the timestamp if it can write the file. Leaving this option set to false will result in a lot of unnecessary recompilations.

Simulating "Change" Permission

Some SMB servers allow you to grant permission to modify existing files, but not to delete these files or create new files in a share. The same result can be achieved on a Samba share if a user or group owns the files in a directory, but does not own the directory the files are stored in. Normal UNIX behavior is then to allow those files to be modified by the file's owner, or, if permissions allow, the group owner. However, these files cannot be deleted, nor can new files be created by anyone other than the owner, or, if permissions allow, the group owner of a directory. An example of this technique can be found on page 240.

Allowing Users to Create Files While Preventing Them from Deleting Other's Files

Windows NT allows you to create a share that will allow files to be created by any of a group of users, but to prevent files from being deleted by anyone other than the creator of a file. This is frequently useful for creating a general storage area while making it hard for users to accidently (or purposely) disrupt the work of another.

Normally this behavior is not possible in a UNIX directory. For a user to be able to create a file in a directory the user must have write access to the directory. However, if a user has write access to a directory he or she will normally be allowed to delete any file in the directory, whether or not it is owned by the user.

Most UNIX flavors allow you to prevent files in such a directory from being deleted by anyone other than the file's owner by setting the sticky bit on the directory. The sticky bit doesn't otherwise have any traditional meaning for a directory. This is how the /tmp directory on most UNIX systems is configured.

An example of this technique can be found on page 242.

File Locking

File locking has never been one of the finer points of UNIX. File locking was ignored for much of early UNIX development. In those days the kernel had to be small and there was little room for nonessential features. By the time people realized that userland was not the best place to implement file locking, a large portion of the "standard" UNIX utilities had been developed. Since many of these programs would break if mandatory file locking were implemented and nobody wanted to rewrite all these programs, a set of simple cooperative file locking commands were added to the UNIX kernel and are accessible through the flock() and fcntl() system calls, originally from BSD and SystemV, respectively. The file locks are called "cooperative" because a program must explicitly choose to check for and honor a file lock. As a result, most programs ignore them. The fcntl() style file locks allow byte-ranges to be locked, not just the whole file.

SMB provides three forms of file locks: byte-range locking, deny modes, and opportunistic locks. All three of these forms of file locks are completely independent of each other. Starting with version 1.9.18, Samba implements all three of them.

Byte-Range Locking

Samba implements the SMB byte-range locking using the UNIX `fcntl()` call. This means if a PC application requests a byte-range lock it will not conflict with a UNIX application that properly honors byte-range locking. However, there are problems. DOS byte-range file locks are specified using a 32-bit unsigned value. The UNIX `fcntl()` supports byte-range locking, but uses a 32-bit signed value, meaning only 31 bits can be used. This would seem to be adequate—who would create a single file 4 gigabytes in size?[13]

After all, the maximum size of a FAT partition is only a little over 2 gigabytes. Unfortunately, OLE2 clients use the thirty-second bit to select a locking range for OLE semaphores. If an OLE2 client is to use a Samba share, this bit must be supported.

Samba works around this problem by compressing the 32-bit range into 30 bits. It compresses to 30 bits because many NFS lock daemons crash if a lock greater than 30 bits is requested. The solution seems to be working (at least, I haven't noticed a problem and I haven't seen a mention of the problem on the Samba mailing list). However, it is far from ideal. Future versions of Samba may provide a better solution, such as supporting byte-range locks using shared memory the same way deny modes are supported.

`locking`

Default: `locking = yes`

Example: `locking = no`

The `locking` option allows you to disable Samba's support for SMB byte-range file locking. If `locking = no` then all client requests for byte-range locks will appear to succeed, though no locking will actually take place. Any time a client checks to see if a byte-range is locked it will appear to be free. If `locking = yes` then real byte-range file locking will take place.

`strict locking`

Default: `strict locking = no`

Example: `strict locking = yes`

---

13. Large database applications and video editing workstations both frequently create single files larger than 4 gigabytes. However, both of these applications almost always handle their own record level locking.

If `strict locking` is set to true Samba will check every read and write access to see if a byte-range file lock exists, and deny access if one does. Otherwise Samba will check only when a client asks to do so. Strict locking can slow the server down and is unnecessary if a client is "well-behaved." Of course, not every client may actually be well-behaved. If you notice data corruption and this parameter is set to false, try setting it to true to see if the problem is solved.

SMB Deny Modes

share modes

Default: `share modes = yes`

Example: `share modes = no`

Setting the `share modes` parameter to true (the default value) will cause Samba to support SMB deny modes. SMB deny modes allow a process opening a file to specify what access it will allow to any subsequent requests to open this file, while it has the file open. When opening the file a client can request that an operation be denied to other clients for the duration of the time the client holds the deny mode. The correct operation of these deny modes is necessary for the proper functioning of most PC applications. Samba implements these deny modes internally since they cannot be simulated with UNIX locking calls.

 SMB Deny Modes

The SMB deny modes are:

DENY_NONE

    Any other opens will succeed.

DENY_READ

    Only opens that are write-only will succeed.

DENY_WRITE

    Only opens that are read-only will succeed.

DENY_ALL

    No other opens will succeed (exclusive use).

DENY_FCB

This is "file compatibility mode." It means do a DENY_DOS open and set the open to be read/write regardless of what the SMB read/write request is set to in the open. This is probably a holdover from the old, ugly DOS FCB (file control block) open API that used to be the only way to open files in MS-DOS.

DENY_DOS

This is MS-DOS compatibility mode. The file may be opened any number of times for both reading and writing by the same client. If the first client has the file open for write in any of its opens, then no other client can open the file in any other way, except for the exception below. If the first client opens the file for reading then any other client may also open it for reading but not writing.

The exception to this is that files ending in the extensions .COM, .DLL, .EXE and .SYM may always be opened even if the above would deny them. Samba forces these to read-only mode, although the spec does not say this.

Once a file is opened in MS-DOS compatibility mode then all other concurrent opens must also be using MS-DOS compatibility mode or they will be denied.

Since UNIX has no concept equivalent to SMB deny modes, Samba implements these lock modes using either lock files or shared memory, depending on how your copy of Samba was compiled. The shared memory implementation is significantly more efficient, and if your system supports it you should use it. Information about shared memory support can be found on page 157. As of version 1.9.18, Samba supports shared memory locks on every major version of UNIX.

Opportunistic Locking

oplocks

Default: oplocks = yes

Example: oplocks = no

fake oplocks

Default: fake oplocks = no

Example: fake oplocks = yes

Opportunistic locking is a relatively sophisticated feature that allows clients to aggressively cache file operations locally. When a client is granted an opportunistic lock it is allowed to do anything to the file that the client wishes. However, if another client tries to open the same file the server will notify the client holding the oplock that the oplock is broken. The client must put the file into a consistent state before access to the file will be granted to the other client.

Opportunistic locks are completely independent of byte-range locks or deny modes. Further, the oplock will be broken before the deny mode is checked. This means that a client can successfully break an oplock on a file only to learn that the client which held the oplock also holds a deny mode that prevents the first client from writing to the file.

The effect of opportunistic locking is to allow a client to cache all file operations locally without unilaterally denying access to other clients. The changes a client has made to the file will be written to the server at the last possible moment, conserving network transactions. Many applications, such as Microsoft Access, exhibit horrible performance if opportunistic locking is not available. Thankfully, Samba offers support for opportunistic locking starting with version 1.9.18. Setting the `oplocks` parameter to true, the default value, enables oplock support.

The approach for previous versions of Samba was simply to refuse all requests for an opportunistic lock. If you set the `fake oplocks` value to true for a resource, Samba will do the opposite, uniformly granting any request for an opportunistic lock while actually doing nothing. This setting was useful for read-only filesystems. The `fake oplocks` parameter is now considered deprecated, since there is little advantage to faking oplocks now that true oplocks are supported. One possible exception to this is a read-only filesystem like a CD-ROM. Setting `fake oplocks` to true on a shared CD-ROM will allow multiple clients to simultaneously cache file operations locally.

Other Miscellaneous Options

These are other miscellaneous options that are rarely used and didn't fit into any other section.

Allowing Clients to Execute Scripts on the Samba Server

`magic script`

Default: none

Example: `magic script = script.sh`

`magic output`

Default: `<magic script name>.out`

Example: `magic output = output.txt`

The `magic script` option sets the name of a file which, if opened, will be executed by the server when it is closed by the client. This is an example of, IMHO, a peculiarly UNIX sort of hack. The output of the script is stored in `<magic script name>.out` unless a different location is specified by the `magic output` parameter. The script will be deleted after it is executed. The effect is to allow arbitrary UNIX remote command execution from any SMB client, and is thus somewhat analogous to the UNIX remote shell command.

Note that many shells will choke on DOS-style cr/lf line endings. In most cases you will need to generate your script file with UNIX-style line endings.

This feature is very experimental and you should be very careful using it, though there is probably no danger if you already grant users shell access. For obvious reasons, don't enable this option on a service which allows guest access unless you really know what you are doing.

Allowing the Digital Pathworks `setdir` Command

`set directory`

Default: `set directory = no`

Example: `set directory = yes`

If true, users of the Digital Pathworks client will be able to use the `setdir` command to change directories. This command is only implemented in the Digital Pathworks clients.

Causing All Writes to be Synchronous

`sync always`

Default: `sync always = no`

Example: `sync always = yes`

If `sync always` is true, then all writes will be followed by a call to `fsync` to ensure the data is written to stable storage before the write call returns. If this parameter is false, then the server will be guided by the client's request with each call. Clients can set a bit indicating that a particular write call should be synchronous.

Printer Services

When a SMB client uploads a file to be printed to a printer service, Samba saves the file in a temporary file located in the directory defined by the `path` parameter. This file will be saved using the userid of the authenticated user, so any user with access to the printer service must have write access to this directory. Samba then executes the UNIX print command, which spools the temporary file to the appropriate spool directory. Note that Samba does not delete this temporary file. Normally this is accomplished by using the `-r` option to `lpr`.

All of the printer-related options appear here for reference. The chapter on setting up printing services provides example configurations for many situations.

Defining a Printer Service

`printable`

Default: `printable = no`

Example: `printable = yes`

Synonym: `print ok`

The printable parameter is what separates filespace services from printer services. If the parameter is set to true then Samba will identify the service as a printer, not a filespace service. When you define a service as `printable` you will also want to make sure that `read only` is true—this is the default behavior for all services. Since an SMB client can access a printer service as a filespace service, if the share were writeable a malicious user could connect as the guest user and disrupt other people's print jobs.

printer

Default: none (which means `lp` on most systems)

Example: `printer = laserwriter`

Synonym: `printer name`

The `printer name` option specifies the local printer name to which the print job will be spooled. This is the name of the printer that will be passed to the local printer command.

printer driver

Default: none

Example: `printer driver = HP LaserJet 5Msi`

The `printer driver` parameter specifies the string a client receives when it asks the Samba server for the name of a driver associated with a given printer. This can be used to automate the process of setting up printers on Windows 95 and Windows NT systems. If the string is left undefined, users will have to manually specify the type of printer driver to use.

This parameter must be set to the exact case-sensitive string that describes the correct printer driver. If you don't know this string then leave this option unset at first. When you set up your first client make note of the correct printer driver name—the string you are looking for will be listed after you select the "manufacturer" in the printer driver setup dialog.

printer driver location

Default: none

Example: `printer driver location = \\%L\PRINTER$`

This specifies the location of the Windows 95 printer driver files to support automatic installation of printer drivers.

Specifying the Print System Type

`printing`

Default: the (hopefully) appropriate value for your system

Example: `printing = sysv`

The value of this parameter controls how Samba interprets the output of your print queue command. It also sets the default values for the `print command`, `lpq command`, `lprm command`, `lppause command` and `lpresume command` parameters.

There are seven possible values for this parameter: `bsd`, `sysv`, `hpux`, `aix`, `qnx`, `plp`, and `lprng`. This value will be set appropriately at compile time. You may find it useful to override this value if you install a printing system different from the standard one for your system.

Defining the Local Printer Commands

SMB includes commands for viewing the printer queue, pausing a print job and deleting a print job after a job has been submitted for spooling. Samba implements all these commands by calling the local command-line printer command to accomplish the appropriate task. Since printer systems vary from system to system, Samba allows you to specify the exact command it will use.

Samba provides seven default printer definitions, for BSD, SystemV, HPUX, AIX, QNX, PLP, and LPRNG. The default printer definitions can be set individually for each printer service using the `printers` parameter.

Each of these parameters can use all the usual macros, plus these printer-specific macros:

`%s`   The full path of the print spool file, unless `%s` is preceded by `/` in your printer string. `/%s` is the same as `/%f`.

`%f`   The spool file name without the full path in front. This is supplied because some print spoolers do not work properly when called with a full path name.

`%p`   The name of the printer to which the job is to be submitted.

%j   The job number of the current print job. This macro has no meaning for the `print command` and `lpq command` options.

print command

Default: The default value depends on the value of the `printing` global parameter:

> bsd, aix, plp, lprng: lpr -r -P%p %s
> sysv, hpux: lp -c -d%p %s; rm %s
> qnx: lp -r -P%p %s

Example: print command = echo Printing %s >> /tmp/ print.log; lpr -P %p %s; rm %s

The `print command` parameter defines the shell command which Samba will use to submit a print job. After Samba has finished spooling a print job to the disk it calls this command. After processing the file this command must remove the spool file, unless you don't mind spool files building up on your system.

The print command can accomplish more than just submitting the print job—it could log the print job or notify the user of the job's completion with a WinPopup message, to name a few examples. There is no reason for the supplied command to actually submit a print job. The spooled file could be imaged with Ghostscript and faxed, emailed to a user, stored to a file, or any other action your imagination comes up with.

lpq command

Default: The default value depends on the value of the `printing` parameter:

> bsd, aix, plp, lprng, qnx: lpq -P%p
> sysv, hpux: lpstat -o%p

Example: lpq command = lpq -P%p

The `lpq command` parameter defines a shell command which, when executed, will return "lpq style" status information about a given printer queue. Samba parses this information to send printer information back to client machines. Currently Samba understands six styles of printer output information, each set by the possible values for the printing parameter. If none of these values correctly parses the status information for your system, you will need to write a script which translates your queue information into something Samba understands.

It is known that Windows for Workgroups does not always request a valid connection number when asking for printer status information. Samba provides a workaround by returning status information about the first printer the client connected to. Thus, if you print to more than one Samba printer from a Windows for Workgroups the printer status box may not always display the correct information.

lprm command

Default: The default value depends on the value of the `printing` parameter:

`bsd`, `aix`, `plp`, `lprng`: `lprm -P%p %j`
`sysv`, `hpux`, `qnx`: `cancel %p-%j`

Example: `lprm command = lprm -P%p %j`

lppause command

Default: A default value exists only if Samba was compiled with `SVR4` defined and `printing = SYSV`.

`sysv`: `lp -i %p-%j -H hold`

Example: (For LPRng) `lppause command = lpc -P%p hold printer %j`

Specifies a shell command to be executed on the server to remove or pause the printing of a given print job.

The LPRng (LPR next generation) and PPR print spool systems both provide a simple way to pause and resume print jobs. Pausing and resuming print jobs may be possible on other systems by manipulating job priority.

lpresume command

Default: A default value exists only if Samba was compiled with `SVR4` defined and `printing = SYSV`.

`sysv`: `lp -i %p-%j -H resume`

Example: (For LPRng) `lppause command = lpc -P%p release printer %j`

Specifies a shell command to be executed to resume a print process that had previously been paused.

Other Miscellaneous Options

Forcing a Printer into PostScript Mode

`postscript`

Default: `postscript = no`

Example: `postscript = yes`

If true this option forces a printer to interpret a print job as a PostScript file. It does this by prepending a `%!` to the beginning of the print output. This is provided to correct for clients which may start a PostScript file with some sort of garbage, like a control-D, which will confuse most printers.

Disabling Printing When Disk Space is Low

`min print space`

Default: `min print space = 0`

Example: `min print space = 2000`

The `min print space` option specifies the minimum amount of free disk space, in kilobytes, that must be available for a print service to be available. This option prevents jobs from being spooled when there is no disk space available, or when disk space is extremely low. A value of zero means no limit.

Chapter 7: Browser Configuration Examples

The Minimum Configuration Necessary
Small Networks (Single Subnets)
Larger Networks (Multiple Subnets)
    A Cross-Subnet Workgroup
    A Cross-Subnet Windows NT Domain
    A Single-Subnet Workgroup or NT Domain With Samba on an
        Isolated Subnet
    Using the LMHOSTS File for NetBIOS Name Resolution

The browser configuration options control whether or not the Samba server will appear in a browse list and what the appearance of the server will be in that list. These options also control whether or not nmbd will participate in browser elections, and what the chance is that nmbd will be a backup browser, master browser, or domain master browser.

The default values for all browser settings are shown below. If you didn't set any parameters, the browser related option would have these settings.

```
; browser naming options
workgroup = WORKGROUP
server string = Samba %v
netbios name = (your hostname)
netbios aliases =

; browser election options
local master = yes
preferred master = no
domain master = no
os level = 0
```

```
; WINS options
wins proxy = no
wins server =
wins support = no
remote announce =

; internal protocol settings
announce as = NT
announce version = 4.2
```

This section will show examples for all but the "internal protocol settings," and the `netbios aliases` option. You should leave the `announce as` and `announce version` unless you really know what you are doing, in which case you probably don't need this book. The `netbios aliases` option is discussed in the section about providing multiple virtual SMB servers from the same host on page 257.

The Minimum Configuration Necessary

Strictly speaking, no browser settings need to be set for Samba to function. With just the default settings you will be able to access the Samba server using the full network pathname (\\SERVERNAME\SHARENAME) from any host on the same network segment as the server. Your server will appear in the browse list as a member of the workgroup called WORKGROUP. Unless your workgroup is called WORKGROUP then this is probably not what you want. Thus, the only parameter you need to set to have Samba appear in the correct workgroup is the `workgroup` option.

```
workgroup = YOUR_WORKGROUP_NAME
```

This will cause Samba to advertise itself as a member of your workgroup. It will appear in the browse list for your workgroup and participate in browse elections. Samba will not become a local master browser unless it is the only SMB server on your network or the other SMB servers on your network are Samba servers. It will lose browser elections against any other servers. It will not register itself with a WINS server, so it will not be accessible to clients on different network segments unless those clients have another way to resolve NetBIOS names. Many clients, such as Windows NT Workstation, are also configured to resolve NetBIOS names using DNS.

Small Networks (Single Subnets)

```
workgroup = YOURGROUP
server string = A Description Of Your Server
local master = yes
preferred master = yes
os level = 17
```

These settings allow your Samba server to become a master browser for your workgroup. Because `preferred master` is true Samba will call a browse election when it first comes on-line. This also give Samba an edge in elections with other potential master browsers that are otherwise equal.

The `os level` of 17 means that it will be considered equal to Windows NT Workstation 4.0 in the election. It will always beat computers running Windows NT Workstation 3.51, Windows 95, Windows for Workgroups, OS/2 and DOS. In turn, the Samba server will always lose to any version of Windows NT Server. Putting Samba on equal footing with Windows NT 4.0 is a good general setting. Samba is a good candidate for local master browser because it is online all the time. Elections should be deferred to Windows NT Server machines because they may also be acting as a primary domain controller. Even in situations where the relevant NT Server machine is not a primary domain controller, possible undocumented features may cause an NT Server to be a better master browser. Note that if you are running a later version of NT Server that has been released since this book was published, you will have to adjust the `os level` accordingly. Later versions of NT will have a higher OS level.

Whether or not Samba is allowed, or even forced, to be the master browser is a matter of taste more than anything. You could set the `os level` higher to put Samba on par with Window NT Server, or set it to 255 to cause Samba to always win browser elections. You may prefer that Samba never be a master browser, leaving your Windows machines to handle browsing. Setting the `os level` back to 0 will cause Samba to lose all elections, except against other Samba servers with their `os level` set to 0. The browser election is explained in detail in the section starting on page 42.

The server string option sets the string that appears next to the Samba server or in the Properties box for the Samba server, in the browse list. Setting it to something descriptive of your server, rather than the default value of something like "Samba 1.9.17p2" is usually helpful to users.

Larger Networks (Multiple Subnets)

The browser configuration is slightly more complex if your Workgroup or NT Domain stretches across multiple TCP/IP subnets. Cross-subnet NetBIOS name resolution relies on a WINS server to resolve NetBIOS names. Using Samba as or with a WINS server is explained in the section starting on page 216. Maintaining the browse list across subnets relies on both the WINS server and a domain master browser. Setting up Samba as a domain master browser is explained in the next subsection. See the section starting on page 46 for details about how cross-subnet browsing works.

A Cross-Subnet Workgroup

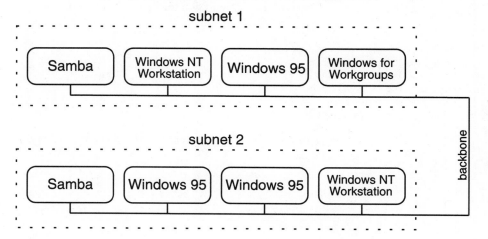

This example considers Samba servers in a multiple-subnet workgroup without any machines running Windows NT Server. Note that a workgroup consisting of Windows for Workgroups, Windows 95, and Windows NT Workstation computers scattered on two subnets will behave not as a single workgroup, but as two workgroups with the same name. This is because Windows for Workgroups, Windows 95, and Windows NT Workstation without a Windows NT Server machine acting as a Primary Domain Controller do not know how to synchronize their local browse list with the domain browse list maintained on the domain master browser.

A UNIX host running Samba on each subnet can be used to glue the two separate workgroups into a single entity. One Samba host needs to be set up as a WINS server and domain master browser. The other Samba host is set up to be the local master browser. All computers in the workgroup must be configured to use the first Samba host as the WINS server. Note that the same Samba host does not need to be both the WINS server and domain master browser. Doing so is simply administratively convenient.

Here is the browser configuration for the host acting as WINS server and domain master browser:

```
workgroup = YOURGROUP
server string = A Description Of Your Server
local master = yes
preferred master = yes
domain master = yes
os level = 31
wins support = yes
```

Here is the browser configuration for the second Samba host:

```
workgroup = YOURGROUP
server string = A Description Of Your Server
local master = yes
preferred master = yes
domain master = no
os level = 31
wins server = DNS name or IP address of the first Samba host
```

In both cases the os level has been set to force the server to always win browser elections.

A Cross-Subnet Windows NT Domain

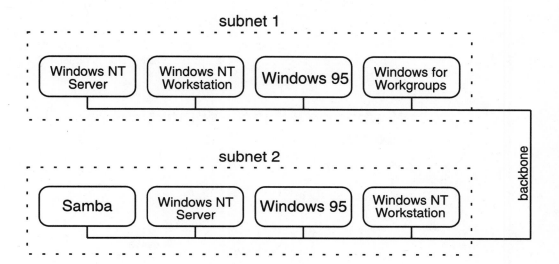

```
workgroup = YOURGROUP
server string = A Description Of Your Server
local master = yes
preferred master = yes
domain master = no
os level = 17
wins server = the DNS name or IP address of your WINS server
```

If you have an established NT domain that stretches across more than one subnet, then you already have at least one machine running Windows NT Server, functioning as your Primary Domain Controller. If this NT domain stretches across more than one subnet, then you also already have a WINS server. You may also have a backup WINS server running. If a Samba server is set up in this situation it makes the most sense to use the WINS server you have already set up.

For similar reasons you should also avoid allowing your Samba server to be the domain master browser. The Windows Browser protocol will prefer to select the Primary Domain Controller as the domain master browser. If the PDC is unavailable, the protocol will select the Backup Domain Controller, if present. If both the PDC and BDC are unavailable, then maintaining the browse list is usually pointless, since users won't be able to log in and use network resources.

Like the small networks example, it is a matter of taste whether or not Samba will be allowed to become a local master browser on a subnet. Putting the Samba server on equal footing with NT Workstation 4.0 is still a good general policy. If you would prefer that Samba never be a master browser, set `local master` to false.

Whenever Samba is integrated into an existing NT domain it makes sense to use the `security = server` setting. This parameter is explained on page 131.

Samba on a Subnet Without Windows NT Server

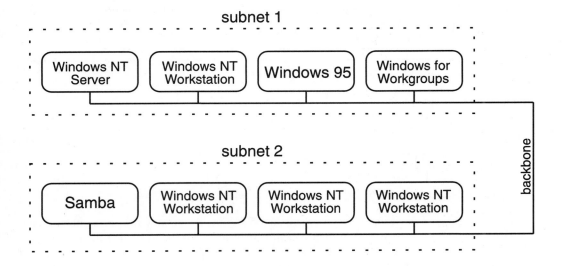

```
workgroup = YOURGROUP
server string = A Description Of Your Server
local master = yes
preferred master = yes
domain master = no
os level = 31
wins server = the DNS name or IP address of your primary WINS server
```

This is a minor variation on the above example. The Samba server is on a subnet with other hosts running only Windows NT Workstation, and the NT Workstation computers are frequently powered on and off. Setting `os level` to 31 or above will cause Samba to always be elected to be the master browser. It will remain the master browser as long as it remains online. When machines are frequently powered on and off it is useful to maintain a single computer as the master browser. In the first example the NT Server computers will remain the master browser.

Note that browse election protocol will defer to the potential browser that has been online the longest. This means that even if Samba has its `os level` set to 17 it will eventually become, and stay the master browser as long as the other machines are regularly powered on and off. Setting the `os level` to 31 just eliminates the possibility that another machine will become the master browser in the period following each election.

Samba on a Subnet With Only Windows 95 or Earlier

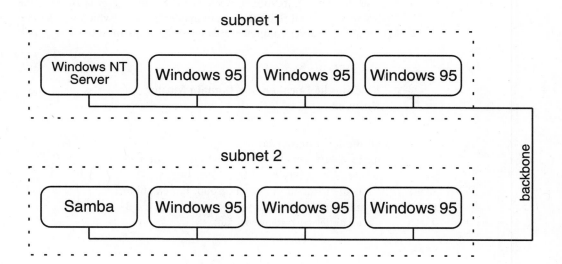

It is a common situation to use a single machine running NT Server to maintain central security account information for a large number of Windows 95 computers. In large networks it is common for a portion of these Windows 95 machines to be located on a subnet different from the subnet containing the Windows NT Server computer. In this situation a WINS server is usually configured on the Windows NT Server computer, allowing hosts on both subnets to resolve NetBIOS names advertised from computers located on the broadcast isolated subnet. However, because a browse master running on a Windows 95 machine does not have the ability to find a domain master browser and synchronize the local browse list with the domain browse list, the browse lists are frequently not correctly maintained.

This problem can be solved by setting up either a computer running Windows NT (Server or Workstation), or a Samba server on the second subnet. Here's the browser configuration for this second Samba server:

```
workgroup = YOURGROUP
server string = A Description Of Your Server
local master = yes
preferred master = yes
domain master = no
os level = 17
wins server = the DNS name or IP address of the WINS server
```

An os level of 17 or higher causes the Samba server to always win browse elections on its subnet. Because the Samba server is aware of the WINS server, it will find the domain master browser, which will be the Windows NT Server computer, and synchronize its browse list.

 Finding the Local and/or Domain Master Browser

You can find the local master browser by querying for the NetBIOS name WORKGROUP<1B>, or find the domain master browser by querying for WORKGROUP<1D>. WORKGROUP is the name of your workgroup. For example, to find the domain master browser for the workgroup UAB-TUCC on the local network segment, run:

```
nmblookup UAB-TUCC#1B
```

A Single-Subnet Workgroup or NT Domain With Samba on an Isolated Subnet

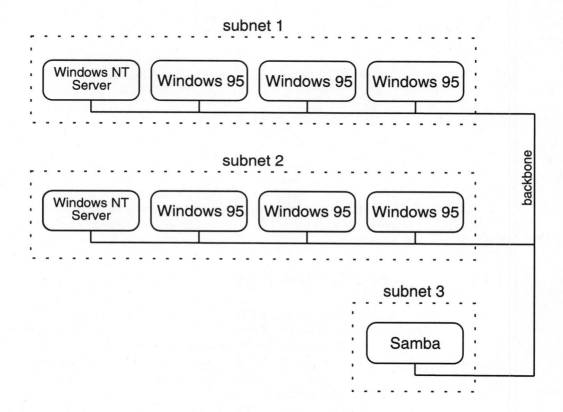

It is a common situation to have a workgroup or NT domain running on a single subnet with a Samba server on a broadcast isolated subnet containing no other SMB servers or clients. Since your workgroup or NT domain is located on a single subnet a WINS server is unnecessary. There are two ways to ensure that the Samba server appears properly in the workgroup's or NT domain's browse list.

Using `remote announce`

The first option is to use the `remote announce` parameter, which lets you specify a remote broadcast address to which the Samba server will periodically announce itself. If you are running an NT domain the Domain Master Browser will almost always be the master browser. You can set `remote announce` to announce Samba to this specific IP address rather than the broadcast address if you wish. Note that the broadcast address for a subnet with the IP address 138.26.25.* is 138.26.25.255.

The complete browser configuration in this situation is:

```
workgroup = YOURGROUP
server string = A Description Of Your Server
local master = no
preferred master = no
domain master = no
remote announce = broadcast address of subnet containing master browser
```

Note that Samba server is configured never to attempt to try and be the master browser. Since there is only one SMB server on the Samba server's network, there's no need to spend any time trying to have an election.

Using a WINS Server

Another way to synchronize the browse list is to use a WINS server and set up a machine to be a domain master browser. First, we'll deal with setting up the WINS server. The easiest way to set up a WINS server in this situation is to make the Samba server the WINS server by setting `wins support = yes`. However, you may wish to use your Windows NT Server computer as a WINS server. Directions for configuring the WINS server component can be found in the "Installing and Configuring WINS Servers" chapter in the *Windows NT Networking Guide*.

It is the domain master browser which allows a local master browser to synchronize its browse list with other computers in the workgroup or NT domain. If your computers participate in an NT domain, then your primary domain controller will automatically become the domain master browser. If you do not have a NT domain you will need to configure Samba to act as a domain master browser. Do not configure your Samba server as the domain master browser if you have an NT domain. Doing so will cause enormous problems.

This is the browser configuration for your Samba server if you've set up an NT domain and your NT Server computer is the WINS server:

```
workgroup = YOURGROUP
server string = A Description Of Your Server
local master = yes
preferred master = yes
domain master = no
wins server = the DNS name or IP address of the WINS server
```

This is the browser configuration if your Samba server is the WINS server and your computers participate in a workgroup, not an NT domain:

```
workgroup = YOURGROUP
server string = A Description Of Your Server
domain master = yes
local master = yes
preferred master = yes
domain master = no
wins support = yes
```

Using the LMHOSTS File for NetBIOS Name Resolution

You can make use of an LMHOSTS file if you wish to avoid using a WINS server to enable NetBIOS name resolution across network segments. The LMHOSTS file is analogous to the /etc/hosts file on UNIX systems. It contains a list of NetBIOS host names and their corresponding IP addresses. When you attempt to access a server from a client and an attempt to resolve the server's name using WINS and broadcast name resolution fails, the LMHOSTS file is consulted.

In general, it always makes more sense to set up a WINS server than to use LMHOSTS. It is very easy to configure Samba to be a WINS server—you just add wins support = yes to the smb.conf file and configure the WINS server setting on all of you client machines as the Samba server's IP address. An LMHOSTS file must be manually maintained, increasing the probability of errors. Further, just because a host appears in your LMHOSTS file does not mean it will appear in the browse list. An LMHOSTS file cannot be used to notify a local master browser of the location of its domain master browser, meaning cross-subnet browsing will not work properly. In other words, servers located on a different network segment will not appear in the Network Neighborhood, even though the servers are defined in your LMHOSTS file. Users will always have to enter the name of the remote machine manually.

An LMHOSTS file can still be useful under some circumstances even if you are using a WINS server. If your client machine needs to be able to access an SMB server at a remote location, you can add the IP address and NetBIOS name of this server to the LMHOSTS file. This remote location can be in a different department that uses their own WINS server, or at a completely different location someplace on the Internet.

Much more detail about the LMHOSTS file can be found in the *Windows 95 Resource Kit* and the *Windows NT Networking Guide*.

Syntax of an LMHOSTS File

The LMHOSTS file is located in the \WINDOWS directory on Windows for Workgroups and Windows 95 machines. Its located in \WINNT\system32\drivers\etc on Windows NT machines. On all three systems you will find a file called LMHOSTS.SAM in these directories. This is a sample LMHOSTS file which explains the syntax of an LMHOSTS file. The syntax of this file is very simple.

1. Each entry must be placed on its own line.

2. Each entry consists of an IP address and a NetBIOS hostname, separated by a space or a tab. The IP address must begin in the first column of the line. The NetBIOS hostname may include spaces if enclosed in double quotes.

3. The "#" character marks the start of a comment unless it marks the beginning of a special keyword (see below).

Six keywords are available on Windows 95 and Windows NT. Five of the keyword starts with a "#", so if you accidently use one on a Windows for Workgroups computer it will be treated as a comment.

#PRE   If this appears after the NetBIOS name in an entry, the entry will be preloaded into the name cache. Normally the LMHOSTS file is consulted after an attempt to use WINS and broadcast name resolution fails. Note that an entry that also appears in an #INCLUDE statement must be preloaded.

#DOM:domain If this appears after the NetBIOS name in an entry, the entry will be associated with the specified NT domain.

#INCLUDE:file name This includes a different file, parsing the contents as if they were part of the normal LMHOSTS file. The file's location can be specified using a UNC name, allowing one central LMHOSTS file to be maintained for a large number of computers. If a UNC name is used, the server's name must have already been specified in the LMHOSTS file using a #PRE tag.

#BEGIN_ALTERNATE, #END_ALTERNATE These two statements can be used to mark the beginning and end of a block of #INCLUDE statements. Only the first file that is successfully accessed will be included. This allows you to specify primary and backup locations for a centrally maintained LMHOSTS file.

\0xnn   This allows nonprintable characters to be used in a NetBIOS name, using hexadecimal notation. Some applications require a server to include a special character in the 16th character of the name. If the NetBIOS name is fewer than 15 characters long you will have to enclose the name in double quotes and pad it with spaces to make sure the special character appears in the 16th character.

An Example Configuration

Creating a central LMHOSTS file is the easiest way to manage LMHOSTS on multiple client machines. We can place a central LMHOSTS file in a share on BASIE, and install an LMHOSTS file on each client that accesses this file. First, let's examine what the LMHOSTS file will look like on the client machines:

```
# client LMHOSTS file
150.34.25.16 BASIE #PRE
#INCLUDE \\BASIE\LMHOSTS\CLMHOSTS
```

For this example, suppose our Samba server is called BASIE. The first entry pre-loads BASIE into the name cache. The next line includes the file CLMHOSTS (for Central LMHOSTS) that is stored in the LMHOSTS share on BASIE. Note that giving the central LMHOSTS file a name other than LMHOSTS let you use the same share to distribute your client LMHOSTS file. If you set up a new machine you just copy the LMHOSTS file out of the share to the appropriate location. Of course, if the new client machine cannot resolve the name of the server without the LMHOSTS file, you may need to use ftp to transfer the file, or just generate it by hand.

Let's suppose you have another server machine, perhaps running Windows NT. You can also create an LMHOSTS share on that machine to distribute the central LMHOSTS file. Your LMHOSTS file can be written to attempt to load CLMHOSTS from COLTRANE if BASIE is unavailable.

```
# more robust client LMHOSTS file
150.34.26.16 BASIE #PRE
150.34.23.3 COLTRANE #PRE
#BEGIN_ALTERNATE
#INCLUDE \\BASIE\LMHOSTS\CLMHOSTS
#INCLUDE \\COLTRANE\LMHOSTS\CLMHOSTS
#END_ALTERNATE
```

The central LMHOSTS file just needs to list all the hosts you want your clients to be able to access:

```
# central LMHOSTS File
150.34.23.3 COLTRANE
150.34.23.4 MONK
150.34.23.5 DAVIS
150.34.23.6 DOLPHY
150.34.25.16 BASIE
150.34.25.17 ARMSTRONG
```

The share from which you distribute the CLMHOSTS file should be read only, but accessible by every client machine. An easy way to do this is to allow guest access. Here's an example section for smb.conf:

```
[LMHOSTS]
        path = /usr/local/samba/lmhosts
        read only = yes
        guest ok = yes
```

Chapter 8: Access Control Configuration Examples

Password Validation
> *Conventional UNIX Password Authentication*
> *Encrypted Password Authentication*
Supporting Windows 95 Network Logons
> *Configuring Network Logons*

These options configure how Samba grants access to services, controlling how user's passwords are authenticated and which users are granted access to services. They also control which hosts will be granted access to the server, as well as how Samba interacts with NIS and supports Windows 95 network logons.

```
; authentication options
security = share
encrypt passwords = no
null passwords = no
password level = 0
smb passwd file = /usr/local/samba/private/smbpasswd
password server =
username map =
unix realname = no

; password program configuration options
passwd chat = *old*password* %o\n *new*password* %n\n *new*password* %n\n
        *changed*
passwd program = /usr/local/samba/bin/smbpasswd

; host based access controls
hosts equiv =
```

```
allow hosts =
deny hosts =

; nis options
homedir map = auto.home
nis homedir = no

; Windows 95 network logon options
domain logons = no
logon path = \\%L\%Uprofile
logon script =
```

Password Validation

Conventional UNIX Password Authentication

The easiest authentication option for Samba is to use plaintext password authentication and the normal UNIX password file, or whatever other authentication method your system uses by default. This has the advantage that your users can continue to use the same passwords they use for other UNIX services. It has the disadvantage that the password will flow over the network in plaintext. If you already allow access to services on your server in this manner, this may not be a problem.

Share Level Authentication

Use these settings to use the UNIX password file and share level authentication:

```
security = share
encrypt passwords = no
```

Both of these settings are the default values—if you had a blank configuration file, Samba would offer non-encrypted share level authentication. When a server tells a client to use share level authentication, the client is expecting passwords to be associated with each share, not with usernames.

Samba doesn't provide a way to just associate a password with a given level of access control. Every non-guest access to a service must be granted as a specific user. To simulate the Windows share level access controls, you can use a service configuration like this:

```
[service]
        path = /some/path
        usernames = readonly readwrite
        only users = true
```

You would then create two accounts—`readonly` and `readwrite`, and set the owner of `/some/path` to `readwrite`. When somebody connects to the service, Samba will test their password against the passwords associated with the `readonly` and `readwrite` usernames. If the supplied password is the correct password for one of these users, the client is granted access under the effective username of that username. Note that this service configuration works the same even if the server is running in user level encryption.

Generally it is not a good idea to use share level access, unless you need to allow guest access to a service. There are ways to provide access using user level authentication, even when you have older clients on your network.

User Level Authentication

Use these settings to use the UNIX password file and share level authentication:

```
security = user
encrypt passwords = no
```

User level authentication associates rights with a username. The server authenticates a user, then grants the appropriate access rights. Further, rather than authenticating each time a client sends a tree connect (`tcon` or `tconX`) command, it authenticates the user during the session setup.

This is generally the easiest mode to run Samba in because it corresponds to the UNIX user-based file access controls. If all of your machines are Windows 95, Windows NT, or OS/2 you shouldn't have any problems using user level authentication.

PAM Configuration

Red Hat, Debian, and Caldera Linux use Pluggable Authentication Modules for user authentication, and other Linux distributions are expected to follow suit. If you installed the Samba Debian or Red Hat package then the appropriate PAM config file was added automatically.

However, if you compiled Samba on your own under one of these distributions you will need to create the /etc/pam.d/samba configuration file, which describes the authentication modules that will by used by Samba. The contents of this file will vary due to the specific authentication modules available on your system as well as individual taste. The file installed by the Samba Red Hat package looks like this:

```
auth required /lib/security/pam_pwdb.so nullok shadow
account required /lib/security/pam_unix_acct.so
```

The file installed by the Debian package looks like this:

```
auth required /usr/lib/security/pam_unix_auth.so
account required /usr/lib/security/pam_unix_acct.so
session required /usr/lib/security/pam_unix_session.so
password required /usr/lib/security/pam_unix_passwd.so
```

You could also add these lines to the /etc/pam.conf file. However, this is not really a good idea—the /etc/pam.conf file is considered obsolete and may disappear from future versions of PAM.

Much more sophisticated configurations are possible, including the ability to notify you of attempts to guess a password. The PAM documentation, stored in the /usr/doc/pam-* directory under most Linux distributions, explains its features in detail.

Encrypted Password Authentication

Encrypted password authentication prevents plaintext passwords from flowing over the network. If you have a very small LAN, setting up encrypted password authentication may not be worth the trouble, especially if your LAN is not connected to the Internet. On the other hand, using encrypted passwords is especially important if clients will be connecting across a large, possibly untrusted network, such as a university network or the Internet.

The problem with using encrypted password authentication is that it is cryptographically incompatible with the UNIX password format. The result is that you need to create a Samba-only password file that mirrors the normal UNIX password file. If you support other services on your system you will need to synchronize user's passwords between both password files. The most common way to accomplish this is to create a script that asks the user for a password and sets both the normal UNIX password and the Samba password. A number of UNIX administrators have been known to run this script as the default shell for their users.

CAUTION!

Make sure the smb-passwd file is not readable by any user other than root.

One can then put an icon on users' desktops for them to double-click on. The icon is just a short-cut to `telnet samba-server.foo.com`.

Step-by-Step Directions for Setting up Encrypted Passwords

The settings necessary in the smb.conf file are:

```
security = user
encrypt passwords = yes
smb passwd file = /usr/local/samba/private/smbpasswd
```

To set up the encrypted password file, follow these steps:

1. If it doesn't exist already, create the `/usr/local/samba/private` directory. If you wish, you may create the private directory at some other location. Be sure to edit the `smb passwd file` parameter, or set the new password file location at compile time. Note that the private directory isn't strictly necessary.

2. Set the access permissions on the private directory to just user read and execute.

```
chmod 500 /usr/local/samba/private
```

3. Generate the `smbpasswd` file using the `mksmbpasswd.sh` script. This script is (oddly) stored in the `source/` subdirectory of the Samba distribution.

```
cat /etc/passwd | mksmbpasswd.sh >/usr/local/samba/private/smbpasswd
```

If your system uses NIS, you should use this command instead:

```
ypcat passwd | mksmbpasswd.sh >/usr/local/samba/private/smbpasswd
```

CAUTION!

Never leave system accounts, like cron and daemon, in the smb-passwd file.

Then use your favorite editor to remove users that should never have Samba access, such as root, cron, and daemon, from the created file.

Alternately, if you wish, you can create the password file by hand. Each entry must have the following structure:

```
username:uid:XXXXXXXXXXXXXXXXXXXXXXXXXXXXXXXX:XXXXXXXXXXXXXXXXXXXXXXXXXXXXXX
XXX:Long name:user home dir:user shell
```

You can use the `mksmbpasswd.sh` script, explained in step 3, to generate a template if you wish.

Note that every userid appearing in the smbpasswd file must have a corresponding userid in the /etc/passwd file. This is because Samba enforces the user's writes by granting access as the corresponding userid. Access will fail if there is no corresponding userid.

4. If you want users to be able to set their passwords themselves from an interactive shell, you need to make the smbpasswd executable setuid root and make sure it appears in your user's path.

```
chmod u+s /usr/local/samba/bin/smbpasswd
```

To make the program appear in users's paths you can either add /usr/local/samba/bin to the default PATH variable, or create a symbolic link from /usr/local/bin/smbpasswd (or some other directory in your user's path).

```
ln -s /usr/local/samba/bin/smbpasswd /usr/local/bin/smbpasswd
```

5. Unless you have especially sophisticated users, you will probably also want to use some technique to synchronize your users' standard UNIX passwords with their Samba passwords.

6. If you have configured Samba to allow users to change their passwords you will have to modify the passwd program and passwd chat parameters to call the smbpasswd program. Note that when clients change their passwords using this technique the password is passed over the network in cleartext! This, obviously, is unfortunate. However, support for the technique that Windows 95 uses for encrypted password changing is slated to be added to Samba in the near future.

Synchronizing smbpasswd with the Windows NT SAM using pwdump.exe

Jeremy Allison[14] of the Samba Team has written a very useful tool called pwdump.exe which will dump the contents of your Windows NT Security Accounts Manager (SAM) into a file with the same syntax as smbpasswd. You can retrieve pwdump.exe from ftp:// samba.anu.edu.au/pub/samba/pwdump/pwdump.exe or the corresponding location on Samba mirror sites, as well as on the Samba distribution included on the CD-ROM that accompanies this book. Also note that the utility is distributed with source code. Non-English-speaking users will need to modify the program before using it because it checks to see if it is being run by Administrator before attempting to dump the database. Jeremy explains that this mostly

---

14. Credit is also due to Paul Ashton for the more difficult task of working out the Windows NT password obfuscation algorithm.

pointless check was added in an attempt to make it clear to the computer press that it was not a "hacking" tool.

By dumping the NT password database at regular intervals and copying it to your Samba server you can keep the passwords between the two systems relatively synchronized. This technique is roughly equivalent to the relatively common technique of using supper (software update protocol) to distribute the passwd files amongst workstations in a UNIX cluster.

Here's one way to accomplish this. First, share the directory containing your smbpasswd file to Administrator.

```
[private]
        path = /usr/local/samba/private
        browseable = no
        allow hosts = your.nt.server
        valid users = root
        username map = /usr/local/samba/lib/private-username-map
```

Since sharing the smbpasswd file is an inherently risky thing to do, several steps were taken to minimize the risk. Setting browseable = no doesn't limit access, but stops the share from appearing in the browse list where curious users can see it. The allow hosts parameter is used to limit access only to the NT Server that will be uploading the password file. The valid users parameter means that only root can connect to the server. Finally, the username map option points to a file that maps the NT Administrator user to root. This file needs to contain this line:

```
root = Administrator
```

Next, use a command scheduler like WINAT or NTCROND to run this command at regular intervals:

```
pwdump.exe > \\SAMBASERVER\PRIVATE\smbpasswd
```

The file generated by pwdump.exe will contain userid values from the NT SAM. To manage the associated file access rights on your UNIX system you will need to create corresponding entries in your /etc/passwd file with the same userid. If this would be inconvenient because you already have the users entered into your /etc/passwd file with different userid values, you will need to create a script to convert the NT userid to the corresponding UNIX userid. Note at this point that the Windows NT POSIX sub-system already defines a method for mapping Windows NT userids to UNIX userids. The UNIX userid is obtained by adding 1,000 to the Windows NT userid.

Note that if a user changes their password, Samba's password file will be out of sync until the next time pwdump is run. Also note that if you change the Administrator password on your NT machine you will have to update the smbpasswd file by hand, since the Administrator password will be out of sync and Samba will refuse the connection.

Supporting Windows 95 Network Logons

 Disabling the Windows 95 Password Cache

The Windows 95 password cache contains a cache of passwords used to connect to recently used network services. The cache is stored in a file under the WINDOWS directory with the form <username>.PWL. Unfortunately, the password cache is really not very secure. This registry setting disables the use of this cache.

```
[HKEY_LOCAL_MACHINE\SOFTWARE\Microsoft\Windows\CurrentVersion\Policies\
      Network]
"DisablePwdCaching"=dword:00000001
```

As of version 1.9.16, Samba supports Windows 95 network logons and roving profiles. This means that a Windows 95 machine can "log onto the network" by authenticating a user's password against the password database in a Samba server rather than an NT Server. It also means that, if configured to do so, Windows 95 will automatically retrieve a user's roving profile from the Samba server. The bottom line is that Samba on a UNIX machine can be used in place of a computer running Windows NT Server to maintain user accounts and user profile.

There is one downside to using Samba to process Windows 95 network logons. Windows 95 has the ability to retrieve a list of domain users from a Windows NT domain controller. Access rights to resources shared from the Windows 95 machine can then be granted using user level access by granting access rights to users selected from the retrieved list. The Samba alternative is to use share level access controls, where each resource is assigned a password for each level of access. It is likely that future versions of Samba will support the domain user list.

Configuring Network Logons

When a Windows 95 machine wishes to log onto the network it broadcasts a request and consults WINS for a logon server for a particular workgroup or NT domain. The first server that replies to the request processes the logon, validating the password using whatever technique Samba has been configured to use (except the share level security mode).

These following options must appear in your [global] section:

```
; security can be either 'user' or 'server'
security = user
local master = yes
domain logons = yes
```

Note that `security` can be set to either `user` or `server`, but not `share`.

Configuring Logon Scripts and Network Wide System Policies

After a user logs onto the network, Samba can provide a batch file called the network logon script. This can be used to map network drives to standard drive letters, run a time-synchronization routine, or to run any other command-line command.

If you plan to configure network logon scripts you'll need to add the `logon script` parameter to your global section. To provide a single network logon script for all users, use something like:

```
logon script = logon.bat
```

To specify a unique logon script for each user, use the `%U` macro:

```
logon script = %U.bat
```

You can use the other substitution macros to create unique logon scripts based on the UNIX user group name (`%G`) or the specific client machine (`%m`, `%M`, or `%I`).

**Policy Downloading Didn't Work Properly
Before 1.9.18**

Prior to version 1.9.18, Samba contained a bug that pre-
vented system policies from being downloaded properly.
nmbd would only announce itself as
SV_TYPE_DOMAIN_MASTER, not as
SV_TYPE_DOMAIN_CTRL.

Next, create a share called [netlogon]. This share will contain the
system policy file (CONFIG.POL) and the network logon script, should
you decide to create either. It must not be writeable by users or
accessible by guest. A user that can write to this directory can modify
the netlogon script to execute arbitrary commands whenever a user logs
onto the network. I like to use /usr/local/samba/netlogon to
hold logon scripts, but you can choose any directory you wish.

```
[netlogon]
        path = /usr/local/samba/netlogon
        writeable = no
        guest ok = no
```

Last, create the logon batch file. Remember that this batch file must
have DOS style line endings. If you don't know how to properly create a
file with DOS style endings on your UNIX machine, you should create
the file using a Windows editor like Notepad. No error will be generated
if you configured logon script to provide a batch but haven't
actually provided a batch file for a particular user. This means you can
create batch files for just a subset of the users of your system. A
technique for generating these scripts on the fly when each user
connects is explained below.

You can create a network wide system policy which controls the
features available to specific users. If you wish to create a network wide
system policy, use the Windows 95 System Policy Editor to create a
CONFIG.POL file. Place this file in the /usr/local/samba/
netlogon directory. For information about using the Windows 95
System Policy Editor, see the *User Profiles and System Policies* chapter
of the *Windows 95 Resource Kit*. Other Windows 95 manuals may also
provide instructions on using the System Policy Editor.

Preventing Long Windows 95 Logon Delay

When supporting network logons from Windows 95 machines on Samba you may notice a very long delay during logon if you have not created a CONFIG.POL file. This is because Windows 95 is attempting to download the CONFIG.POL file and can wait as long as 10 seconds before timing out. Either create a CONFIG.POL file or set these registry settings on your Windows 95 machines:

```
[HKEY_LOCAL_MACHINE\System\CurrentControlSet\control\Update]
"UpdateMode"=3Ddword:00000001
"NetworkPath"=3D""
"LoadBalance"=3Ddword:00000001
```

Dynamically Generating Network Logon Scripts

The network logon script can be generated on the fly each time a user connects by using the root preexec or preexec parameter. The command specified by the root preexec or preexec command will be executed when a client requests a connection to a particular share. The connection request will not return until the script has exited. Thus, as long as your script is not executed in the background it can create files that will be available in the share without risk of a race condition. You can also use the root postexec command to delete the file after the client has disconnected from the service. Note that the root preexec parameter is necessary since the directory containing the netlogon scripts should not be writeable by a normal user.

The bottom line is that you can specify a script to create the appropriate logon script in the [netlogon] service when a user logs onto the network from a Windows 95 PC.

```
[netlogon]
        path = /usr/local/samba/netlogon
        writeable = no
        guest ok = no
        root preexec = /usr/local/samba/bin/
        makelogonscript %U %m
        root postexec = rm /usr/local/samba/
        netlogon/%U.bat
```

Below is a simple perl script, "logon-script," that creates a logon batch file that maps the user's home directory to the U: drive and syncronizes the PC's clock with the Samba server. It also logs which user logged into which machine to a log file. Much more sophisticated scripts are possible. Just make sure your script does not take long to execute since the logon process will pause while it is executed. A long pause may be annoying to users. Each line in the generated file must be ended with DOS style line endings. Failing to do so will cause problems when the script is executed on the client machine. Also note that the root postexec command is used to delete the logon script after the client PC has disconnected from the [netlogon] share.

```perl
#!/usr/bin/perl
#
# log when a user "logs into the network"
# and generate a custom logon script
#

($sec,$min,$hour,$mday,$mon,$year,$wday,$yday,$isdst) = localtime(time);
$month = ('Jan', 'Feb', 'Mar', 'Apr', 'May', 'Jun', 'Jul', 'Sep', 'Oct',
'Nov', 'Dec')[$mon];
open LOG, ">>/usr/local/samba/var/netlogon.log";
print LOG "$month $mday $hour:$min:$sec\ $ARGV[0] logged into $ARGV[1]\n";
close LOG;
open LOGON, ">/usr/local/samba/netlogon/$ARGV[0].bat";
print LOGON "@echo off \r\n";
print LOGON "NET USE U: \\FRODO\$ARGV[0]\r\n";
print LOGON "NET TIME \\FRODO /YES /SET\r\n";
close LOGON;
```

Setting up Windows 95 Roving Profiles

A roving profile allows each user to store the contents of their Desktop and Start Menu on the Samba server (or any other SMB server, for that matter). This means that no matter which specific Windows 95 machine is being used, a user will see the same desktop settings and Start Menu configuration.

First, decide where you want to store the roving profile information. This location is specified using the logon path parameter. The default setting is:

```
logon path = \\%L\%U\profile
```

Note that this is the full network path as viewed from the Windows 95 client machine, not the absolute pathname on the Samba server. The %L macro will be replaced with the NetBIOS name of your Samba server, and the %U macro with the username of the authenticated user. This means that users' Windows 95 profiles will be stored in the `profile` directory in each user's home directory. In many situations, this path will be appropriate.

If your users also have shell access to your Samba server, it is a good idea to store profile information in a hidden directory, using a setting like this:

```
logon path = \\%L\%U\.winprofile
```

You can choose to store the roving profile outside of the user's UNIX home directory. This is especially useful if different users than those granted shell access to your system may log into the Samba server. First, set the logon path to this:

```
logon path = \\%L\profiles\%U
```

Next, create the `[profiles]` service:

```
[profiles]
        path = /usr/local/samba/profiles
        writeable = yes
        browseable = yes
```

The `browseable` parameter has explicitly been set to true because roving profiles will fail if the profile directory is not visible in the browser. This is because Windows 95 checks to see if each component of the path is visible before accessing the profile.

CAUTION!

The `profiles` share must be browseable to work properly.

Obviously, edit these lines properly if you want to use a share name other than `profiles`. Finally, create a directory for each user inside of whatever location you decided would be the best place to store the profiles. Make sure each directory is owned by the appropriate user, and has only user read, write, and execute (700) permission. One way to make sure this directory is prepared for each user is to add this parameter to your `[profiles]` section:

```
root preexec = /bin/mkdir /usr/local/samba/profiles/%U; \
        /bin/chown %U /usr/local/samba/profiles/%U; \
        /bin/chmod 700 /usr/local/samba/profiles/%U
```

You could remove this parameter after all of your users have logged in for the first time.

Note that roving profiles will not work correctly unless you select the "Users can customize their preferences..." option under the "User Profiles" tab of the Passwords control panel.

Finally, you should never use the `homes` service in a logon path. A bug (or is it a feature?) in Windows 95 can cause the client machine to maintain a connection to a `homes` service after a user has chosen the "Close all Programs and Logout" option from the Restart menu.

Storing the NT User Profile on the Samba Server

The Windows NT "User Manager for Domains" allows you to specify a path describing the location of a user's profile. You can manually specify any directory on any SMB server that supports encrypted passwords and share level security, which includes Samba. One possibility is to create a directory in each user's UNIX home directory called "`.ntprofile`". The NT profile is a directory, not a file as it is under Windows 95. The first time a user logs in this directory will be created inside the specified path.

In order to store profiles on a Samba server you must be configured to use user level security (`security = user`) and encrypted password (`encrypt passwords = yes`). Windows NT will refuse to download the profile otherwise. Also note that creation of the profile directory will fail if the directory containing the profile directory is not browseable. You can avoid this problem by creating the directories ahead of time. Each has the form `<NT username>.PDS`.

With the addition of the experimental code being developed in parallel with Samba, and first available in the 1.9.18alpha series, it has become possible to do what is possible with Windows 95: to "log in" to a Samba Server from an NT 3.5, 3.51 or 4.0 Workstation. This new feature is no small feat. Since Microsoft will not publish the protocol it uses to implement its NT domain authentication protocol, the feature has been coded by reverse-engineering the protocol from packet dumps. If you are interested in this feature, consult the `DOMAIN.txt` and `NTDOMAIN.txt` files in the Samba documentation directory.

Chapter 9: Service Configuration Examples

Filespace Services

Sharing Home Directories

This is a good general purpose home directory sharing configuration:

```
[homes]
    comment = Home Directories
    browseable = no
    writeable = yes
    valid users = %S
```

CAUTION!

Use the `valid users = %S` option to prevent clients from attaching to home directories other than their own.

Note that even though `browseable = no` in this example, a user's home directory will still show up when he or she browses the server. It will appear as a folder with the user's username as its title.

Most UNIX installations are generally trusting and allow world read privileges on user's home directories. This makes sharing files between users convenient. However, it also means that, with the simple (and common) configuration above, a valid user on the system can read the contents of any other user's home directory from any client that can access your server! In other words, world read access suddenly really does mean anybody in the world may gain read access.

The problem is that just because something doesn't appear in the browse list doesn't mean it can't be accessed. If a user with the username jane has world read privileges on her directory, another user can gain read-only access to jane's file by accessing `\\SERVERNAME\jane`, even if logged in as the guest user. This potentially malicious user cannot write to this share unless jane has granted world write access on her directory,

Granted, this user would be able to do this from a shell account as well. This side effect is emphasized here because many Samba servers have disabled shell access and are intended to be used only as a Windows file server. This, and the example below, may be a little on the paranoid side, but its a healthy paranoia!

The `valid users` parameter in the example above prevents this sort of access. It works by taking advantage of the `%S` macro, which is replaced with the current name of the service. In the case of the `[homes]` service, the `%S` macro will be replaced with the username used to access it. In the above example another user can attempt to access `\\SERVERNAME\jane`, but will be turned back because the valid users list just contains "jane".

You may be working in an environment where you purposely grant world read access to everyone's home directory, and you would like this to extend over the network through Samba. If this is the case, you should use the following configuration:

```
[homes]
comment = Home Directories
browseable = no
writeable = no
write list = %S
```

This configuration uses the combination of `writeable` and `write list` with the same %S macro to prevent a user from accidentally granting write access to other users.

If you want to provide a filespace on the server for each user, but would prefer not to use their home directories, add a path statement like this:

```
path = /sambahome/%u
```

You can use the `root preexec` parameter to create these directories as they are needed, rather than creating all of them ahead of time.

```
root preexec = if [ ! -e /home/%u/.samba ]; \
        then /bin/mkdir /home/%u/.samba; chown %u \
        /home/%u/.samba; fi
```

You could hide a user's Samba directory inside their home directory like this:

```
path = /home/%u/.samba
```

Since, in this case, the shared directory will be created inside the user's home directory, you can use the `preexec`, rather than the `root preexec` parameter. The `chown` command is not needed anymore.

```
preexec = if [ ! -e /home/%u/.samba ]; \
        then /bin/mkdir /home/%u/.samba; fi
```

Sharing a Different Directory for Each Client Machine while Using the Same Service

This example uses the `%m` macro to create a unique filespace for each client machine that is accessible under a single share name.

```
[pchome]
        comment = PC Specific Directory
        path = /usr/pc/%m
        public = no
        writeable = yes
```

Presumably only one person will be accessing all the files in a given directory via this share at one time. This is because, even though Windows NT is something of a multiuser operating system, in almost all cases only a single user uses a specific machine from the console at a time. As a result, in most cases, you can get away with:

```
fake oplocks = yes
```

This can result in a significant performance boost, since clients can aggressively cache file operations locally. Remember that if more than one user does access the same file you run the risk of file corruption.

Here's a variation on the `root preexec` configuration used in the [homes] example. This configuration example will create the appropriate directory if one doesn't already exist, then set the file access mode on this new directory to world read/write/execute with the sticky bit set. This allows anybody to create files, but prevents people from deleting each other's files.

```
root preexec = if [ ! -e /usr/pc/%m ]; \
        then /bin/mkdir /usr/pc/%m; chmod 1777 /usr/pc/%m; fi
```

Read Only Shares

Since file lock information is irrelevant on a read only share, you can turn off file locking and enable fake oplocks. Turning off file locking results in a small performance increase, especially if you are not using shared memory file locking. Setting the fake oplocks parameter to true allows clients to cache file information aggressively, resulting in potentially enhanced performance.

```
[cdrom]
        comment = Shared CD-ROM Directory
        path = /cdrom
        read only = yes
        locking = no
        fake oplocks = yes
```

For a CD-ROM in particular you can save a small amount of server resources by mounting and unmounting the drive as it is needed. The `root preexec` and `root postexec` parameters make this possible. Probably this isn't really necessary.

```
root preexec = /bin/mount /dev/cdrom /cdrom
root postexec = /bin/umount /cdrom
```

Providing a Temporary File Space

Sharing the /tmp directory can provide a useful temporary file space, especially if your Samba server has a large amount of disk space and your clients have a small amount of local space. This example grants guest read/write access.

```
[tmp]
        comment = Temporary File Space
        path = /tmp
        read only = no
        public = yes
```

Preserving the Archive, Hidden, and System Bits

This example uses the `map archive`, `map hidden`, and `map system` options to preserve DOS file attributes by mapping them to the user, group, and other execute bits. This is best used when a share is only accessed by SMB clients. The unusual changes in execute permissions may disrupt the use of files from UNIX users.

```
[someshare]
        comment = A Share Only Accessed From SMB Clients
        path = /usr/somedir
        writeable = yes
        map archive = yes
        map hidden = yes
        map system = yes
        create mask = 755
        directory mask = 755
```

Note that the create mask and directory mask parameters must be set to allow the execute bits to be set. Put another way, every digit in the create mask and directory mask must be odd. By default the directory mask allows all three execute bits to be set, but the create mask only allows the user execute bit to be set on files.

Access Control Examples

Limiting Access to Specific Users

This example only grants access to the user with username bob.

```
[bobsfolder]
        comment = Bob's Stuff
        path = /some/random/path
        valid users = bob
        public = no
        writeable = yes
```

Granting Read Access to All and Write Access to Some

This example grants read access to any user, but limits write access to only the members of the UNIX group "editors."

```
[newsletter]
        comment = Weekly Newsletter
        path = /some/random/path
        public = yes
        read only = yes
        write list = @editors
```

> This works because the members of the write list are given write access regardless of the fact that the share is set to read only. This lets you set a general read only policy and override it in specific cases.
>
> This example is a variation on the above. It grants access to all valid users on the Samba system, not all users in general. It still grants access to members of the "editors" group.

```
[newsletter]
        comment = Weekly Newsletter
        path = /some/random/path
        read only = yes
        write list = @editors
```

Granting Read Access to Some and Write Access to Some Others

This example limits access to a subset of all the valid Samba users with the valid users parameters, and grants write access only to members of the "editors" group.

```
[newsletter]
        comment = Weekly Newsletter
        path = /some/random/path
        valid users = @staff @editors
        read only = yes
        write list = @editors
```

Allowing Users to Modify, But Not Delete, Each Other's Files

This example creates a project space where all users who are granted access can create new files and modify files created by others. However, a user cannot delete a file or directory that the user did not originally create.

The /usr/project directory must have world read/write/execute permission with the sticky bit set. The UNIX group "project-group" must exist. All users who will be granted access to the service must be members of this group.

```
[project]
        comment = Shared Project Space
        path = /usr/project
        writeable = yes
        public = no valid
        users = @project-group
        force group = project-group
        force create mode = 764
        force directory mode = 775
```

Access to the share is limited to members of the project-group by using the valid users option. The featured properties of this example are created by setting the effective groupid of every user granted access to the share to project-group. The `force create mode` and `force directory mode` ensures that every file and directory created in the share will grant group read and write access. The combination of those three commands ensure that everybody can modify any file in the share, while the user who created the file retains ownership of the file. Finally, setting the sticky bit on the `/usr/project` directory prevents a user from deleting a file that the user does not own.

This is an alternative configuration which would grant read access to any valid user, but only grant write access to members of the project-group. Note that the valid users parameter is replaced with the write list parameter, and writeable is changed to false.

```
[project]
        comment = Shared Project Space
        path = /usr/project
        writeable = no
        public = no
        write list = @project-group
        force group = project-group
        force create mode = 764
        force directory mode = 775
```

This works because the write list parameter grants write access to the listed users regardless of whether or not the entire share is "writeable."

Simulating the Windows "Change" Permission

This example is a variation on the previous example. Windows filesharing servers allow you to grant permission to change existing files but not to create new files. You can accomplish the same effect under UNIX if a user is granted write access to a file but not the directory containing the file.

For example, suppose you wish to create a directory in which an member of the group "editors" can modify existing files, but only the user "writer" can add a new file. Here's one way to do so:

```
[edit-directory]
        comment = Simulating Change Permission
        path = /home/edit-directory
        force group = editors
        force create = 764
        force directory = 775
        valid users = @editors writer
```

The directory /home/edit-directory must be owned by "writer" with the permissions set to 755. The valid users option allows only "writer" or members of the group "editors" to access the share. Because only "writer" has write access to the directory, only "writer" can create new files. However, the force group parameter causes any new files to be owned by the group "editors" while the force create parameter causes group write access to be granted to any new created file. The force directory parameter accomplishes the same thing for directories. As a result, any member of the group "editors" will be able modify any file created by "writer."

Allowing Users to Create Files But Not Modify or Delete Files

```
[drop-off-box]
        comment = Drop Off Box
        path = /usr/somepath
        create mode = 444
        delete readonly = no
```

This unusual configuration can be very useful for implementing a drop-off box where users can store files, but then not modify or delete the file that was just created. The create mode = 444 setting makes it impossible to set the write bit on any file in the directory. Normal DOS behavior is to allow a user to delete a file even if the Read-Only attribute is set. The delete readonly = no setting prevents Samba from simulating this behavior. This is the default setting for this option.

Printer Services

Samba's print services are simple, but effective. All they do is accept a print job from an SMB client, write the print job to a temporary file, then call your native UNIX printing system to process the job. As long as your standard UNIX print services work correctly, very little configuration is necessary.

A Simple Setup: Sharing All Available Printers

In your global section, add:

```
load printers = yes
printcap name = /etc/printcap
```

Add the following service section:

```
[printers]
        writeable = no
        path = /tmp
```

If a `[printers]` section exists Samba will make all the printers that are listed in your `printcap` file available to SMB clients, working in much the same way as the `[homes]` section. If a client attempts to access a service that isn't listed in the smb.conf file, but does match the name of a printer in the `printcap` file, the client is given access to a printer service with the settings in the `[printers]` section. Setting the `load printers` global parameter to true causes all the printer names in the `printcap` file to be added to the browse list returned when a client browses the Samba server. Note that each name given to a printer will appear in the browse list.

If you would prefer to make only a subset of your printers visible in the browse list, or if your printers have multiple names and you only want one of them to appear in the browse list, use the `auto services` global parameter, which adds additional service names to your browse list. Note that the printers not listed will still be accessible to people who know their names.

```
auto services = bishop-laser green-bar third-floor
```

The `printcap name` global parameter is only necessary if your printcap file is stored someplace else, or if, like AIX, your system doesn't have a `printcap` file. In the latter case you can create a substitute printcap file. This process is explained in the next section.

Setting `writeable` to false is a slightly paranoid step that prevents clients from writing to the spool directory by accessing the printer service as a filespace service. The `path` parameter is not necessary if you choose to use the `/tmp` directory as your temporary printer spooling location. If you choose to use a different directory make sure it is writeable by the guest user.

Sharing a Subset of Available Printers

The easiest way to make a significant subset of the printers on your system available for use through Samba is to create a substitute `printcap` file. Since Samba only uses the `printcap` file to determine the valid names of printer services, you can create a simple `printcap` file containing the names of printers to which you wish to grant access. In other words, this file doesn't need to be a valid printcap file—it only needs to contain the names of the printers you wish to make available. This means the names only need to appear in the substitute `printcap` file in a single line separated by vertical bars (|).

For example, to share printers called `bishop-laser`, `comm-laser`, and `room324-laser` through Samba, create a file that contains:

```
bishop-laser|comm-laser|room324-laser
```

If you stored it at `/usr/local/samba/lib/printcap`, then you would need to add this setting to your global section:

```
printcap name = /usr/local/samba/lib/printcap
```

This technique is also useful if your system doesn't have a standard `printcap` file.

Explicitly Defining Printer Services

Unless you have an enormous number of printers spooled on your Samba server, it probably makes sense to explicitly define each printer you want to make available. This allows you to define specific access controls for each printer. It also allows you to specify specific features of each printer, such as a comment describing each printer, share the printer under a different name than its defined name on your system, or the name of the Windows printer driver needed to print to the printer.

A printer service definition is the same as other sections in the `smb.conf` file, except that it has the printable parameter set to true.

This example grants guest access to the `bishop-laser` printer spool:

```
[bishop-laser]
        printable = yes
        comment = Bishop Laser Printer
        public = yes
        browseable = yes
        printer driver = HP LaserJet 5Si MX
```

Specifying the Windows Printer Driver Name

The `printer driver` parameter specifies the exact name of the Windows printer driver needed to print to the printer. Determining the correct string for the printer driver associated with a particular printer is easy. The first time you set up a printer, don't include the printer driver parameter. Set the printer up on one of your Windows clients. When you reach the dialog box that asks you to select an appropriate printer driver, find the correct driver, then record the exact string used to describe it. This string will be the name of the printer that you choose from the list on the right side of the dialog box. Use this string to set the printer driver parameter. Test your setting by setting up the printer on a different computer, or by deleting and re-adding the printer to the client you used to determine the printer driver name. This time you should not be asked to choose a printer driver.

If you make a typo when specifying a driver name, or specify a driver that does not exist on a client, the printer service will still work, though you will be required to specify the correct printer type when installing the printer.

Forcing a Printer to Print in PostScript Mode

```
postscript = yes
```

Some clients insist on sending a leading control-D to the printer when printing a file. Unfortunately, this can cause some printers not to recognize the incoming data as PostScript, usually causing many pages of postscript data to be printed instead. Setting the `postscript` parameter to true prevents this from occurring by adding a `%!` to the beginning of the data sent to the printer.

Setting a Printer Service Name Different From the Printer Spool Name

The name of the printer spool to which print jobs are sent is normally set to be the same as the name of a printer service. The printer name parameter allows you to specify a printer spooler name that is different from the service name. This is especially useful if your default printer spooler is only accessible under the name `lp`, but you would like to share it to your SMB clients using a more meaningful name. For example,

```
[unix-printer]
        comment = UNIX lp printer
        printer name = lp
```

Printer Access Controls

The same parameters used to control access to filespace services are used to control access to printer services. However, while all the access control parameters are allowed, only two forms of access controls are relevant. The allow hosts and deny hosts parameters, explained on page 169 can be used to limit access to a printer service to specific clients. The valid users and invalid users parameters, explained on page 171, can be used to grant or deny access to specific users. All other access control parameters control the type of file access granted, or the userid under which the client is granted access. Neither of these types of controls have any relevance to printer services, since no files are accessed and all printer operations are executed under the effective userid of the guest account.

For example, this printer definition grants access only to users in the group "printer-users":

```
[color-laserjet]
        comment = Color Laser Printer
        valid users = @printer-users
```

This example grants access to all clients with a hostname that ends in `tucc.uab.edu`:

```
[unix-printer]
        comment = accessible from the tucc subdomain
        allow hosts = .tucc.uab.edu
```

Chapter 10: Other Tricks and Techniques

This chapter contains examples of techniques and situations which didn't fit into the other configuration example chapters.

Using a Windows Tape Drive to Back Up a UNIX Share

Believe it or not, there are instances where it is useful to use a tape drive installed on a Windows or OS/2-based server to back up a share from a UNIX system. This is most common in Windows dominated environments where a few rebels choose to run Linux. I used this technique to backup my home directory and a few other key directories using a tape drive on an NT server and the NTBackup program until I found a better backup solution. I do not recommend using a tape backup program that does not understand long file names. Any backup program that properly stores NTFS (on Windows NT) or HPFS (on OS/2) filesystems should properly store nearly all UNIX long file names.

Other than possible problems with the file name, there are a few major problems with storing a UNIX share on a Windows tape drive. The biggest problem has to do with retaining UNIX file permissions and ownerships. When the file is stored on a Windows tape drive, the UNIX file permissions will be mapped to Windows file permissions, and the user and group owner will be completely lost. To be a useful backup technique, this information must be retained.

The second problem has to do with hard and symbolic links. Hard links cannot be properly reproduced, since the Windows backup system will have no knowledge of the internal structure of the UNIX filesystem. Each hard link to a single file will be stored on the Windows tape drive as a separate, independent file. If you later restore the files in the shared directory, each instance of a hard link to a single file will be restored with independent, separate files. The way symbolic links behave will depend on your Samba settings. If you have Samba configured to follow symlinks, each symlink will be stored separately. If you restore you will encounter the same problem as with hard links. If you set the follow symlinks option to false, the symlinks won't even be stored.

All but the problem with hard links can be overcome. The trick is to store the UNIX file permissions and ownerships in a text file in each directory using a pretty simple perl script. This text file will be properly restored if you ever have to restore a share from the Windows backup tape. After a restoration you can run another perl script to restore the UNIX file information with another script. Yes, it's a kludge, but what did you expect?

Configuring the Share You Plan to Back Up

The share you plan to backup must have the following permissions:

```
follow symlinks = no
map archive = no
map hidden = no
map system = no
; If you plan to back up files owned by more than one user
admin users = Administrator
; If you are backing up the entire root filesystem
dont descent = /proc,/dev
```

The map archive, map hidden, and map system options prevent the Windows machine from modifying the UNIX file permissions. The only one of these that is actually important is the map archive option—the others conform to default options and are just here in case you've set either to true in the [global] section. The map archive parameter is set to true by default, and causes the user execute bit to be turned off on any file written to tape. The first time I stored my home directory using NTBackup I was a little annoyed to discover that all my executable files were no longer executable.

The admin user option is necessary to make sure that the backup user on the Windows NT or OS/2 system has full access to share if contents in the share are owned by more than one user. Since the "admin user" will have full access to all files in the share, I think you should only grant access to the NT Administrator, or a user that is equally well trusted. If all the files in a share are owned by a single user, you can avoid the admin user option.

If you plan to back up your entire root filesystem, you will need to use the dont descend option to prevent attempting to backup non-file sections of the filesystem, like the /dev or the /proc directory (on System V and Linux machines). Since hard links won't always be properly reproduced, this technique is probably not a good way to restore an entire UNIX filesystem.

Preserving Permissions, Ownerships, and Symbolic Links

Two perl scripts can be used to store and then later restore file permissions, file ownerships, and symbolic links. The `savestats` script stores all the relevant information in a file called `.filestats` in each directory. The `restorestats` script reads these files and restores file permissions, file ownerships, and symbolic links. Each script recursively descends each directory specified as a command line argument. You'll need to run `savestats` at some point shortly before you run a backup. One way to do this would be with the `root preexec` or, if permissions will allow, `preexec`.

```
root preexec = /usr/local/samba/bin/savestats %P
```

If you do this you should create a share that is used only for running backups, since the `savestats` script will be run each time the share is opened. If you run backups automatically you could also schedule a cron job to run it automatically. Both these scripts are quick and dirty, but they work.

Using `smbclient` and `smbtar` to Back Up a Windows Share

It is probably much more common that a UNIX machine has a tape drive that you would like to use to back up a share from a Windows or OS/2 machine. The `-T` option and `tar` command, which are part of the `smbclient` tool, make doing this as easy as using tar to backup or restore a normal UNIX volume (of course, the `tar` command is not the easiest way to manage backups under UNIX, so your mileage may vary). The `smbtar` shell script wraps up the smbclient command, simplifying the process of running backups.

All DOS file attributes will be lost on any files restored using smbtar.

`smbtar` Examples

To get you started quickly here are some examples of varying complexity.

To run a full backup of the share `\\BAGGINS\Public` onto the tape in tape drive `/dev/rmt0`, use:

```
smbtar -s BAGGINS -p password -x Public -t /dev/rmt0
```

To backup only files with the archive attribute set, use:

```
smbtar -s BAGGINS -p password -x Public -t /dev/rmt0 -i
```

To restore all the files stored in a tar file, use:

```
smbtar -s BAGGINS -p password -x Public -t /dev/rmt0 -r
```

To perform a backup of all files that have changed since the last backup, regardless of the state of the archive bits, use a shell script like this:

```
#!/bin/sh
smbtar -s BAGGINS -p password -x Public -t /dev/rmt0 \
       -N /usr/local/backup/BAGGINS.lastbackup
touch /usr/local/backup/BAGGINS.lastbackup
```

This works because smbclient will compare the modification date of the files in the SMB share to the modification date of an arbitrary UNIX file. Rather than just updating the modification date of an empty file, you could generate a simple log file of your backups. To do so, use a shell script something like this:

```
#!/bin/sh
smbtar -s BAGGINS -p password -x Public -t /dev/rmt0 \
       -N /usr/local/backup/BAGGINS.log
date '+%b %d %H:%M:%S%t finished backup of \\BAGGINS\Public' \
       >> /usr/local/backup/BAGGINS.log
```

If you want to backup or restore only a subdirectory, use the -d option. This option stores the \\BAGGINS\work directory:

```
smbtar -s BAGGINS -p password -x Public -t /dev/rmt0 -d work
```

Remember that you can string multiple tar files together on the same tape by using the non-rewinding tape device. For example, under BSDish systems the /dev/rmt0.1 device doesn't rewind the tape device.

Finally, note that the Linux SMB filesystem can greatly simplify the process of running a backup of a Windows share. Since a mounted filesystem appears to a normal part of the UNIX filesystem you can use your favorite UNIX backup program (dump, taper, BRU, Legato, whatever) to backup and restore Windows shares. The SMB filesystem is explained in detail on page 280.

Synchronizing Your PC's Clocks with the Samba Server

Windows and OS/2 clients can synchronize their clocks with the Samba server by using the `NET TIME` command. Executing this command:

```
NET TIME \\SERVERNAME /YES /SET
```

will synchronize your PC's clock with the clock in the Samba server. You just need to find a way to have this command executed regularly. One way is to put this command into a batch file, called perhaps `TIMESYNC.BAT`, and then place this file in all your PC's Startup directories.

If you are using domain logins, you can add the command to your logon script. On a Windows NT machine you can use the `WINAT` command scheduler, or a similar cron-like service, to execute the command at regular intervals (such as once a day).

By running a Network Time Protocol client on your Samba server you can synchronize your PC's clocks with all other systems on your network, or even with the global time standard, without installing NTP clients on all of your PCs. This is especially useful if you are running a time-sensitive application on your PCs, such as a Kerberos authentication client.

Note that your PC and your Samba server must agree on when the timezone offset starts and stops. There are some Slackware Linux distributions that had timezone files that specified the wrong offsets. This problem may exist on other UNIX systems. If you're having problems with time synchronization, make sure you have a known good timezone file.

Also note that `nmbd` only advertises itself as a timeserver if the `time server` parameter is true. However, the time synchronization will work whether or not this parameter is true.

Printing From a UNIX Machine to a Windows Printer Server

The `smbprint` shell script that is included in the Samba distribution makes it easy to configure `lp` to print to a Windows or OS/2 printer service. This is especially useful when a UNIX system is integrated into an already Windows dominated environment, or to allow users of a UNIX system to print directly to printers attached to their PCs. These instructions apply only to systems which use an `lpd` style `printcap` file to configure printers. Most newer print spoolers are backwards compatible to `lpd printcap` files.

The `smbprint` script works by acting as a print filter for `lpd`. Normally a print filter accepts a data stream from `lpd`, processes it, then returns it back to `lpd`. This data is then sent to the appropriate printer device. The `smbprint` script, instead of returning the data back to `lpd`, uses the `smbclient` command to send the print file to a remote SMB printer service.

Create the printcap Stanza

First add a stanza similar to the following to your printcap file:

```
win-printer:\
        :cm=Laser Printer Spooled on NT Server: \
        :sd=/var/spool/lpd/win-printer: \
        :af=/var/spool/lpd/win-printer/usage.log: \
        :if=/usr/local/samba/bin/smbprint: \
        :mx=0: \
        :lp=/dev/null: \
```

The only parameters which are absolutely necessary are `sd`, `af`, `if`, and `lp`.

The `sd` parameter specifies the directory that will be used to spool data before transmitting them to the SMB printer service.

The `af` parameter specifies the printer accounting file. In this case it is actually not used to specify an accounting file. Since `lpd` passes the `af` argument to the `smbprint` script, it is used in this case to describe the location of the spool directory to the `smbprint` script. Note that this argument must specify a file, not a directory, though the file need not exist. This is because some implementations of `lpd` require this entry to reference a file.

The `if` parameter specifies the print filter, and should contain the full path to wherever you've installed `smbprint`.

The `lp` parameter specifies the print device. In this case the file will never leave the print filter, so the device should be set to `/dev/null`.

The remaining parameters in this example are useful, but not required. The `cm` parameter specifies a comment string describing the printer. The `mx` parameter sets the maximum size of a file that can be printed. In this case it should be set to 0, which means unlimited.

Create the Spool Directory

The next step is to create the spool directory. Your spool directory may not be in the same location as this example. You can look at other stanzas in your printcap file if you are not sure.

```
$ mkdir /var/spool/lpd/win-printer
```

Even if the files are never spooled locally this directory is required to hold lpd's locking information and the configuration file for `smbprint`.

Create the `smbprint` Configuration File

To allow more than one printer service to use the same print filter, `smbprint` stores the configuration information for each printer service in the spool directory, in a file called `.config`.

If you intend to connect to your printer service as the guest user, use a `.config` file containing these entries:

```
server=SERVERNAME
service=Printer-Service-Name
user=guest
```

Obviously, this won't work correctly unless you grant access to the guest user on the Windows or OS/2 server.

If you need to connect to your printer service with a different username, use a .config file like this:

```
server=SERVERNAME
service=Printer-Service-Name
user=username
password=password-for-username
```

If the user's password expires you will have to modify the `.config` file to reflect the new password.

Setting the Log File Location

CAUTION!

Depending on the permissions that your print spooler has, leaving `logfile` set to `/tmp/smb-print.log` is also a potential security hole. An attacker could create a link from `/tmp/smb-print.log` to some system file and damage the file.

The `smbprint` script writes all the output from `smbclient` to `/tmp/smb-print.log`. This file is very useful for debugging printing problems. However, it can grow quite large if left alone. Once you have the printer service operating correctly you should turn off this logging option. Open the `smbprint` script in your favorite editor and find this line:

```
logfile=/tmp/smb-print.log
```

Change it to:

```
logfile=/dev/null
```

Logging Printer Usage

If you wish to log all use of your printer service, you can add a line like this to the end of the `smbprint` script:

```
date "+%b %d %H:%M:%S%t$5 sent a print job to $service on $server" \
    >> $acct_file
```

You may need to create the log file and `chown` it to the userid used to run the filter, which is usually `lp`.

```
$ touch /var/spool/lpd/win-printer/usage.log
$ chown lp /var/spool/lpd/win-printer/usage.log
```

Using Ghostscript With `smbprint`

 Magic Filter

The Magic Filter software package is a relatively painless way to correctly print a wide range of file types, like GIF, JPEG, Postscript, and even compressed files.

It is possible to use ghostscript to turn a non-postscript printer being shared from a Windows machine into something that behaves like a postscript printer from the perspective of your UNIX machine. This example assumes you already have ghostscript installed on your system.

Create a copy of the `smbprint` script called something like `smbprint-gs`. You will need to modify this script to process the input stream through ghostscript before using `smbclient` to transmit the file to the remote SMB printer service. For example, to print to an HP DeskJet printer attached to a Windows machine, change these lines at the end of `smbprint`:

```
(
# NOTE You may wish to add the line 'echo translate' if you want automatic
#       CR/LF translation when printing.
#       echo translate
        echo "print -"
        cat ) | /usr/local/samba/bin/smbclient "\\\\$server\\$service" \
                $password -U $server -N -P >> $logfile
```

to this:

```
cat | /usr/bin/gs -q -dSAFER -dNOPAUSE -sDEVICE=deskjet \
        -sOutputFile=- - | /usr/local/samba/bin/smbclient \
        "\\\\$server\\$service" $password -U $server -N -P -c \
        'printmode graphics;print -' >> $logfile
```

The `-q`, `-dSAFER`, and `-dNOPAUSE` options tell ghostscript to operate in a manner appropriate for use as a filter rather than an interactive command. The `-sDEVICE=deskjet` option tells ghostscript to produce output appropriate for printing on a Hewlett-Packard DeskJet printer. Other printer formats are available. Consult the gs man page for more information about the ghostscript command-line options.

Note the use of the `printmode graphics` command passed to `smbclient`. This command is necessary whenever you print graphics information, rather than an ASCII file, through a Windows printer service.

Creating Multiple Virtual Servers Running on the Same Host

NetBIOS aliasing takes advantage of the `include` parameter and macro substitutions to create a conditional configuration file. Specifically, it uses the `%L` macro, which is replaced with the name that the client called the server. This technique has the advantages that it does not require an IP address for each virtual server, it can be used if you wish to start `smbd` and `nmbd` using `inetd`, and it is simpler to configure. However, the IP aliasing technique will offer better performance for a server with high usage.

This example uses three configuration files: `smb.conf`, `smb.conf.yin`, and `smb.conf.yang`. The `smb.conf` file contains global settings common to both virtual servers. This file must contain:

```
[global]
        netbios aliases = YIN YANG
        include = /usr/local/samba/lib/smb.conf.%L
```

The `netbios aliases` parameter causes nmbd to advertise the Samba server under two names. Both names are also registered as NetBIOS names with your WINS server, if you are using one.

When a client connects to the server, the `%L` macro is replaced with the name of the server to which the client claimed to be connecting, causing either the `smb.conf.yin` or the `smb.conf.yang` file to be included after the include parameter. Both of these files can contain additional global parameters unique to each virtual server, as well as all service definitions. Note that the `%L` macro presents the server's NetBIOS name in all lowercase.

Using Share Level and User Level Security at the Same Time

There are many situations where it is useful to provide some services to guest users and other services to specific authenticated users. One such situation is a public computer lab where any user can access shares containing applications, like word processor software, or printers. However, one would usually also wish to provide additional access rights to certain users, such as administrators or lab monitors.

Unfortunately, SMB does not provide a simple way to provide traditional guest access when using user level security. Likewise, authenticating specific users is difficult when using share level security. A relatively elegant way out of this bind is to create two virtual servers using NetBIOS aliasing.

This example will create two virtual servers. One, called Public will be used to provide services to guest users. The second, called Admin will be used to grant read/write access to the same filespace service.

First, create the main `smb.conf` file.

```
[global]
        netbios name = ADMIN
        netbios aliases = PUBLIC
        include = /usr/local/samba/lib/smb.conf.%L
```

Second, create each specific configuration file. Here is a possible `smb.conf.admin` file, which will contain the configuration for the Admin server. It grants read/write access to the Apps share to members of the UNIX group labadmins.

```
security = user

[apps]
        comments = Administrative Access to Apps Share
        path = /shares/apps
        guest ok = no
        valid users = @labadmins
        read only = no
```

Here is a possible `smb.conf.public` file, which contains the configuration for the Public server. It grants guest access to the Apps share and to the Lab-Printer printer. When allowing guest access, it is also important to use some sort of host-based access control to prevent abuse, especially if your network is connected to the Internet.

```
security = share
allow hosts = .lab.watsamatau.edu

[apps]

        comments = General Use Applications
```

```
        path = /shares/apps guest
        ok = yes read
        only = yes

[lab-printer]
        comments = General Use Printer
        guest ok = yes
```

Some organizations find it useful to always share some resources, such as printers, from virtual servers. This allows the administrators to move the print service to a different host without affecting service from the perspective of the user.

Handling WinPopup Messages

Sending WinPopup Messages Using `smbclient`

The `smbclient -M` command provides a facility for sending WinPopup messages to a Windows or OS/2 machine. Here's a short example:

```
(~)$ smbclient -M SOMESERVER
Connected. Type your message, ending it with a Control-D
Wanna leave for lunch?
sent 24 bytes
(status was 0-0)
```

If you can't resolve the address of the target machine using broadcast name resolution, you may have to use the `-I` switch to specify the IP address or hostname of the target machine.

Note that for a Windows for Workgroups or Windows 95 machine to receive a WinPopup message it must be running WinPopup. A Windows NT machine must have Windows Messaging installed and enabled.

Sending a WinPopup Message to All Connected Machines

The `examples/misc` directory of the Samba distribution contains a perl script called `wall.perl`. I like to rename `wall.perl` as `smbwall` and install it in `/usr/local/samba/bin`. This script uses the `smbstatus` command to determine the machines with an open connection to the Samba server, and sends a WinPopup command to each of these machines. It can be used to send users messages, such as a warning that the system is going down for maintenance. It can also be scripted, which would be useful if you plan to disconnect all users before scheduled backups.

To use the script manually, just type `smbwall`.

```
$ smbwall
Enter message for Samba clients of this host
(terminated with single '.' or end of file):
The system will be going down for maintenance.
.
Added interface ip=138.26.25.10 bcast=138.26.255.255 nmask=255.255.0.0
Connected. Type your message, ending it with a Control-D
sent 48 bytes (status was 0-0)
```

You can use `smbwall` in a script by piping messages into it:

```
echo 'Backups will start in 5 minutes' | smbwall
```

Receiving WinPopup Messages

The `message command` parameter allows you to specify a command which will be executed to process a received WinPopup message. The parameter supports three extra macro substitutions:

`%s` The path of the file containing the WinPopup message.

`%t` The destination of the message (usually the server's NetBIOS name).

`%f` The user the message is from.

The specified command needs to somehow deliver the contents of the file described by %s to the user. Each of these suggestions use the "&" to invoke the command in the background. This is very important that this command return immediately. There are a few techniques that could be used.

You could mail the message to root, or another user:

```
message command = sh -c '/bin/cat %s | \
       /bin/mailx -s WinPopup\ message\ from\ %f root' &
```

You could write the message to the console:

```
message command = sh -c '(echo WinPopup\ message\ from\ %f | cat %s) \
    > /dev/console' &
```

The `smb.conf` man page suggests using `xedit` to display the message. This would be useful if you run X on the machine running Samba.

```
message command = csh -c 'xedit %s; rm %s' &
```

The problem with this is that if you use Xauthentication on your X server, since the message command is executed with the effective userid of the guest user, the xedit will not be allowed to contact your X server.

I have written a Tcl/Tk script called TkPopup that takes care of this problem. This script is included in the `scripts/` directory on the CD-ROM included with this book.

Being Very Cautious (Paranoid?) About Security

Except in rare cases, a healthy paranoia is usually appropriate when considering the security of your server. Many Samba hosts are connected to TCP/IP networks which are completely exposed to the Internet. Since Samba uses SMB over TCP/IP, your Samba server is available for use, and thus exposed to attack, from anywhere on the Internet. On the other hand, having a healthy paranoia about security doesn't mean you should be scared. There are a few simple steps you can take to help make your system more secure.

Don't Use a Samba Version Prior to 1.9.17p2

A method was found to exploit a buffer overrun in Samba version 1.9.17p1 and earlier which allows an attacker to gain root access to your system. This technique has been widely disseminated on the Internet. If you are running a susceptible version of Samba you can expect somebody to try to break into your system sooner or later.

Use Encrypted Passwords

It is usually a good general policy to use encrypted passwords instead of plaintext passwords. Setting up encrypted password authentication is described in detail on page 224.

Limit Access to Clients From Specific IP Addresses

In almost all cases a Samba server is intended for access from a specific set of client machines, usually located on the same LAN as the Samba server. It doesn't hurt to specify a global `allow hosts` and `deny hosts` parameter which allows access from only your own IP addresses. These parameters are described in detail on page 169. They allow describing ranges of hosts by IP address, hostname, network/netmask pairs, and NIS netgroups.

For example, suppose your LAN is allocated the first 64 IP addresses in the class C domain 150.39.28.*. This setting would allow access only from addresses 150.39.28.0 to 150.39.28.63:

```
allow hosts = 239.39.28.0/255.255.255.192
```

Rather than describe the netmask explicitly, you can just specify the number of leading ones in the netmask.

Unfortunately, it may sometimes be necessary to grant access to machines outside of this range of IP addresses. You may have employees who wish to access the server from home, or you may be collaborating with people at another institution. You can add additional specific IP addresses or ranges of IP addresses to the list. This would allow access from the same range of machines, as well as from the single IP address 138.26.25.10.

```
allow hosts = 239.39.28.0/255.255.255.192 138.26.25.10
```

Since allow hosts is a service option, you could add this extended `allow hosts` configuration to the specific service the remote site needs to access, rather than extend access to all of your SMB services.

Alternately, suppose you are in a large organization, like a university, that has control of an entire class B domain. Initially, you grant access from every other computer on campus with this statement:

```
allow hosts = 145.34.
```

However, you discover that bored students are using the publicly available terminals in the library to mount attacks on your server. If all of these machines have DNS hostnames that end in `.lib.watsamatu.edu`, you could use this statement to block access:

```
deny hosts = .lib.watsamatau.edu
```

As you can see, quite complex rules can be developed. Note that you can also grant and limit access by hostname and NIS groupname, if you are using NIS for distributed authentication.

Use root Directory to Limit Access to Your Server

The root directory parameter uses the `chroot()` system call to change the perceived root level of the filesystem. This would be useful if you are running Samba on a particular sensitive server, or in an extremely exposed location. Otherwise, using the root directory parameter will probably be more trouble than its worth.

Setting `root directory = /usr/local/` means that the Samba server will be unable to access any portion of the filesystem that is not underneath the `/usr/local/` directory. If you created a server with `path = /` it would share only the `/usr/local/` directory, not the entire filesystem.

The benefit of using `root directory` is that even if an intruder finds a bug in Samba that allows arbitrary files to be manipulted, only files under the location specified by `root directory` will be accessible.

The downside of this technique is that you have to provide copies of all the files outside of the new root directory that Samba may need access to. This includes system files like `/etc/hosts`, devices like `/dev/null`, `/bin/sh` so Samba can launch a shell, the printer spooler, and more. To sum up, this technique is not for the faint of heart. It is not a good idea unless you absolutely need it and you know what you are doing.

Dealing with Older Clients

You can make use of the `include` parameter to include special configuration options for Windows for Workgroups clients on your network. This allows you to specify settings that would be desirable for Windows for Workgroups clients, but not for new clients. First add the `include` parameter to the end of your `[global]` section:

```
include = /usr/local/samba/lib/smb.conf.%a
```

The `/usr/local/samba/lib/smb.conf.WfWg` file could contain the following:

```
; settings for Windows for Workgroups clients
protocol = COREPLUS
max xmit = 8192
```

Setting the maximum protocol extension to `COREPLUS` has the unusual effect of causing Windows for Workgroups to not convert passwords to all uppercase before transmitting them to the server. If you would rather not use `COREPLUS` as your maximum protocol then you will probably have to set the `password level` parameter to a non-zero value. See page 135 for details about `password level`.

Depending on the settings in the rest of your configuration file, you may wish to adjust the `mangled names`, `mangle case`, `preserve case`, and `short preserve case` settings so the client only receives uppercase 8.3 file names. See page 186 for details about each of these parameters. In most cases, the default settings will work properly.

Chapter 11: Diagnosing Problems

While it would be impossible to explain a solution to every possible problem you could encounter, it is possible to describe some helpful techniques for narrowing down the source of a problem. In the end each problem will be solved by your own problem-solving skills, but these hints can help you get started.

The Samba Diagnosis Procedure

This is the diagnosis procedure written by Andrew Tridgell and included with the Samba documentation in the file DIAGNOSIS.txt. This section contains the information in that file with added detail and examples.

Assumptions

All of these tests assume that you are running Samba version 1.9.16 or later. They also assume that your SMB client machine is running Windows for Workgroups, Windows 95 or Windows NT (either Workstation or Server).

You need to have this share available on your server:

```
[tmp]
comment = temporary files
path = /tmp
read only = yes
```

If you don't, you need to add it to your smb.conf file.

The Procedure

Test 1: Is smb.conf free from errors?

In the same directory in which you store your smb.conf file, run:

```
testparm smb.conf
```

If testparm reports any errors then your smb.conf file is faulty. You should receive a description of what part needs to be fixed.

Test 2: Is TCP/IP configured properly on both the client and the server?

On the client machine, open up an MS-DOS prompt and run:

```
ping samba.server.hostname
```

If you receive a "command not found" error, then TCP/IP may not be correctly installed on the client.

On the Samba server, also run

```
ping client.hostname
```

If you get an error message on either the PC or the UNIX machine saying "host not found," then your domain name server (DNS) configuration is incorrect, or the hostname is not properly entered into your DNS server.

If `ping` fails to reach the other host, then you may have a physical network problem between the two machines, or the TCP/IP software on the other machine may not be properly configured.

I've also noticed that Windows 95 clients sometimes drop their network connections for no apparent good reason. If you've checked your TCP/IP settings and you know they are correct, this may be the problem. A quick way to find out is to try and ping the Windows 95 host from itself. On the Windows machine run:

```
ping localhost
```

If you get a "network not accessible" error, then your Windows 95 machine has "dropped" its network interface. This is the most common Windows 95 networking problem that I encounter. Sometimes making sure the latest Windows 95 service pack is installed seems to solve the problem, but not always. Unfortunately, the only solution I've found is to reboot the Windows machine.

Test 3: Is `smbd` running and accessible?

On the UNIX machine run:

```
smbclient -L SAMBASERVER -U '' -N
```

You should be shown a list of shares available on the server like this:

```
Server=[FRODO] User=[ftp] Workgroup=[UAB-TUCC] Domain=[UAB-TUCC]
```

Sharename	Type	Comment
tmp	Disk	Temporary Directory
IPC$	IPC	IPC Service (John Blair's Linux Box)

```
NOTE: There were share names longer than 8 chars.
On older clients these may not be accessible or may give browsing errors
```

```
This machine has a browse list:
```

Server	Comment
FRODO	John Blair's Linux Box
TUCCSTER	UAB-The University Computer Center

You may receive an error containing one of the following:

1. Bad password - name/password pair in a Tree Connect...

You probably have an incorrect `valid users` or `invalid users` definition in your global section. Temporarily comment out all instances of `valid users` and `invalid users` and try again. You could also have an invalid guest account. Verify that you guest account allows minimal access to your system.

2. The requester does not have the necessary access rights...

You probably have an incorrect `hosts allow` or `hosts deny` setting in your global section. Either comment out all instances of `hosts allow` and `hosts deny` and try again, or use `testparm` to test your host-based access controls. This example demonstrates that a given hostname is denied access:

```
# testparm smb.conf frodo.tucc.uab.edu 138.26.25.10
Load smb config files from smb.conf
Processing section "[tmp]"
Loaded services file OK.
Deny connection from frodo.tucc.uab.edu (138.26.25.10) to tmp
Deny connection from frodo.tucc.uab.edu (138.26.25.10) to IPC$
```

Note that both the DNS hostname and the IP address must be supplied to testparm for it to test your `hosts allow` and `hosts deny` settings.

If you are using `inetd` to start nmbd, check to see if you are using tcpwrappers. If you are, then make sure that your `hosts.allow` and `hosts.deny` files contain an entry for nmbd and allow access from the PC. Alternately, you could remove the tcpwrappers from the nmbd entry and use Samba's host-based access controls.

3. Connection refused

If you have configured `inetd` to start `smbd`:

You probably have a problem with your settings in `inetd.conf`, or the NetBIOS services are not properly listed in your `services` file, or in your services yp database if you are using NIS. The `netbios-ssn` service must be in your `services` file, or in your service yp database if you are using NIS.

```
netbios-ssn 139/tcp
```

Your `inetd.conf` file must contain an entry for smbd like this:

```
netbios-ssn stream tcp nowait root /usr/local/samba/bin/smbd smbd
```

Some versions of inetd have trouble with command line options. If you are starting smbd with several command line options you may need to create a small wrapper script to start it up properly. A better solution is to avoid using command line options by setting the corresponding parameter in smb.conf.

If you are running smbd as a stand-alone daemon:

First check to see that smbd is running:

```
$ ps aux | grep smbd
```

or

```
ps -ef | grep smbd root 12375 0.0 0.7 1252 592 ? S 00:08 0:00 smbd -D
```

If it isn't, start it up. It may be failing to start because of invalid command-line options or errors in the smb.conf file. Use testparm, as in step 1, to check the latter.

Next check that the netbios-ssn service is in the LISTEN state:

```
$ netstat -a |   grep netbios
tcp          0               0 *:netbios-ssn      *:*              LISTEN
udp          0               0 *:netbios-ns       *:*
udp          0               0 *:netbios-dgm      *:*
```

If smbd is running and netbios-ssn is not in the LISTEN state, you may have configured smbd to bind to the wrong port.

4. Session request failed...
or your server software is being unfriendly...

You may have invalid command-line options on smbd, a problem in smb.conf, or a similar problem that causes smbd to fail when it is started. Check your inetd.conf for typos and use testparm to check your smb.conf file. Alternately, you may already have something running on port 139, such as smbd in daemon mode or Digital's Pathworks server.

Test 4: Is `nmbd` running?

On the UNIX machine run:

```
nmblookup -B SAMBASERVER __SAMBA__
```

You should receive back the address of your Samba server, like this:

```
138.26.25.10 __SAMBA__
```

If this fails, then nmbd is not running to service the request.

If you have configured `inetd` to start `nmbd`:

You probably have a problem with your settings in `inetd.conf`, or the NetBIOS services are not properly listed in your `services` file. The `netbios-ns` service must be in your `services` file, like this:

```
netbios-ns 137/udp
```

Your `inetd.conf` file must contain an entry for nmbd like this:

```
netbios-ns dgram udp wait root /usr/local/samba/bin/nmbd nmbd
```

Some versions of `inetd` have trouble with command line options. If you are starting nmbd with several command line options you may need to create a small wrapper script to start it up properly. A better solution is to avoid using command line options by setting the corresponding parameter in `smb.conf`.

If you are running `nmbd` as a stand-alone daemon:

First check to see that nmbd is running:

```
$ ps aux | grep nmbd
```

or

```
ps -ef | grep nmbd root 12375 0.0 0.7 1252 592 ? S 00:08 0:00 nmbd -D
```

If it isn't, start it up. It may be failing to start because of invalid command-line options or errors in the `smb.conf` file. Use `testparm`, as in step 1, to check the latter. Also make sure you have not configured nmbd to listen to the wrong port.

Test 5: Can the client's NetBIOS name be resolved?

On the UNIX host, run:

```
nmblookup -B ACLIENT '*'
```

You should see something like:

```
138.26.25.25 *
```

If you don't, then the software on the PC isn't installed correctly, the PC isn't running, you got the name of the PC wrong, or the PC is on a different network segment and its name cannot be resolved. The last problem could be caused by an incorrect setting in the PC's WINS server configuration. If you are using a NetBIOS hosts file to resolve hostnames on different network segments, then the PC isn't in the file or its entry in set improperly.

Test 6: Has `nmblookup` properly determined your broadcast address?

On the UNIX host, run:

```
nmblookup -d 2 '*'
```

This causes `nmblookup` to conduct the same test as test 5, but by using a broadcast to the default broadcast address. You should see a list of hosts that have responded. Note the list may not contain all available hosts, since they may not all respond in the short time `nmblookup` listens for responses. You should see something like this:

```
Added interface ip=138.26.25.10 bcast=138.26.255.255 nmask=255.255.0.0
Got a positive name query response from 138.26.25.10 (138.26.25.10)
Got a positive name query response from 138.26.25.12 (138.26.25.12)
Got a positive name query response from 138.26.24.253 (138.26.24.253)
Got a positive name query response from 138.26.25.17 (138.26.25.17)
Got a positive name query response from 138.26.25.25 (138.26.25.25)
Got a positive name query response from 138.26.25.20 (138.26.25.20)
Got a positive name query response from 138.26.25.28 (138.26.25.28)
```

If you don't, then `nmblookup` hasn't properly determined your broadcast address. Experiment with the `interfaces` parameter in the `smb.conf` file to manually set the host address, broadcast address, and netmask. The interfaces parameter is explained on page 123.

Note that if the client machine and your Samba server are not on the same network segment, and your router will route broadcast packets, you can use the -B option to specify the broadcast address of the remote segment.

Test 7: Is user authentication working properly?

On the UNIX host, run:

```
smbclient '\\SAMBASERVER\TMP'
```

You will be asked for the password for the username you are currently logged into the UNIX machine as. If you would like to connect with a different username use the -U option. After you enter the password you should be presented with the "smb: \>" prompt. You may receive one of these errors:

1. Invalid network name in tree connect.

   This means the mp service is not properly defined in your smb.conf file. The testparm command may help you find the error. A common error is to have the path parameter set to a nonexistent directory.

2. Bad password - name/password pair...

   There are several possible causes of this problem:

   a. Your system uses a nontraditional password authentication system, like shadow passwords or Kerberos, and you didn't compile the support into smbd.

   b. You have an incorrect valid users setting.

   c. You have a mixed case password and the password level parameter is not set high enough.

   d. You enabled encrypted password authentication but you haven't created the SMB encrypted password file, or you haven't set your password in this file with smbpasswd yet.

   e. On Red Hat Linux, or another system which uses pluggable authentication modules (PAM), you may not have configured Samba's authentication options correctly.

   f. You entered the wrong password.

Test 8: Is `nmbd` responding to the PC?

This test is really the same as test 4, only you're checking that you can list the available shares from the PC. On the PC machine, at an MS-DOS prompt, type:

```
net view \\SAMBASERVER
```

You may receive an error containing one of the following:

1. `network name not found`

   This error means that the PC cannot resolve the NetBIOS name of the Samba server. This could be caused by several problems.

   If you are running `nmbd` as a stand-alone daemon, then `nmbd` may not be running or it may not be binding to the correct port. If you are using `inetd` to start `nmbd`, then a misconfiguration may be causing `nmbd` to not successfully start. Use the solutions described in test 4.

   If you are not in the same network segment as `SAMBASERVER`, you need to be running WINS or have `SAMBASERVER` listed in your `LMHOSTS` file. If you are using either technique, check that you have not misconfigured the WINS settings, or made a typo in the LMHOSTS file. Note that you cannot use tabs in the LMHOSTS file! Also note that no errors will be generated if your LMHOSTS file fails to load.

2. `invalid network name...` or

   `bad password...`

   You probably have an incorrect `hosts allow` or `hosts deny` setting in your global section. Either comment out all instances of `hosts allow` and `hosts deny` and try again, or use `testparm` to test your host-based access controls. This example demonstrates that a given hostname is denied access:

```
# testparm smb.conf pchost.tucc.uab.edu 138.26.25.30
Load smb config files from smb.conf
Processing section "[tmp]"
Loaded services file OK.
Deny connection from frodo.tucc.uab.edu (138.26.25.30) to tmp
Deny connection from frodo.tucc.uab.edu (138.26.25.30) to IPC$
```

   Note that both the DNS hostname and the IP address must be supplied to testparm for it to test your `hosts allow` and `hosts deny` settings.

   If you are using `inetd` to start `nmbd`, check to see if you are using tcpwrappers. If you are, then make sure that your `hosts.allow` and `hosts.deny` files contain an entry for nmbd and allow access from the PC. Alternately, you could remove the tcpwrappers from the nmbd entry and use Samba's host-based access controls.

Test 9: Can the PC access a share on the Samba server?

On the PC machine, at an MS-DOS prompt, type:

```
net use X: \\SAMBASERVER\TMP
```

You will be prompted for a password. After you enter a correct password, you should see `command completed successfully`. If you don't, then there are a few things that could be wrong. This assumes that you've demonstrated in test 8 that the PC can resolve the `SAMBASERVER` NetBIOS name and that you entered the correct password.

It is possible that the server can't work out the correct username to validate your password with. One way to check this is to add `user = username`, where "username" is the username you wish to connect to the service as. If you then successfully connect to the server, you may need to create a username map file or use the `SERVICE%USERNAME` notation to communicate your username to Samba.

It is also possible that nmbd improperly determined the name of your server. You can test this by setting the `netbios name` option in your smb.conf file, or using the -N command line option for nmbd to specify a name.

Another possibility is that you are using one of the more recent revisions of Windows 95 and Windows NT which refuses to connect to a server using non-encrypted password authentication. You can correct this by editing the registry to re-enable the use of plaintext passwords. This process is explained on page 134 for Windows NT and page 134 for Windows 95. Alternately, you can configure your Samba server to use encrypted passwords. This may require you to recompile the server to support encrypted passwords, or to add a Samba encrypted password file. This process is explained in detail on page 224.

Another possibility is that your client software is not installed properly, or that you have errors in your smb.conf file. Use `testparm` to verify that the smb.conf file is correct and that your host-based access controls aren't blocking access.

Test 10: Can you browse the Samba server?

On the PC, use the File Manager, Windows Explorer, or Network Neighborhood to try and browse the server. When you double click on the server you should be presented with a list of shares. If you receive an "invalid password" error at this point, and you have your Samba server configured to use plaintext passwords, then you are probably connecting from one of the more recent revisions of Windows 95 and Windows NT which refuses to connect to a server using non-encrypted password authentication. Of course, if this were the problem, then Test 9 would have also failed. Apply the same solution as explained in Test 9.

Diagnosing Printer Problems

Do you have access to the printer?

On the UNIX host, run:

```
smbclient '\\SAMBASERVER\TMP' -P
```

If you get an error, apply the same diagnostic procedure as in Test 3 of the diagnosis procedure.

Is /dev/null world writeable?

Check to see what the permissions are on /dev/null. A surprisingly common problem is that /dev/null is not world writeable. Samba's printing services will not function properly unless they can discard the output of print commands in /dev/null.

Is lpr working properly?

Change the print command parameter for the printer service in question to:

```
print command = /bin/cp %s /tmp/tmp.print
```

Print a file to the printer service. The `/tmp/tmp.print` file should now exist. Try to print it with `lpr` to the printer the service is associated with. If that succeeds, then you either have a configuration problem on your client machine, or you have the `print command` parameter set improperly.

A common problem is that the specified printer command is not in the path that Samba searches. Try re-writing your `printer command` parameter with the full path of `lpr` or the corresponding command. You also may have the wrong `printer` setting, which would cause Samba to try and use the wrong defaults. Depending on your system, and any changes you've made to the default printing system, Samba may incorrectly guess what printer settings to use. Use the `testparm` command to examine the contents of the print command parameter. Try printing a file with those commands to see if they are correct. The default values for the print command on various systems are explained on page 203.

Increasing the Log Level for Specific Machines

Increasing the log level to 3 or 4 can shed light on the cause of most problems. However, log levels this high generate prodigious amounts of information. On a busy server it may be very difficult to separate the information that explains your problem from all of the normal dialog.

The `include` command and macro substitutions are the solution to this problem. Suppose you're having problems with logging in from you Windows for Workgroups machines. Add this to the end of your `[global]` section:

```
include = /usr/local/samba/lib/smb.conf.%a
```

Then create the `/usr/local/samba/lib/smb.conf.WfWg` file containing this parameter:

```
log level = 3
```

Because the `include` is at the end of your [global] section, it will override any other log level setting you have for the machine you are examining, but leave that setting intact for all other machines.

You can use the same technique to increase the log level for specific machines. For example, to examine a problem from the machine called **BADBOY**, create a file called `/usr/local/samba/lib/smb.conf.BADBOY` containing the log level setting, then add this to the end of your global section:

```
include = /usr/local/samba/lib/smb.conf.%m
```

I'm sure by now you get the picture.

The Windows `nbtstat` Command

```
nbtstat [-a remotename] [-A IP address] [-c] [-n] [-R] [-r] [-S] [-s]
        [interval]
```

The `nbtstat` command, provided under both Windows 95 and Windows NT, allows you to query some attributes of other hosts and current connections using NetBIOS over TCP/IP. This command is only available if TCP/IP is installed. If TCP/IP isn't installed on your client I doubt you would have made it this far.

options:

-a remotename Lists the NetBIOS name table available on a remote machine referenced by NetBIOS name.

-A IP address Lists the NetBIOS name table available on a remote machine referenced by IP address. DNS names cannot be used in place of the IP address.

-c Lists the contents of the NetBIOS name cache on the host on which `nbtstat` is invoked.

-n Lists NetBIOS names being made available from the host on which `nbtstat` is invoked.

-R Reloads the `LMHOSTS` file after purging all names from the NetBIOS name cache.

-r Displays NetBIOS name resolution statistics for name resolution attempts from the host on which `nbtstat` was invoked.

-S Displays both NetBIOS client and server connections to and from the host on which `nbtstat` was invoked. Hosts are shown by IP address.

`-s`   The same as the `-S` option, except an attempt is made to resolve the IP address of each host into a DNS name.

`interval` Causes the selected statistic to be automatically redisplayed every `<interval>` seconds. Pressing CTRL+C causes `nbtstat` to stop redisplaying the statistics.

Chapter 12: The Linux SMB Filesystem

The standard Linux source tree now contains an SMB filesystem. This filesystem allows you to mount a remote SMB file-share over a local directory in much the same way a remote NFS export can be mounted locally. The contents of the remote share can then be manipulated as if it were a normal part of the Linux filesystem.

Since the SMB filesystem loadable module, called `smbfs`, is usually included as a part of most Linux distributions, very little work will be required to use it. If the module is present on your system and you are running `kerneld`, the module will be loaded automatically when you try to mount a volume from an SMB server.

A quick way to see if `smbfs.o` is present on your system is to use `modprobe -l -t fs` to list the available filesystem modules. For example:

```
$modprobe -l -t fs
/lib/modules/2.0.32/fs/fat.o
/lib/modules/2.0.32/fs/hfs.o
```

279

```
/lib/modules/2.0.32/fs/minix.o
/lib/modules/2.0.32/fs/msdos.o
/lib/modules/2.0.32/fs/nfs.o
/lib/modules/2.0.32/fs/smbfs.o
/lib/modules/2.0.32/fs/vfat.o
```

The SMB Filesystem Compared with the Network Filesystem (NFS)

There are major differences between a remote volume mounted using the Network Filesystem and a volume mounted using the SMB filesystem. Since NFS was designed to share a UNIX volume, it makes accessing the remote filesystem completely transparent, preserving permissions, ownerships, and links. On the other hand, SMB was designed for sharing DOS files. As a result, it has no concept of file owner and a completely different permission structure (DOS attributes).

Access control is also handled completely differently on the two systems. NFS uses host-based access control, and for the most part leaves user-based access control up to the remote system. If a file is owned by userid 500 on the NFS server, it will be owned by userid 500 on the client. This can cause an obvious problem if the passwd files are not synchronized between the two systems—write access can be granted to a completely unrelated user. As a result, in most cases write access can only be granted to completely trusted hosts. In these situations some sort of distributed authentication management, such as NIS or Kerberos is usually used to enforce access controls properly across the network. In contrast, user-based access control is completely integrated into the SMB protocol. To mount a shared volume, the server must either grant guest access or the client must present a valid username and password.

As a result of these differences, the normal UNIX mount command cannot be used to mount an SMB volume. A userspace tool, called smbmount, is provided allows you to specify a username and password to use to connect to the remote service. It also allows you to control the permissions and ownerships assigned to the files and directories in the smbmounted filesystem.

smbmount to Be Integrated into smbclient

The creator of the Linux SMB filesystem, Volker Lendec, has explained that `smbmount` and `smbumount` will eventually be dropped in favor of a modified version of `smbclient`. However, the plan is to include a command-line compatible shell script so the end user sees no difference.

Compilation Notes

This is not the appropriate place to provide a tutorial on building the Linux kernel. If you haven't built a Linux kernel and you want to, read the Kernel-HOWTO or consult one of the many good books about Linux.

The SMB filesystem component can be compiled into the kernel, or compiled as a loadable module. In most situations it makes the most sense to compile the SMB filesystem as a loadable module, since it is not likely to be in use most of the time.

If you are adding the SMB filesystem to the kernel, there's only one option which you will have to decide whether or not to use. Windows 95 SMB servers have exhibited a bug which makes listing directories unreliable. There is a workaround for this bug which slows down the speed at which the SMB filesystem requests a directory listing. This seems to make accessing a Windows 95 shared volume more stable.

Windows 95 Workaround May Be Dropped

The Windows 95 workaround may be dropped as a compile-time option in Linux 2.2. Instead, a run-time switch to `smbmount` or `smbclient` would be used.

Here are the relevant listings in the command line configuration tool for kernel version 2.0.32, the latest non-development kernel at the time of writing.

```
SMB filesystem support (to mount WfW shares etc..) (CONFIG_SMB_FS)
        [Y/m/n/?] m
SMB Win95 bug work-around (CONFIG_SMB_WIN95) [Y/n/?] Y
```

Older kernels offered an experimental option to support Windows 95 long file names. This option is no longer experimental, or even an option anymore. If you are still using one of these older kernels you should consider upgrading to a recent version.

Mount Management Tools

Since the conventional mount utility does not provide enough information to mount an SMB share, the smbmount tool is provided. This command must be installed setuid root to allow non-root users to mount a shared volume.

smbmount

```
smbmount servicename mount-point [ -h ] [ -C ] [ -n ] [ -P password ]
        [ -s server name ] [ -c client name ] [ -I hostname/IP ]
        [ -U user name ] [ -D domain name ] [ -u uid ] [ -g gid ]
        [ -f file mode ] [ -d dir mode ] [ -m max xmit ] [ -p port ]
```

Required parameters:

servicename The name of the SMB service you want to mount. The service name takes the form //SERVER/SERVICE, where SERVER is the name of the SMB server, and SERVICE is the service name. Note that the man page, which states you can specify a subdirectory to mount, is incorrect. The subdirectory option does not work.

Unlike the smbclient command, the servicename uses forward slashes, not DOS style backslashes. This conveniently avoids the need to escape the backslashes in the shell. Further, the servicename can be started with a single slash, rather then two slashes. This makes smbmount compatible with the Berkeley automounter daemon. Using AMD with smbmount is explained on page 286.

In order to mount the remote filesystem smbmount needs to resolve the NetBIOS name into an IP address. smbmount cheats, resolving the hostname using DNS, rather than using NetBIOS name resolution.

Unfortunately, this will fail in two situations:

1. If the NetBIOS name of the host is different from the first component of the DNS name, or

2. If the server's DNS name is in a different DNS domain or subdomain, causing an attempt to resolve just the first part of the name to fail.

In either of these two situations you will need to use the -I option to specify the remote host's IP address manually.

`mount-point` This is the directory you wish to mount the remote filesystem over. Just like the mount command, this directory must already exist and must grant write permission to you, unless you are root.

Important Options:

`-C`   Normally passwords are converted to uppercase before being transmitted to the server. Most SMB servers require this. This option causes your password to be transmitted exactly as it was entered.

`-c client name` Allows you to specify the NetBIOS name of the client—that is, the machine that smbmount is being run on. This is useful if your NetBIOS name is the same as your hostname, or if the local hostname returned is the fully-qualified DNS name, not just the hostname.

`-D domain name` Sometimes a server will require a domain name to authenticate your username and password. This is especially true when you are connecting to a remote service located in an NT domain that is authenticating your username & password by contacting a different trusted NT domain.

`-f file mode, -d dir mode` These options describe the permissions which will be assumed by directories and files in the mounted filesystem. These parameters are necessary because the smb filesystem makes no attempt to translate the DOS attributes into UNIX file permissions, as the Samba server does.

It is possible for a non-root user to successfully set the user and group owners to something other than themselves. I consider this a bug, though a minor one, since the `-f` option does not allow you to set the user or group setuid bits in the mounted filesystem. However, paranoid administrators may wish to not make smbmount available to normal users because of this feature.

The defaults for these values are determined from the current umask. File permissions are set to the current umask, and directory permissions adds execute permission to the current umask.

-h   Displays a short description of the command-line options.

-I DNS name/IP address of the server This option is used to manually specify the DNS name or IP address of the server.

-n   Causes smbmount to not ask for a password. This behaves the same as smbclient's -N option.

-P password Allows you to specify a password on the command line, which is useful (but potentially dangerous) in scripts. The -n option is assumed if you specify a password.

-s server name Allows you to specify a NetBIOS name different from the one you described in the servicename parameter. Note that this does not change the way smbmount resolves the NetBIOS name into an IP address, it just uses this value instead of the value in the servicename.

These rights can be assigned arbitrarily, and as a result, can differ from the actual rights assigned by the server. In other words, you can cause the files in the mounted filesystem to have the write bit set even if the server has granted you read-only access. In this situation, attempts to write to the files will fail since you cannot override the restrictions imposed by the server.

-u uid, -g gid These options determine the userid and groupid that the mounted SMB filesystem will be owned by. This is required because SMB tells us nothing about the owner of individual files. The defaults for these values are the current user's userid and groupid.

-U username This option specifies the username to use when accessing the SMB service. This is useful if your current UNIX username differs from the username you wish to use to access the SMB service.

Hacker Options:

-p port Specifies the TCP port to connect to on the server. Normally this value is set to 139. The only reason to use this option is if you have a test environment where an SMB server is running on a non-standard port.

-m max xmit This option sets an upper limit on the packet size that is negotiated with the server. Don't use this option unless you know what you're doing.

Environment Variables:

USER/LOGNAME If the -U option is not specified on the command line, smbmount will check to see if the USER environmental variable exists. If it does, its contents will be used as the username. If USER does not exist, smbmount will check for LOGNAME.

smbumount

```
smbumount mount-point
```

mount-point The pathname of the directory the SMB share is currently mounted over.

The smbumount command is provided to allow non-root users to unmount an SMB filesystem. It is essentially just a wrapper around umount that allows non-root users to unmount an SMB filesystem that the user previously mounted. Filesystems mounted by other users cannot be unmounted.

Examples

In an ideal situation, this will allow you to mount an SMB share:

```
smbmount //SERVER/SHARENAME /some/mount/point
```

This will allow you to connect to a service which grants guest access:

```
smbmount //SERVER/SHARENAME /some/mount/point -U guest -n
```

I find the most common option I use is the -c tag, since on my system smbmount attempts to use the fully qualified domain name as the client's NetBIOS name.

```
smbmount //SERVER/SHARENAME /some/mount/point -c CLIENTNAME
```

You will need to provide the username and password to use smbmount in a non-interactive script.

```
smbmount //SERVER/SHARENAME /some/mount/point -U jdblair -P xxxxx
```

In all of these cases, unmounting is easy:

```
smbumount /some/mount/point
```

Alternately, if you are root, you can use the conventional umount command:

```
umount /some/mount/point
```

Using the Automount Daemon (AMD) with the SMB Filesystem

Why Use the Automounter?

The Berkeley Automounter can be used to automatically mount and unmount a remote SMB share. That this is possible is really a testament to the rather amazing flexibility built into the automount daemon's map file.

The AMD provides a "program" filesystem type which will call an arbitrary command-line program to mount a filesystem. You just need to configure the map file to call smbmount with all the appropriate options. However, there are some potentially serious problems with this technique. Remember that the automounter is designed chiefly for NFS mounts, which require no access control information. As a result, the automounter has no way to ask a user for a username and password to use to access the SMB service on a case-by-case basis. The username and password must be "hard-coded" into the AMD map file. Because of this limitation, using AMD to mount and unmount an SMB filesystem is probably only appropriate in two situations.

1. Your Linux machine is, for all intents and purposes, a single user machine. It is very common for a Linux machine to be used this way. Even though Linux is a multi-user operating system, if you are the only person with access to your system there will be little danger in hard-coding the passwords needed to access SMB shares you use

frequently. Of course, if your machine is broken into, someone may be able to steal your Windows password.

2. You are automounting public (or public to all users of your Linux system) shares. If anybody can access the share as the Guest user already, there will be little danger in adding the option to your AMD map file.

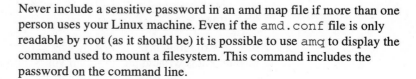

Be very cautious when using a sensitive password in an AMD map file.

Never include a sensitive password in an amd map file if more than one person uses your Linux machine. Even if the amd.conf file is only readable by root (as it should be) it is possible to use amq to display the command used to mount a filesystem. This command includes the password on the command line.

Also note that the Linux version of the Berkeley Automount Daemon is notoriously flakey. The current development kernel (2.1.xx) has a completely re-written automount service that is integrated into the kernel. This new automounter promises to correct the bugs in the current version. Since this new automounter should be backwards compatible to the Berkeley AMD, the example map file should continue to work properly.

Configuring AMD

A common default automounter map file in Linux distributions allows NFS filesystems exported from other hosts to be transparently accessible under the AMD mountpoint. This is the default map file installed by Red Hat's AMD package:

```
/defaults fs:=${autodir}/${rhost}/root/${rfs};opts=nosuid,nodev
*         rhost:=${key};type:=host;rfs:=/
```

The default AMD mountpoint under Red Hat Linux is /net. The result is that an NFS export "export" on server "server" can be transparently accessed in the directory /net/server/export.

The following configuration will allow the SMB share //SERVER/SERVERNAME to be accessed transparently under /net/ sharename (or wherever your default AMD mountpoint is).

Add this definition to your /etc/amd.map file:

```
sharename type:=program;fs:=${autodir}/${key};\
        mount:="/usr/sbin/smbmount smbmount //SERVER/SERVERNAME ${fs} \
        -P password -U USER -c CLIENTNAME"; \

unmount:="/bin/umount umount ${fs}"
```

Note that you will need to replace these generic entries with the appropriate values for your configuration. You need to reference smbmount and umount using their full path names. The full path on your system may be different.

You need to create the directory that AMD will mount the filesystem over. Create this directory inside whatever your mount point directory is. Red Hat uses `/.automount`, so I need to create `/.automount/sharename`.

If `amd` is running, there is an easy way to figure out what your mountpoint is without picking apart your configuration files—look at the command line options used to start AMD:

```
$ ps auxww | grep amd
root      2141  0.0  0.7  1056    584    ?  S  16:44  0:00
      /usr/sbin/amd -a /.automount -l syslog -c 1000 /net
      /etc/amd.conf
```

The argument following the `-a` switch is the mountpoint. The `-l` option describes where amd logs error messages (in this case, it uses syslog). The `-c` option describes the period of inactivity, in seconds, before a filesystem will be unmounted. Other options are possible. Read the AMD man page or the more detailed techinfo documentation (look in `/usr/doc/amd-*/doc`).

Following all the switches and their arguments will be pairs of arguments, each describing the automount directory and its corresponding configuration file. The example above shows that the `/net` directory is used as the automount directory and the `/etc/amd.conf` file configures its behavior.

An Example

The following is an excerpt from my `amd.conf` file:

```
/defaults fs:=${autodir}/${rhost}/root/${rfs};opts=nosuid,nodev
*        rhost:=${key};type:=host;rfs:=/
tucc-public type:=program;fs:=${autodir}/${key};\
      mount:="/usr/sbin/smbmount smbmount //TUCCSTER/TUCC-Public ${fs} \
      -P xxxxx -c FRODO -U jdblair";\
      unmount:="/bin/umount umount ${fs}"
```

I've also created the mount directory `/.automount/tucc-public`.

First, lets see what filesystems are mounted:

```
(~)$ mount
/dev/hda2 on / type ext2 (rw)
/dev/hda3 on /usr/local type ext2 (rw)
/dev/hda4 on /var type ext2 (rw)
none on /proc type proc (rw)
frodo:(pid2477) on /net type auto(intr,rw,port=1023,timeo=8,retrans=110,\
      indirect,map=/etc/amd.conf)
```

Note the last line describing the automount directory. Next, I list the contents of the tucc-public directory:

```
.(~)$ ls /net/tucc-public
```

3270	Internet	Win95 Patches	qws3270
3270-install	Networker	library-install	tcl
Antivirus	Public	ph	
Install Shortcuts	Remote	printer-drivers	

If I show the currently mounted filesystems, I see that /TUCCSTER/ TUCC-Public is now listed.

```
(~)$ mount
/dev/hda2 on / type ext2 (rw)
/dev/hda3 on /usr/local type ext2 (rw)
/dev/hda4 on /var type ext2 (rw)
none on /proc type proc (rw)
frodo:(pid2477) on /net type auto
(intr,rw,port=1023,timeo=8,retrans=110,indirect,map=/etc/amd.conf) /
TUCCSTER/TUCC-Public on /.automount/tucc-public type smbfs (0)
```

After a period of inactivity (1000 seconds in my case) the remote SMB filesystem will be unmounted.

Index

NOTICE:

By opening the CD-ROM packaging, you are agreeing to be bound to the following terms: